KEY

MATH

D0531632

First edition published in 1995 by:
Stanley Thornes (Publishers) Ltd
Second edition 2000

Reprinted in 2002 by:
Nelson Thornes Ltd
Delta Place
27 Bath Road
CHELTENHAM
GL53 7TH
United Kingdom

02 03 04 / 10 9 8 7 6 5

A catalogue record for this book is available from the British Library

ISBN 0-7487-5525-X

Illustrations by Maltings Partnership, Mark Dunn, Clinton Banbury and Mike Gordon
Page make-up by Tech Set Ltd

Printed and bound in China by Dah Hua Printing Press Co. Ltd.

Acknowledgements
The publishers thank the following for permission to reproduce copyright material:
Ace Photo Agency, spine, p. 220 (Anthony Price); Aerofilms, p. 274; British Museum, p. 291; British Shoe Council, p. 376; Buxton Micrarium, p. 43 (bottom); Collections/Brian Shuel, p. 237; Colorsport, p. 370; Genesis Space Photo Library, pp. 286, 356 (NASA); George Wimpey PLC, p. 382; Images, p. 32, 323; John Walmsley, p. 212; Lincolnshire County Council, p. 40; Mary Evans Picture Library, p. 171; Ordnance Survey, p. 274 (top right – reproduced from 1990 Ordnance Survey 2 cm to 1 km West London area map), p. 317 (from 1992 Ordnance Survey map 2 cm to 1 km Hexham, Haltwhistle and surrounding area) with the permission of the Controller of Her Majesty's Stationery Office © Crown Copyright; OSF, p. 282 (top left – G I Bernard, top middle – Barry Walker, bottom right – Mark Hamblin); Paul Smith, pp. 176, 177, 178, 179; Reed Consumer Books, p. 337; Sally and Richard Greenhill, p. 194; Science and Society Picture Library, p. 245; Science Photo Library, pp. 126, 251 (Dr Jeremy Burgess), 274 (bottom left – Claude Nuridsany and Marie Perennou); 336 (Manfred Kage); Tony Stone Images, front cover, back cover (Lori Adamski Peek); Zefa, pp. 43 (top), 147, 282 (top right – Mehner, bottom left – Reinhard).
All other photographs by Martyn F Chillmaid.

The publishers'have made every effort to contact copyright holders but apologise if any have been overlooked.

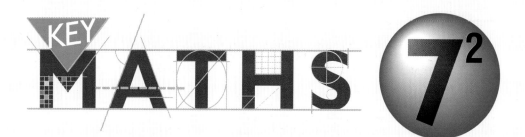

KEY MATHS 7²

▶ **David Baker**
The Anthony Gell School, Wirksworth

▶ **Peter Bland**
Huntingdon School, York

▶ **Paul Hogan**
Fulwood High School, Preston

▶ **Barbara Holt**
Churchdown School, Gloucester

▶ **Barbara Job**
Christleton County High School, Chester

▶ **Renie Verity**
Pensby High School for Girls, Heswall

▶ **Graham Wills**
The Dyson Perrins CE High School, Malvern

Contents

Statistics: about our school

QUESTIONS

EXTENSION

SUMMARY

TEST YOURSELF

The size of your school is measured by the number of pupils.
These pie-charts give information about secondary schools in the UK.

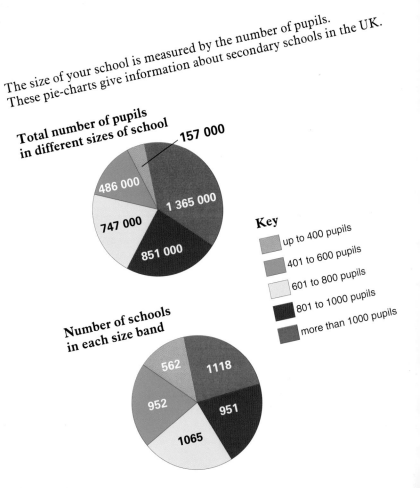

Total number of pupils in different sizes of school

157 000

486 000

1 365 000

747 000

851 000

Key

up to 400 pupils

401 to 600 pupils

601 to 800 pupils

801 to 1000 pupils

more than 1000 pupils

Number of schools in each size band

562 1118

952 951

1065

CORE

1 Surveys

In a **survey** we collect information. This information is also called **data**. The data can be sorted and shown on a diagram.

Statistics	
	The study of facts about numbers is called **statistics**. Governments were the first collectors of statistics. (The name statistics came from the word **states**.) They counted things like the number of people who should pay taxes.

Exercise 1:1

Sarah is doing a survey. She is asking her friends how they come to school. Is it by car, bus, train or bike, or do they walk?
Numbers on their own may look dull. Sarah wants to show her results in a diagram. She can use a bar-chart, a pictogram or a pie-chart.

Bar-chart	
	A **bar-chart** is a diagram made up of bars. Each bar **represents** part of the data.

1   Sarah has drawn a bar-chart.

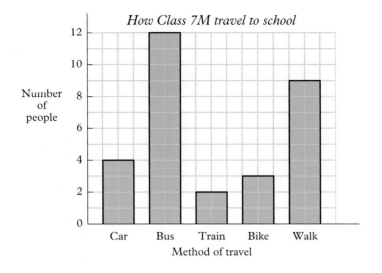

How Class 7M travel to school

a How many children walk to school?
b What is the most common way to travel? How can you tell this from the bar-chart?
c How many children are in this class?

2   Andrew has one brother and one sister. This means that there are three children in his family.
He has done a survey for his class to find the number of children in each family.

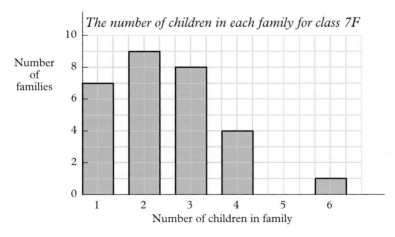

The number of children in each family for class 7F

a How many families have just one child?
b Which is the most popular number of children for a family to have?
c How many families have five children?
d How many families were in the survey?

3 Kevin has done a survey on favourite colours. He has drawn his diagram with horizontal bars.
This is another way of drawing a bar-chart.

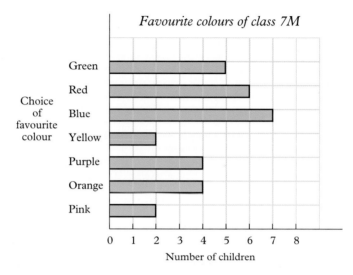

a What is the most popular colour?
b How many people chose red?
c How many people were in Kevin's survey?

. . . .

| Pictogram | A **pictogram** is a diagram which uses pictures instead of bars. |
| Key | A pictogram must always have a **key** to show what each small picture represents. |

Example   ⚲   represents 2 children.

         ⚲   represents 1 child.

         ⚲ ⚲ ⚲ ⚲   represents 2 + 2 + 2 + 1 = 7 children.

4 Pupils at Stanthorn High live in different districts. Daniel has done a survey of where the boys live. He has drawn a pictogram of his results.

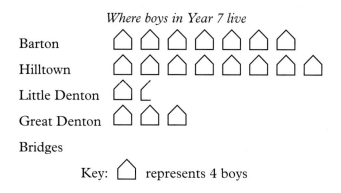

Where boys in Year 7 live

Key: ⌂ represents 4 boys

a How many boys live in Hilltown?
b How many boys live in Little Denton?

c Three boys live at Bridges. Using ⌂ represents 4 boys, show how Daniel could draw 3 boys on his pictogram.

5 Here are the results of a survey on where people went on holiday:

England	Scotland	Wales	Ireland	France	Spain	Other
9	4	5	1	5	4	1

Jaswinder has drawn a pictogram:

Jaswinder's pictogram is not very good.
Write down two things which you think are wrong.

6 Draw a correct pictogram for the results in Question **5**.

7 **a** Draw a bar-chart for Jaswinder's survey in Question **5**.
   b Did you find the pictogram or the bar-chart easier to draw?
   c Write down your reasons.

8 Alix has done a survey. She asked the girls in Year 7 which primary school they used to attend.

She used **tally marks**. Tally marks are done in groups of 5. The fifth tally mark goes across the other four. This makes them easier to count.

School	Tally	Total
St Bridget's	||||| ||||| ||	12
Mill Junior	||||| ||||| ||||| ||||| |||	
Canal Road	||||| ||||| ||||| ||||	19
Church Junior	||||| ||||| ||	
Other	|||||		6

Total _____

a How many Year 7 girls went to Mill Junior?
b How many went to Church Junior?
c What is the total number of girls in the survey?

· ·

Some surveys are difficult to do.
Would it be difficult to do a survey of hair colour or of eye colour?
What problems might you find?

Exercise 1:2

1 a Choose a subject for your own survey.
  b Look at the tally-table in Question **8** above. You will need a tally-table like that for your own survey.
  c Decide who you are going to ask in your survey. These are the people in your **sample**.
   Do not ask the same person twice. You could keep a record of names to help you.
   You could get a friend to help.
  d Draw a pictogram and then a bar-chart to show your results.
  e Write about what you did. Say who you asked.
   Write about any problems you had.
  f At the end put the heading **Conclusions**.
   Say what you found out:
     What was the most common?
     What was the least common?
     Did you notice anything else?

2 Pie-charts

· ·

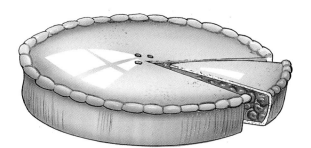

| Pie-chart | Another type of diagram is a **pie-chart**. The **angle** of the slice represents the number of items. |

Exercise 1:3

1 7B had a choice of lunchtime clubs.
The pie-chart shows how they chose.
Seven chose the computer club.
a Write down the fraction of the pie-chart that is the computer club.
b Write down the number of pupils in 7B.

Lunchtime clubs in 7B

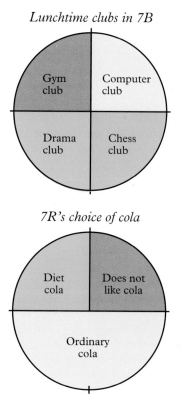

2 Hitesh has drawn a pie-chart.
He asked boys in 7R whether they preferred diet cola or ordinary cola.
There are 16 boys in 7R.
a Write down the number of boys who prefer ordinary cola.
b Write down the number of boys who prefer diet cola.

7R's choice of cola

3 Chantelle's pie-chart for 7B shows favourite subjects.
14 people chose Maths.
  a Write down the most popular subject.
  b Write down the number of people who chose Art.
  c Write down the number of people in the survey.

Favourite subjects

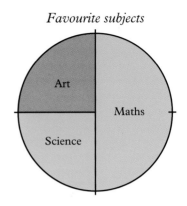

4 This pie-chart shows how 7D have lunch.
  a Write down the largest slice of the pie-chart.
  b Write down the fraction of the class that has sandwiches.
  c Eight pupils in 7D have sandwiches.
  Write down the number of pupils in the class.

How 7D have lunch

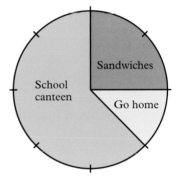

5 Andrew has drawn a pie-chart. It shows how his class, 7P, travel to school.
There are 32 children in Andrew's class.

How Andrew's class gets to school

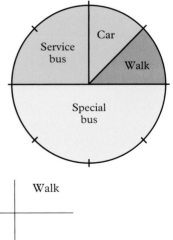

Copy this table and fill it in.

Travel	Service bus	Special bus	Car	Walk
Number of children				

3   Tallying in groups

· ·

How long did it take you to get to school this morning? Was it five minutes, half an hour or even longer?

Suppose we wanted to put the times for the whole class on a tally-table. A table showing every minute would be too long.

This sort of data needs to be tallied in **groups**.

Groups

Bar-charts for **groups** have their *bars touching*. A bar-chart for groups might look like this:

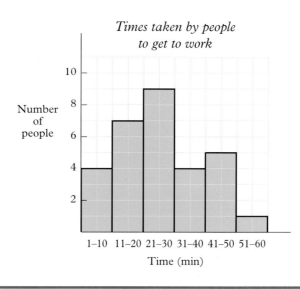

Times taken by people to get to work

Exercise 1:4

1 Here are the times the pupils in 7M took to get to school this morning.
The times are in minutes, correct to the nearest minute.

15	5	8	22	12	10	30	25	27	22
35	8	18	17	22	15	44	35	45	55
12	28	35	48	48	30	40	19	25	50

a Copy the tally-table.
Fill it in by tallying the times.

Time (min)	Tally	Total
1–10		
11–20		
21–30		
31–40		
41–50		
51–60		

Total _____

b Write down the group that has the most pupils in it.
c Copy the axes on to squared or graph paper.
Draw a bar-chart. Remember not to leave gaps between the bars.

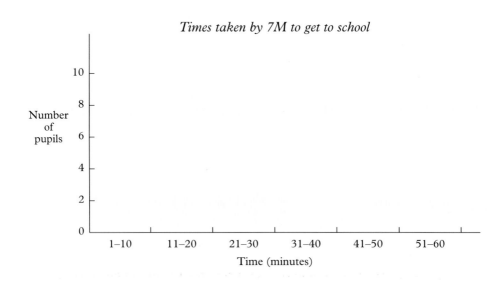

Times taken by 7M to get to school

2 A class measured their armspans from fingertip to fingertip.
Here are their results. The measurements are in centimetres, correct to
the nearest centimetre.

132	129	147	127	128	124	134	139
138	136	144	143	133	141	139	130
142	143	140	137	148	136	146	151
123	131	135	135	130	140	138	133

a Copy the tally-table and fill it in.

Armspan (cm)	Tally	Total
120–124		
125–129		
130–134		
135–139		
140–144		
145–149		
150–154		

                          Total _____

b Copy the axes on to squared or graph paper.
Draw a bar-chart of the results.

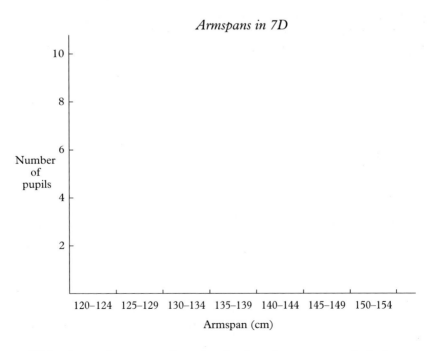

Armspans in 7D

c Write down the group of results that has the most people in it.

3 Class 7B had a day out. They recorded how much they each spent on the trip.

Here are their results. The figures are pounds (£).

0.99	1.26	3.05	0.45	3.26	1.42	1.15
1.40	0.58	0.20	0.90	0.25	0.75	1.75
2.41	1.80	2.85	1.80	1.30	1.88	0.48
0.77	2.40	2.30	1.64	1.93	1.26	1.30

a Copy the tally-table and fill it in.

Amount (£)	Tally	Total
0.01–0.50		
0.51–1.00		
1.01–1.50		
1.51–2.00		
2.01–2.50		
2.51–3.00		
3.01–3.50		

Total _____

b Draw a bar-chart of the results on squared or graph paper.

4 Mr Jones runs the school library. He has done a survey of the number of books borrowed each day.

Here are the results:

34	48	20	22	25	33	14	23	17	12
14	24	39	27	18	36	46	34	43	30
26	26	29	32	45	18	28	31	29	23
13	40	16	19	28	25	21	36	27	35

Make a tally-table. Count in fives starting with 11–15. Go up to 46–50.

Number of books borrowed	Tally	Total
11–15		
16–20		
21–25		
26–30		

5 Class 7M collect for charity.
Here are the amounts collected for the first half term.

36p	18p	53p	10p	20p	4p	39p	65p	£1.25	24p
47p	63p	7p	68p	94p	49p	41p	0	30p	45p
0	50p	£1.17	42p	16p	56p	£1.05	70p	61p	3p
75p	5p	59p	38p	65p	22p	83p	44p	37p	£1.34

Make a tally-table using groups 0–19p, 20–39p, etc.

6 Do a survey of your own. Try this idea.
  a Choose a book or magazine of your own.
  b Count the number of words in each of the first 50 sentences.
  c Make a tally-table like this:

Number of words	Tally	Total
1–5		
6–10		
11–15		
16–20		
21–25		
26–30		
31–35		
36–40		
Over 40		
	Total	____

  d Use your tally-table to record your results.
  e Draw a bar-chart of your results.
  f What can you say about your results?
  g Compare your results with the results of a friend.
     Which book do you think is easier to read? Give reasons for your
     answer.

4   Location

Have you travelled on a train? People often book seats on long train journeys. You get a card with a letter and a number on it. The coaches have letters on them and the seats have numbers.
The card tells you where to sit.

Have you flown in an aeroplane? You are given a boarding card with a letter and a number. This tells you where your seat is.

In a theatre the rows are given letters and the seats have numbers.

This is a ticket for *Phantom of the Opera*.
You would be in row D, seat number 4.

Exercise 1:5

1   The diagram shows the seats in a theatre.
There are six rows, A to F. Each seat is numbered.
Mrs Ellis and her two small children have seats A7, A8 and A9.

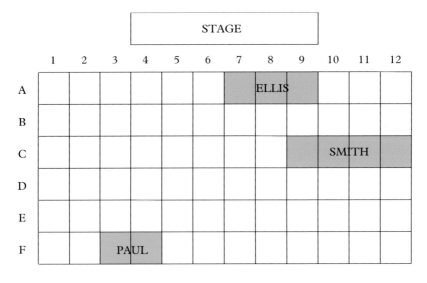

a   Mr Smith has bought four seats for his family.
Write down his seats.
b   Paul has bought two seats in the back row.
Write down his seats.

| **Co-ordinates** | In maths, we need to mark the positions of things at points. |
| **x axis** | We use two numbers. These numbers are called **co-ordinates**. |

y axis

We draw a horizontal line and a vertical line known as **axes**.
The horizontal line is called the **x axis**.
The vertical line is called the **y axis**.

The **x co-ordinate** (across number) is given **first**.
The **y co-ordinate** (up number) is given **second**.

In the diagram, A has co-ordinates (3, 2).
B has co-ordinates (1, 0).

2 List the co-ordinates of the vertices (or corners) of these shapes:
  a the square ABCD
  b the rectangle PQRS
  c the triangle LMN

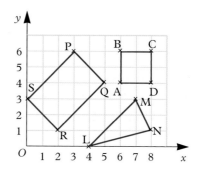

3 Draw a pair of axes like those in Question **2**. Use squared or graph paper. Do not copy the shapes.
  a Plot E (3, 0), F (0, 2), G (3, 4), H (6, 2).
  b Join the points to get a **rhombus**.
  c Draw a line from E to G. This line is called a **diagonal**.
  d Draw the other diagonal FH.
  e Write down the co-ordinates of the point where the diagonals cross.

5 Scatter diagrams

Bill has taken a job as an ice cream man.

When will he sell the most ice cream?

Bill expects it will be on a hot day. On a cooler day he will sell less. Bill will sell very little ice cream on a very cold day. Bill calls that common sense.
In maths it is called **correlation**.

Correlation

A hot day means a lot of ice cream sold. A lot of ice cream sold means a hot day. It works both ways.
There is **correlation** between the two.

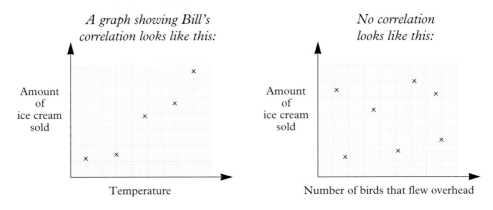

A graph showing Bill's correlation looks like this:

Amount of ice cream sold

Temperature

No correlation looks like this:

Amount of ice cream sold

Number of birds that flew overhead

Scatter diagrams

Graphs like these are called **scatter diagrams**.
The points are scattered about.

Big hands often go with big feet.
Little hands often go with little feet.
That sounds like **correlation**.

Exercise 1:6

1 **a** Collect the hand length (to the nearest half centimetre) and the
shoe size of people in your class.
Write them in a table like the one below.

You do not have to collect from
everybody. About twelve people
should be enough.

length
of
hand

Name											
Shoe size											
Hand length (cm)											

  b Plot your results on graph paper.
Use axes as shown below.

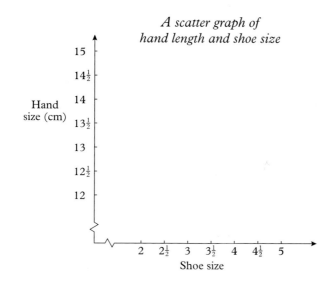

*A scatter graph of
hand length and shoe size*

  c Write down what you notice.

17

2 Some children have been weighed and measured as part of a medical examination.
The results are shown in the table.

Height (cm)	143	131	125	122	132	138	134	136	139	124
Mass (kg)	78	64	55	51	60	76	69	72	68	58

a Draw a pair of axes on graph paper as shown below.
Remember to label the axes and give your graph a title.
b Plot the points.
c Do the results show good correlation?
Explain your answer.

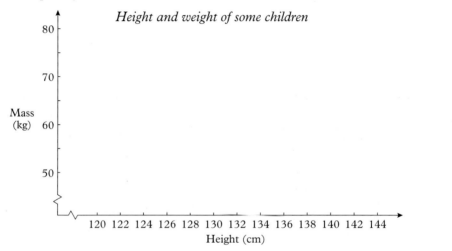

3 The length from beak to tail and the wing span of some birds of prey are shown in the table.
The measurements are given in inches.

Length (in)	25	42	34	28	26	19	21	14	17	14	11	42
Wing span (in)	58	97	85	65	59	44	50	28	40	35	25	100

a Draw a pair of axes on graph paper.
Length goes on the horizontal axis. Use a scale of 2 cm to 10 inches and go from 0 to 50.
Wing span goes on the vertical axis. Use a scale of 1 cm to 10 inches and go from 0 to 110.
Remember to label the axes and give your graph a title.
b Plot the points.
c Do you think there is good correlation? Explain your answer.

1 The school tuck shop has done a survey of Year 7. They want to know the most popular flavours of crisps.
Here are the results.

Flavour	Ready salted	Cheese and onion	Salt and vinegar	Barbecued beef	Prawn cocktail
Number of pupils	25	40	35	45	20

  a Write down the most popular flavour.
  b Work out the number of Year 7 pupils who took part in the survey.
  c Draw a bar-chart of the survey results.
     Number the axis which goes up the page 5, 10, 15, ..., up to 50.

2 **a** Draw a pictogram for the survey results in Question **1**.

    Use ☥ represents 5 pupils.
  b Pictograms can be hard to draw.
    What would be the problem if 38 and not 35 chose salt and vinegar?

3 Sian has asked her class, 7D, what sort of bikes they have.
There are 32 children in the class.

Choice of bike in my class

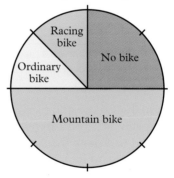

  a Write down the most popular sort of bike.
  b Write down the number of children who do not have a bike.

  c Copy this table and fill in the numbers of pupils.

Bike	Mountain	Racing	Ordinary	None
Number of pupils				

4 Class 7M decided to see how good they were at estimating one minute. They shut their eyes and counted. They opened their eyes on the count of 60 and wrote down what they saw on the clock.
The results, in seconds, are given below.

72 70 52 48 52 48 63 71 63 70
61 62 59 62 50 64 46 65 69 65
58 64 61 48 63 68 67 73 55 51

a Make a tally-table. Count in fives starting with 46–50.
Go up to 71–75.

Time (sec)	Tally	Total
46–50 51–55 56–60		

b Draw a bar-chart of the results.
c How good do you think 7M were at estimating?

5

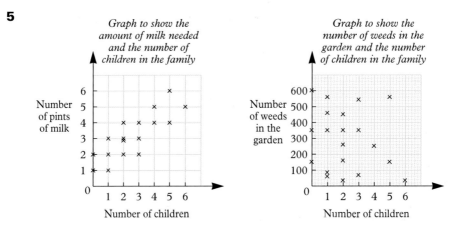

Graph to show the
amount of milk needed
and the number of
children in the family

Graph to show the
number of weeds in the
garden and the number
of children in the family

a Which of these graphs shows correlation?
Explain how you can tell from the patterns of the crosses.
b If you had done the surveys, would you have expected the graphs of
the results to look like this? Explain your answer.

6 Some Year 7 pupils had been studying statistics. They each did a survey
and wrote about their results. They also had a test.
The marks for the survey and the test are shown in the table. All marks
are out of 20.

Test	16	12	18	15	6	14	18	4	16	8	13	16
Survey	14	13	15	15	8	12	19	6	17	5	11	19

a Draw axes on graph paper or squared paper.
Make both axes go from 0 to 20.
Label the axes and give the graph a title.
b Plot the points.
c Is there correlation? Explain your answer.

1 Do a survey to discover the most popular girl's (or boy's) name in Year 7.
It would be helpful if your teacher could provide form lists for this.
Do you need all the Year 7 names on your tally-table?
Would you get the same result if you surveyed Year 11?
Do you think there are fashions in names?

2 A Year 7 class were weighed by the school nurse. She wrote down the
weights to the nearest kilogram.
Iona weighed 37.7 kg and her twin sister Kirsty weighed 37.9 kg. Both
Iona's and Kirsty's weights were put down as 38 kg by the nurse.
  a What is the smallest weight that could be rounded to 38 kg?
  b Here are the results for all the children.
      Decide on suitable groups and construct a tally-table.

38	43	38	35	36	51	30	38	37	43
39	36	34	41	33	42	37	40	49	42
38	31	36	32	34	36	46	45	46	44

  c Draw a bar-chart to illustrate the results.

3 Here are the results of Sarah and Naseem's survey on how children in
their class come to school:

Car	Bus	Train	Bike	Walk
4	12	2	3	9

Sarah has started to draw a pie-chart of the survey results.

The 30 children are represented by 360°

1 child is represented by 360 ÷ 30 = 12°

Means of travel	Number of children	Angle
car	4	12° × 4 = 48°
bus	12	12° × 12 = 144°
train	2	12° × 2 =
bike	3	
walk	9	
Total	30	

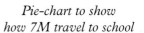

*Pie-chart to show
how 7M travel to school*

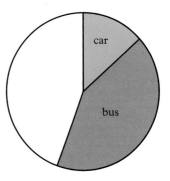

  a Copy the table and fill in the angles.
  b Copy the pie-chart and complete it.

4 Eighteen pupils listed their favourite sports.
The table shows the results.

Athletics	Ball games	Cycling	Swimming
2	9	3	4

a Work out the angles which represent each type of sport.
b Draw a pie-chart.

5 A table for road deaths of young people of school age in a particular
area is shown below. The deaths took place during one year.

Pedestrians	Pedal cyclists	Motor cyclists	Motor cars
23	12	17	8

Draw a pie-chart to illustrate these results.

6 The table gives the top speeds in miles per hour of different cars and
their insurance groups. The higher the insurance group, the more the
car owner has to pay for insurance.

Top speed (m.p.h.)	98	117	87	101	90	92	119	122	102	121	100	124	119	91	120	93	123	93
Insurance group	5	10	3	10	3	6	15	12	8	10	8	13	13	3	11	7	14	5

a Plot a graph of insurance group against top speed.
Make top speed the horizontal axis.
Use a scale of 2 cm to 10 m.p.h. Start at 80 m.p.h.
Make insurance group the vertical axis.
Use a scale of 1 cm to 2 groups.
b Do you think this graph shows good correlation?
Explain your answer and why you think this may be so.

7 Rearrange each of these groups of letters to get a word used in this
chapter.
  a EPI
  b ARB
  c TAAD
  d EVURSY
  e TREASCT
  f PLEAMS
  g MARGIPCOT
  h LYTAL
  i QUYFENCER
  j SACTITTISS
  k ADOORSTINCE
  l NOORLATERIC

- Data is collected in a survey.
  Tally marks are used to record data.
  Data can be represented in diagrams.
  Pictures are used to represent data in a pictogram.
  Pictograms should have a key.
  Bars are used to represent data in a bar-chart.
  All diagrams should have a title.

School	Tally	Total
St Bridget's	|||| |||| ||	12
Mill Junior	|||| |||| |||| |||| |||	23
Canal Road	|||| |||| |||| ||||	19
Church Junior	|||| |||| ||	12
Other	||||		6
	Total	72

- Angles are used to represent data in a pie-chart.

- Some data is tallied in groups.
  Bar-charts for groups are drawn with their *bars touching*.

- Co-ordinates are used to locate a point.
  The *x* co-ordinate is written first, then the *y* co-ordinate.
  Co-ordinates must always be put inside a pair of brackets.
  A is (3, 2)
  B is (1, 0)

- Scatter diagrams compare two sets of data.
  Scatter diagrams can show correlation.

1 The pie-chart shows where a group of pupils spent their family holiday. Ten pupils spent their holiday in the USA.

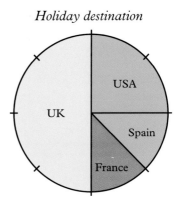

Holiday destination

   a How many spent their holiday in the UK?

   b How many spent their holiday in France?

   c Which was the most popular country for a holiday?

   d How many pupils took part in the survey?

   e Copy the table and fill it in.

Country	UK	USA	Spain	France
Number of pupils				

2 Draw a pictogram of the survey in Question **1**.

Use  to represent four pupils.

3 Pupils' results for a Science exam in school are:

```
20   32   48   67   89   91   13   55
12   74   56   77   25   90   42   61
15   87   41   55   20   16   91   49
48   63   51   38   57   75   64   70
```

   a Make a tally-table. Count in twenties: 1–20, 21–40, etc.

   b Draw a bar-chart from your tally-table.

4 Fourteen pupils got the following results in Maths and English.

Maths	10	40	60	70	58	24	75	44	33	28	66	71	14	33
English	30	50	55	81	48	36	62	29	54	14	55	62	22	46

   a Draw a scatter diagram.
Put Maths on the horizontal axis and English on the vertical axis.
Number both axes 0, 10, 20, …, up to 90.

   b Is there correlation? Explain your answer.

2 Symmetry

QUESTIONS

EXTENSION

SUMMARY

TEST YOURSELF

1 Lines of symmetry

This picture of a house has a line of symmetry. It can be split down the middle so that one half is the reflection of the other.

Line of symmetry	A **line of symmetry** divides a shape into two equal parts. Each part is a reflection of the other. If you fold the shape along this line, each part fits exactly on top of the other.

Exercise 2:1

1 **a** Copy the shapes on the next page on to 1 cm squared paper.
  b Cut them out.
  c Fold them along the dotted line to check that this is a line of symmetry.
  d Stick them into your exercise book like this:

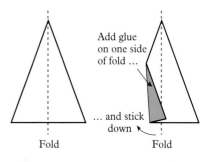

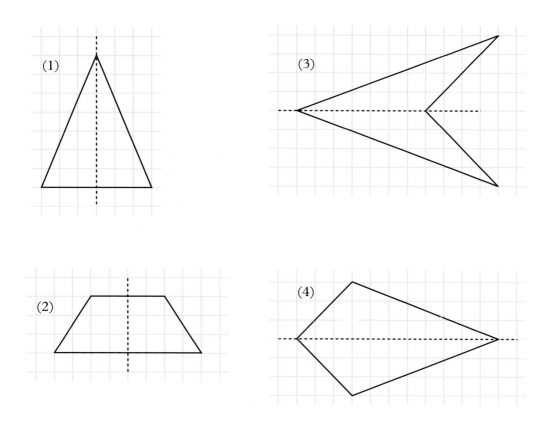

(1)

(2)

(3)

(4)

Some shapes have more than one line of symmetry. We usually show all the lines on one diagram.

A square has 4 lines of symmetry.

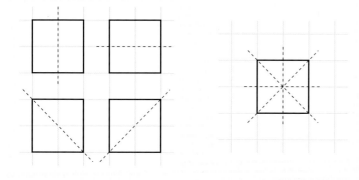

Exercise 2:2

1　**a**　Copy these shapes on to squared paper.
　　b　Mark on **all** the lines of symmetry using dotted lines.
　　c　Cut out each shape.
　　d　Fold the shapes along your broken lines to check that they are lines of symmetry.

(1)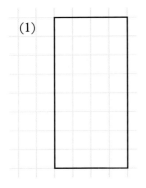

(4)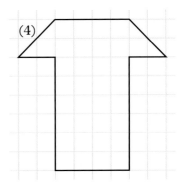

(2)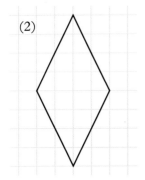

(5)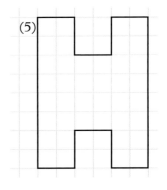

(3)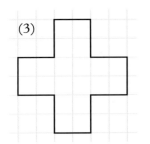

(6)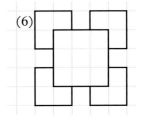

You can only see half of this shape:

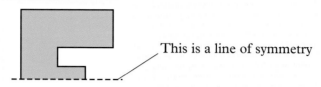

This is a line of symmetry

We can use the line of symmetry to complete the shape.
It now looks like this:

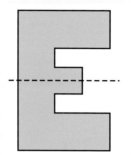

Place a mirror along the line of symmetry.
The reflection completes the shape.

Mirror line   A line of symmetry is often called a **mirror line**.

Exercise 2:3

1 Copy this diagram *and* diagrams **b**–**g** on the next page on to squared paper.
Draw their reflections in the line of symmetry.

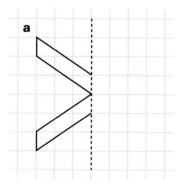

b

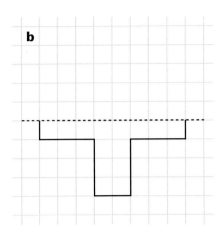

e

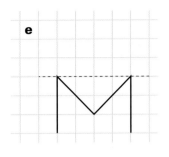

c

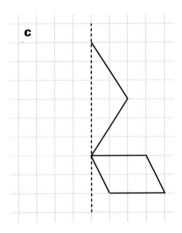

f

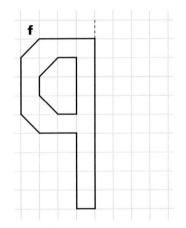

d

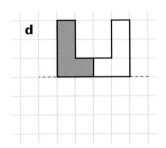

g

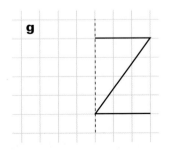

2 The points

A (2, 0) B (2, 4) C (4, 8) D (1, 7) and E (5, 6) are shown on the grid.

a Copy the grid on to squared paper.
Draw the mirror line.

b Mark the reflection of each point in the mirror line.

c Write down the co-ordinates of the reflections.

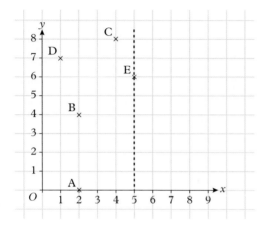

3 **a** Copy the grid.
Draw in the mirror line on your grid.
Plot the points
P (1, 5) Q (3, 2) R (6, 2) S (8, 5)

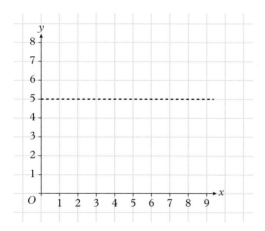

b Mark the reflection of each point in the mirror line.

c Join P → Q → R → S with straight lines.

d Join the reflections in the same way.

e The new shape has another line of symmetry.
Mark it on your diagram.

2 Symmetry in everyday life

Here are some letters of the alphabet. We have marked their lines of symmetry.

The letter   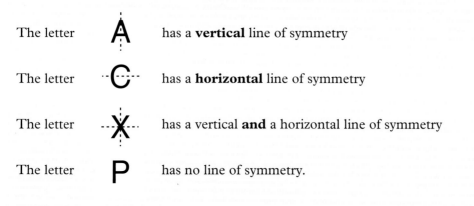   A   has a **vertical** line of symmetry

The letter   C   has a **horizontal** line of symmetry

The letter   X   has a vertical **and** a horizontal line of symmetry

The letter   P   has no line of symmetry.

Exercise 2:4

1 Write down the capital letters of the alphabet.
Mark the lines of symmetry on each letter.

Write down the letters that have:
a a vertical line of symmetry.
b a horizontal line of symmetry.
c a vertical **and** a horizontal line of symmetry.

2 This word has a line of symmetry

MUM

Write down two other words that have a line of symmetry.

3 For each of the following:
  a Plot the points on a grid.
  Join them as you go.
  b Mark on all the lines of symmetry.

(1) (2, 7) (3, 5) (4, 3) (5, 5) (6, 7)
(2) (2, 1) (3, 3) (4, 5) (5, 3) (6, 5) (7, 3) (8, 1)
(3) (3, 7) (3, 1) (5, 1) (6, 2) (7, 4), (6, 6), (5, 7) (3, 7)

On black and white television a pattern looked like this:

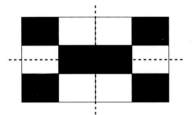

It has two lines of symmetry.

On colour television the same pattern looked like this:

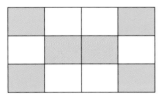

In colour the pattern has no lines of symmetry.

Colour can affect symmetry.

Exercise 2:5

1 Look at these flags.
Copy and complete the table.
Write 'yes' or 'no' in each box.

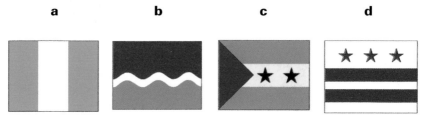

	a	**b**	**c**	**d**

Nigeria Seychelles São Tomé-Principe District of Columbia

Flag	Horizontal line of symmetry	Vertical line of symmetry
a		
b		
c		
d		

2 How many lines of symmetry do these road signs have?
Write down your answers.

a   **b**   **c**   **d**

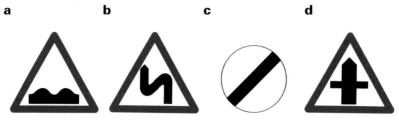

3 These symbols are called logos. You see them on cars.
They have line symmetry.

a   **b**   **c**   **d**   **e**

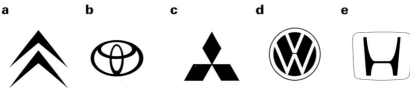

Sketch the logos and mark on the lines of symmetry.

4 Words are sometimes shown by symbols.
Write down the numbers of lines of symmetry for each symbol.

a   **c**   **e**

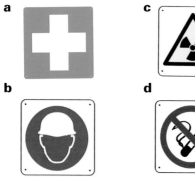

b   **d**

5 **a** Copy these four tiles on to squared paper.

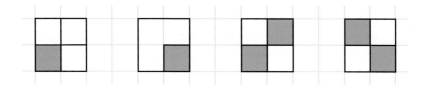

b Cut out the tiles.
c Put the tiles together to make a larger tile.
For example:

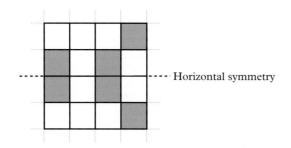   Horizontal symmetry

d Copy your new tile on to squared paper.
Mark the lines of symmetry.
e Make five more patterns that have vertical symmetry or horizontal symmetry.
Copy each of your patterns on to squared paper.
Draw in the lines of symmetry.
f Make two patterns that have a diagonal line of symmetry.

6 The following diagrams show chemical bonding.
Copy the diagrams and draw in any lines of symmetry.

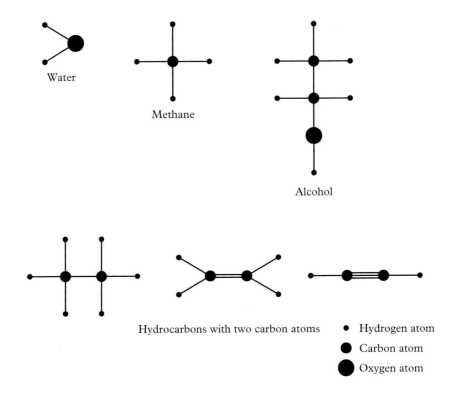

Water

Methane

Alcohol

Hydrocarbons with two carbon atoms

• Hydrogen atom

● Carbon atom

⬤ Oxygen atom

7 The outlines of leaves can show symmetry.
Bring in to school a collection of different leaves.
Which leaves have outlines with lines of symmetry?

Oak

Ash

Horse chestnut

3 Turnings

'Tighten the screw another half turn'

'Turn right at the crossroads'

'The wind changed, turning from North to North-East'

| **Turn** | We use the word **turn** to describe something that moves round in a circle. |

Start   Start   Start

1 full turn   Half turn   Quarter turn

| **Clockwise Anti-clockwise** | We use **clockwise** and **anti-clockwise** to say which way to turn. |

Clockwise   Anti-clockwise

Exercise 2:6

The clock shows 3 o'clock.

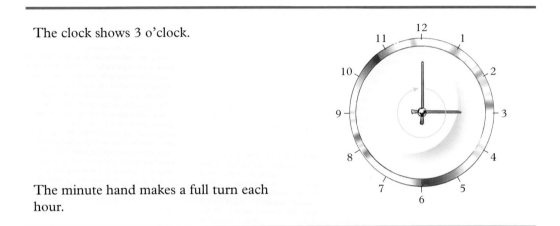

The minute hand makes a full turn each hour.

1 What part of a turn does the minute hand make in:
    a 30 minutes?
    b 45 minutes?
    c 15 minutes?
    d 20 minutes?

2 What time passes when the minute hand makes:
    a a quarter turn?
    b a half turn?
    c four full turns?

3 What time passes when the hour hand makes:
    a a quarter turn?
    b a half turn?
    c four full turns?

4 What size of turn does the hour hand make in:
    a 3 hours?
    b 6 hours?
    c 4 hours?
    d 1 hour?

Points of the compass

The diagram shows the **points of the compass**.

If you face East and make a half turn clockwise, you end up facing West.

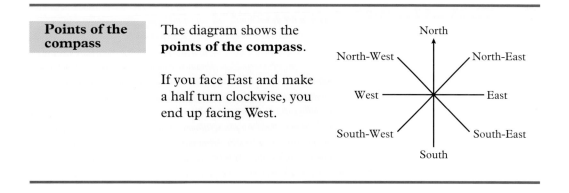

5 Copy and complete this table.

Start facing	Turn	Direction	End up facing
N	$\frac{1}{4}$	clockwise	
N	$\frac{3}{4}$	clockwise	
E	$\frac{1}{4}$	clockwise	
S	$\frac{3}{4}$	anti-clockwise	
E	$\frac{1}{8}$	anti-clockwise	
SW	$\frac{3}{8}$	anti-clockwise	
E	$\frac{5}{8}$	clockwise	
SE	$1\frac{1}{8}$	clockwise	
	$\frac{3}{8}$	clockwise	W
	$\frac{5}{8}$	anti-clockwise	NE

4 Rotational symmetry

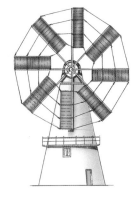

Kelly visited a windmill.
She saw that one sail of the windmill pointed down the line of the windows.

This sail was back at its starting position after 8 equal part-turns.

The diagram shows what Kelly saw.
The green sail is the one that she watched.

Start

1 part-turn

2 part-turns

3 part-turns

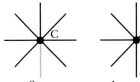

4 part-turns

5 part-turns

6 part-turns

7 part-turns

8 part-turns

Start again

The windmill has **rotational symmetry of order 8 about its centre** (marked C).

Rotational symmetry	A shape has **rotational symmetry** if it fits on top of itself more than once as it makes a complete turn.
Order of rotational symmetry	The **order of rotational symmetry** is the number of times that the shape fits on top of itself. This must be 2 or more. Shapes that only fit on themselves once have no rotational symmetry.
Centre of rotation	The **centre of rotation** is the point about which the shape turns.

Exercise 2:7

1 For each shape:
   a Trace the shape.
   b Use your tracing to see how many times the shape fits on top of itself in one complete turn.
   c Write down the order of rotational symmetry.
   If a shape has no rotational symmetry, write 'none'.

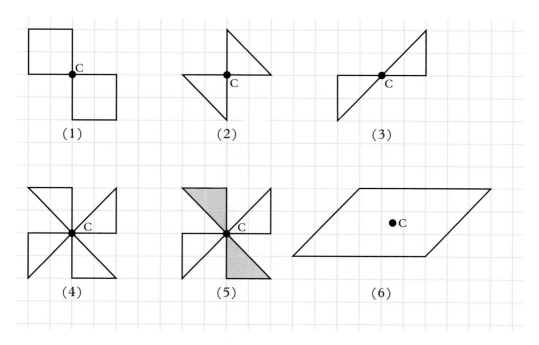

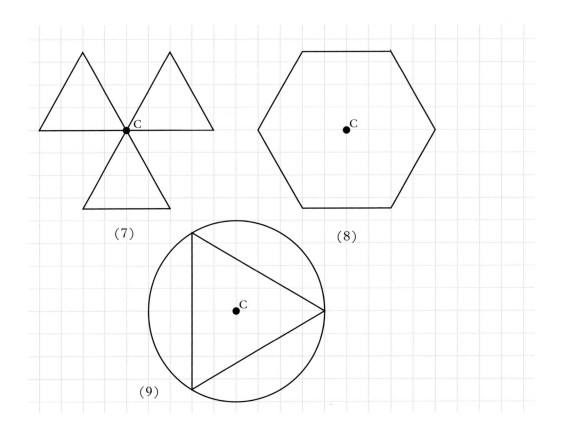

(7)

(8)

(9)

2 Rachel saw that the hubcaps of cars have rotational symmetry.
Write down the order of rotational symmetry of each of these hubcaps.
Ignore the maker's logo in parts **c**, **d** and **e**.

a

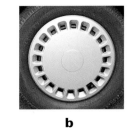

b

c

d

e

3 Write down the order of rotational symmetry of these road signs.
If a sign has no rotational symmetry, write 'none'.

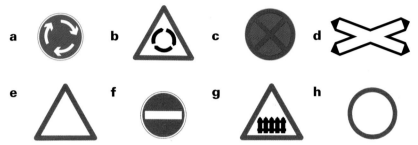

4 These are photographs of snowflakes.
No two snowflakes are the same.
Write down the order of rotational symmetry of each snowflake.

5 Diatoms are tiny cells with beautiful ornate outer shells.

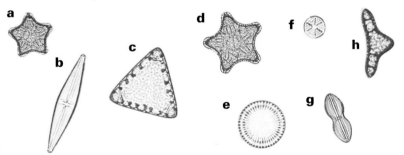

Write down the order of rotational symmetry of each diatom.

6 Obaid cut two oranges in half.
He made the cut in two different
ways.
He found two patterns.

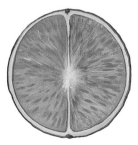

Describe the symmetry of each pattern.

1 Copy these shapes on to squared paper.
Mark on **all** the lines of symmetry.

a   **b**

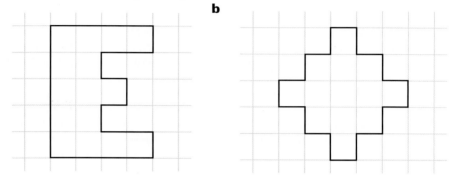

2 Copy these diagrams on to squared paper.
Draw their reflections in the lines of symmetry.

a   **b**

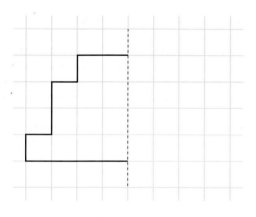
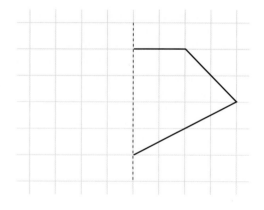

c

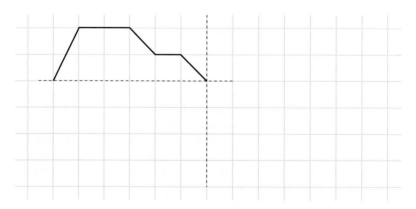

3 M J A E T V P D
Write down the letters in the list that have:
a a vertical line of symmetry.
b a horizontal line of symmetry.

4 Write down the number of lines of symmetry for each
information symbol.

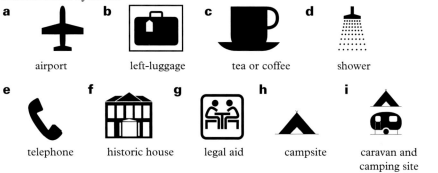

a airport **b** left-luggage **c** tea or coffee **d** shower

e telephone **f** historic house **g** legal aid **h** campsite **i** caravan and camping site

5 These are old-fashioned science symbols.

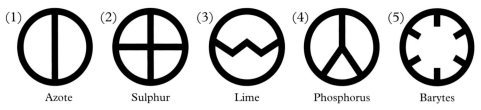

(1) Azote (2) Sulphur (3) Lime (4) Phosphorus (5) Barytes

a Write down the number of lines of symmetry for each symbol.
b Write down the order of rotational symmetry for each symbol.
   If a symbol has no rotational symmetry, write 'none'.

6 a Copy each of these shapes on to squared paper.
   Leave plenty of space between them.
b Complete your shapes so that they have rotational symmetry of
   order 4 about C.

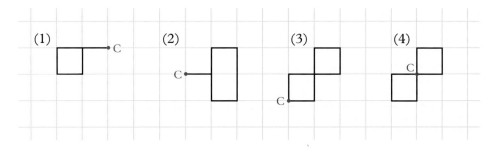

(1)   (2)   (3)   (4)

1 Copy these diagrams on to squared paper.
Draw their reflections in the line of symmetry.

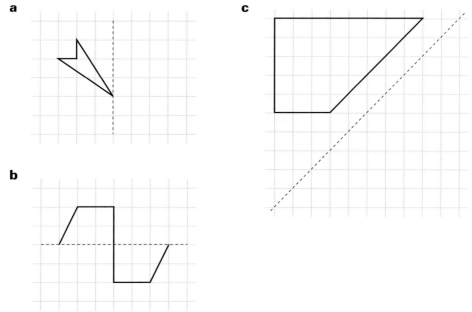

a

c

b

2 Write down the number of lines of symmetry for each symbol.

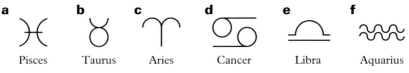

a	**b**	**c**	**d**	**e**	**f**
Pisces	Taurus	Aries	Cancer	Libra	Aquarius

3 **a** Copy each of these diagrams on to triangular dotty paper.
Leave plenty of space between them.

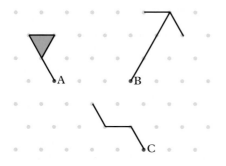

b Use the centre of rotation marked to complete each shape so that it
has rotational symmetry of order 3.
Tracing paper may help.

4 a Copy this grid on to squared paper.
Draw in the lines of symmetry.
Letter the points as shown.

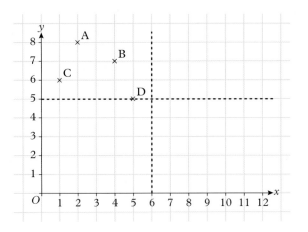

b Reflect the points in the vertical line of symmetry.
Mark them on your diagram and label them A_1, B_1, C_1, D_1.
c Reflect the points A, B, C, D in the horizontal line of symmetry.
Mark them on your diagram and label them A_2, B_2, C_2, D_2.
d If you reflected $A_1B_1C_1D_1$ in the horizontal line and $A_2B_2C_2D_2$ in the vertical line, would the reflections be in the same place?

5 a Copy this grid on to squared paper.
Draw in the mirror line.
Letter the points as shown.
b Reflect points P, Q, R, S, T in the line of symmetry.
Mark them on your diagram and label them P_1, Q_1, R_1, S_1, T_1.

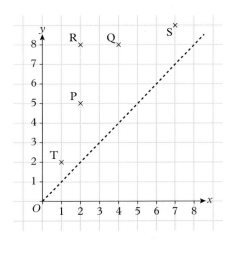

c List the two sets of co-ordinates in your book like this:

P (2, 5) P_1 (   )
Q (4, 8) Q_1 (   )
R (   ) R_1 (   )
S (   ) S_1 (   )
T (   ) T_1 (   )

d Describe how the points have changed when they have been reflected.

- **Line of symmetry**

  A line of symmetry divides a shape into two equal parts. Each part is a reflection of the other.

  If you fold the shape along this line, each part fits exactly on top of the other.

- Some shapes have more than one line of symmetry.
  A square has 4.

  We usually show all the lines on one diagram:

- **Turn**

  We use the word '**turn**' to describe something that moves round in a circle.

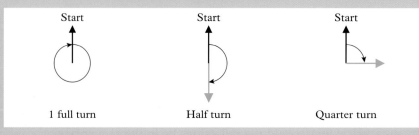

| Start | Start | Start |
| 1 full turn | Half turn | Quarter turn |

  We use clockwise and anti-clockwise to say which way to turn.

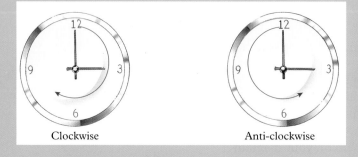

Clockwise   Anti-clockwise

- A shape has **rotational symmetry** if it fits on top of itself more than once as it makes a complete turn.

  The **order of rotational symmetry** is the number of times that the shape fits on top of itself. This must be 2 or more.

  Shapes that only fit on themselves once have no rotational symmetry.

  The **centre of rotation** is the point about which the shape turns.

1 Copy these shapes on to squared paper.
Mark on **all** the lines of symmetry.

a   **b**

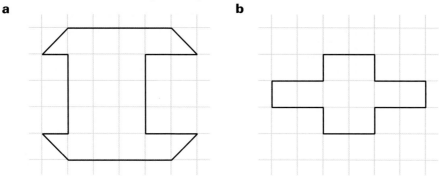

2 Copy these diagrams on to squared paper.
Draw their reflections in the line of symmetry.

a   **b**

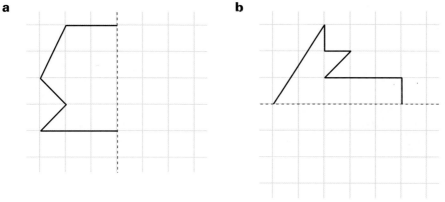

3 L W J S U D
Write down the letters in this list that have:
a a vertical line of symmetry.
b a horizontal line of symmetry.
c no line of symmetry.

4 Write down the number of lines of symmetry for each symbol.

a   **b**   **c**   **d**   **e**

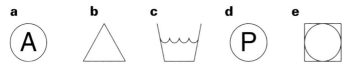

5 Write down the order of rotational symmetry of each of these shapes.
If a shape has no rotational symmetry, write 'none".

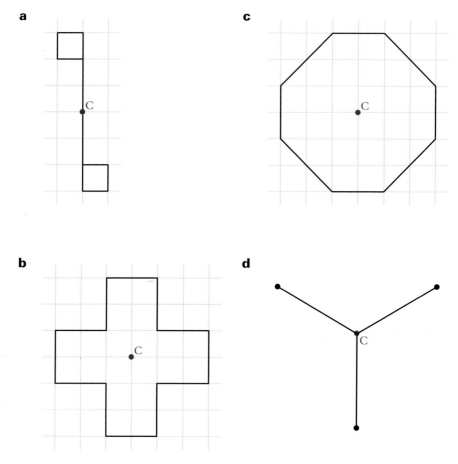

a

c

b

d

6 Copy this diagram on to squared paper.
Complete it so that it has rotational symmetry order 4 about C.

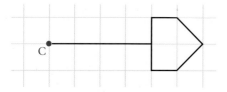

3 Number patterns

This is a Chinese version of the number pattern known as 'Pascal's Triangle'. It appears in a manuscript dated 1303; Blaise Pascal was born in 1623.

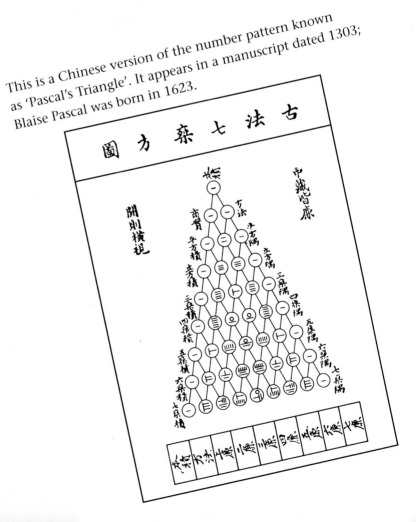

1   Factors, multiples and primes

Sometimes we cannot
see any order or pattern.

Sometimes we can
see order.

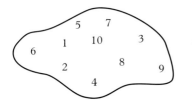

$\Rightarrow$

1 2 3 4 5 6 7 8 9 10

Counting numbers	The **counting numbers** are: 1 2 3 4 5 6 7 8 9 10 11 12 ...
Odd numbers	The red numbers have a pattern. They start the **odd numbers**.
Even numbers	The blue numbers also have a pattern. They start the **even numbers**. The rule is 'add 2' to get the next number.

Exercise 3:1

1 **a** List the even numbers from 20 to 50.
   b Copy and complete:
      An even number always ends in 0, 2, ..., ..., ...

2 **a** List the odd numbers from 51 to 81.
   b Copy and complete:
      An odd number always ends in ..., 3, ..., ..., 9

Example   Write down the rule for each of these patterns.
             Find the next two terms.
             a 1, 4, 7, 10, 13, ...
             b 22, 20, 18, 16, 14, ...

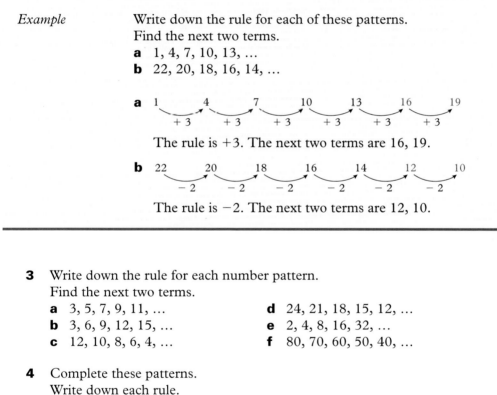

             The rule is +3. The next two terms are 16, 19.

             The rule is −2. The next two terms are 12, 10.

---

3 Write down the rule for each number pattern.
   Find the next two terms.
   a 3, 5, 7, 9, 11, ...   **d** 24, 21, 18, 15, 12, ...
   b 3, 6, 9, 12, 15, ...   **e** 2, 4, 8, 16, 32, ...
   c 12, 10, 8, 6, 4, ...   **f** 80, 70, 60, 50, 40, ...

4 Complete these patterns.
   Write down each rule.
   a 1, 7, 13, ..., 25, ...   **d** 128, 64, ..., 16, 8
   b 3, 9, 27, ..., ...   **e** 243, 81, ..., 9, 3
   c 5, ..., 15, ..., 25   **f** 42, ..., 28, 21, 14

5 Each pattern has a rule and a starting number.
   Write down the next four numbers in each pattern.
   a +5, start with 7   **d** ×3, start with 1
   b −3, start with 21   **e** ÷2, start with 48
   c ×10, start with 2   **f** ÷10, start with 100 000

6 Joel added two odd numbers
$$3 + 7 = 10$$
He tried two more
$$5 + 3 = 8$$
and two more
$$9 + 9 = 18$$

Joel decided that 'an **odd** number added to another **odd** number is an **even** number'.

Use different odd numbers to check Joel's idea.
Choose odd and even numbers to investigate these.
Write down your results in words.

a	even + even	**d**	odd − odd	**g**	even × even
b	even + odd	**e**	odd × odd	● **h**	odd ÷ odd
c	even − odd	**f**	odd × even	● **i**	odd ÷ even

If we multiply each counting number by 2 we get

$$1 \times 2 \quad 2 \times 2 \quad 3 \times 2 \quad 4 \times 2 \quad 5 \times 2 \quad 6 \times 2 \quad 7 \times 2$$

or   2   4   6   8   10   12   14

Multiples

The **multiples** of 2 are 2, 4, 6, 8, 10, 12, 14, …

The multiples of 3 are 3, 6, 9, 12, 15, …
The multiples of 4 are 4, 8, 12, 16, 20, …

All numbers are multiples of 1.

Exercise 3:2

1 List the first five multiples of

a 5	**b** 6	**c** 7	**d** 8	**e** 9	**f** 12

2 Copy these lists of multiples.
Fill in the missing numbers.

a 3, 6, 9, …, 15, 18, …

b 4, 8, …, 16, 20, …, 28

c 15, 20, …, 30, 35, …, 45

d 21, …, 35, 42, 49, …, 63

e 12, …, 36, 48, …

f 18, …, …, 45, 54, 63

3 The Mayans were an ancient South American people. These are their counting numbers or numerals.

Our counting numbers	Mayan numerals
1	•
2	• •
3	
4	• • • •
5	———
6	——•———
7	
8	• • • ———

Copy the table.
Draw the Mayan numerals for the counting numbers 3 and 7.

Factor

A number that divides exactly into **another number** is called a **factor** of that number.

Examples

1 $10 = 1 \times 10$
$10 = 2 \times 5$
1, 2, 5 and 10 are the factors of 10.

2 $3 = 1 \times 3$
1 and 3 are the factors of 3.

Exercise 3:3

1 List the factors of:
   a 12   **b** 20   **c** 7   **d** 35   **e** 29

2 **a** List the factors of 18.
   b List the factors of 24.
   c Write down the factors which appear in both lists.
   d Write down the largest number in **c**.

Highest Common Factor

The largest factor shared by two numbers is their **Highest Common Factor**.

The highest common factor of 18 and 24 is 6.

---

3 **a** List the factors of 36.
   b List the factors of 45.
   c Write down the highest common factor of 36 and 45.

4 **a** List the factors of 32 and 48.
   b Write down the highest common factor of 32 and 48.

Exercise 3:4

▼ 1 You will need a *new copy* of the
1–100 number square for *each*
part of this question.

1	2	3	4	5	6	7	8	9	10
11	12	13	14	15	16	17	18	19	20
21	22	23	24	25	26	27	28	29	30
31	32	33	34	35	36	37	38	39	40
41	42	43	44	45	46	47	48	49	50
51	52	53	54	55	56	57	58	59	60
61	62	63	64	65	66	67	68	69	70
71	72	73	74	75	76	77	78	79	80
81	82	83	84	85	86	87	88	89	90
91	92	93	94	95	96	97	98	99	100

a Shade all the squares that
contain multiples of 2.

b Shade all the squares that
contain multiples of 3.

c Shade all the squares that
contain multiples of 5.

d Shade all the squares that
contain multiples of 7.

e On another copy of the 1–100
number square:
(1) Cross out number 1.
(2) Circle the numbers 2, 3, 5 and 7
Do not cross them out.
Cross out all the other numbers you shaded in parts **a, b, c** and **d**.
(3) 2, 3, 5 and 7 have already been circled.
Circle all the other numbers that are not crossed out.
(4) Make a list of all your circled numbers.
They are called **prime numbers**.

Prime numbers **Prime numbers** have only two factors, themselves and 1.
Examples of prime numbers are 2, 3, 11, 19.
1 is not a prime number.

---

2 There is only one even number that is prime.
Write down this number.

3 Use the list of prime numbers that you made at the end of Question **1**.
a The number 1 is not prime, but many prime numbers end in 1.
List the prime numbers up to 100 ending in 1.
b 3 is prime and many prime numbers end in 3.
List the prime numbers up to 100 ending in 3.
c 5 is prime.
Explain why no other prime numbers end in 5.

d 7 is prime.
List the prime numbers up to 100 ending in 7.
e (1) Explain why 9 is not prime.
(2) List the prime numbers up to 100 ending in 9.

• **4** Find all the prime numbers between 100 and 110.

Prime factors

The factors of 12 are 1, 2, 3, 4, 6, 12.
The factors 2 and 3 are also prime numbers.
They are **prime factors**.

Example

Find the prime factors of 28.

The factors of 28 are
1, 2, 4, 7, 14, 28
The prime factors of 28 are 2 and 7.

Exercise 3:5

1 Find the prime factors of:
a 20   **b** 33   **c** 42   **d** 39

A number can be written as the product of its prime factors.

Example   Write 24 as a product of prime factors.

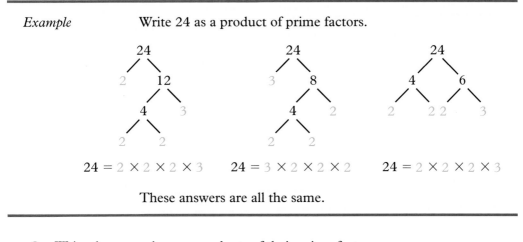

$24 = 2 \times 2 \times 2 \times 3$ $24 = 3 \times 2 \times 2 \times 2$ $24 = 2 \times 2 \times 2 \times 3$

These answers are all the same.

---

2 Write these numbers as products of their prime factors:
a 21   **c** 36   **e** 48
b 28   **d** 32   **f** 68

2   Patterns in number

Some number patterns have special names because of the shapes that they make.

Exercise 3:6

1   Copy the square patterns.
Complete the multiplications.

$1 \times 1 = \ldots$ $2 \times 2 = \ldots$ $3 \times 3 = \ldots$

2   Draw the next two patterns.
Write down their multiplications.

Square numbers   1, 4, 9, 16, 25, ... are called **square numbers**.

---

3   Write down the next two square numbers after 25.

4   a   Copy and complete:

1 $= 1$
$1 + 3$ $= 4$
$1 + 3 + 5$ $= \ldots$
$1 + 3 + 5 + 7$ $= \ldots$
$1 + 3 + 5 + 7 + \ldots = \ldots$

b   What special numbers are your answers?

• **5**   **a**   What is the fourth square number?
  b   What is the tenth square number?

Exercise 3:7

1

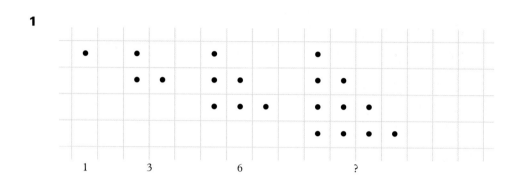

1   3   6   ?

Copy these triangle patterns on to squared paper.

2   Draw the next two patterns.
Count the dots.

Triangle numbers   1, 3, 6, 10, 15, 21, ... are called **triangle numbers**.

---

3   **a**   Copy and complete:

1   = 1
1 + 2   = 3
1 + 2 + 3   = 6
1 + 2 + 3 + 4   = ...
1 + 2 + 3 + 4 + 5   = ...
1 + 2 + 3 + 4 + 5 + ... = ...

  b   What special numbers are your answers?

4   **a**   What is the fourth triangle number?
  b   What is the tenth triangle number?

5

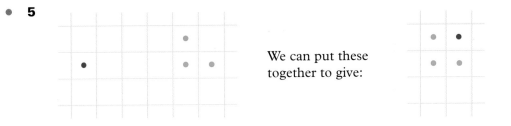

We can put these together to give:

The sum of the first two triangle numbers gives the second square number $1 + 3 = 4$

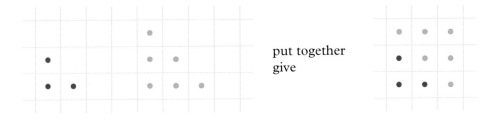

put together give

The sum of the second and third triangle numbers gives the third square number $3 + 6 = 9$

a Which two triangle numbers will give the fifth square number? Draw a diagram to illustrate your answer.

b Which two triangle numbers will give
   (1) the seventh square number?
   (2) the tenth square number?
   (3) the twelfth square number?

6 Find a quick way of adding the numbers 1 to 40 without using a calculator.

Patterns from tables

1 Write out the two times table:

$$1 \times 2 = 2 \qquad 6 \times 2 = 12$$
$$2 \times 2 = 4 \qquad 7 \times 2 = 14$$
$$3 \times 2 = 6 \qquad 8 \times 2 = 16$$
$$4 \times 2 = 8 \qquad 9 \times 2 = 18$$
$$5 \times 2 = 10 \qquad 10 \times 2 = 20$$

2 Some of the answers have two digits.
Add these digits together to give a single digit.
This gives the red numbers.

2	2
4	4
6	6
8	8
10	$1 + 0 = 1$
12	$1 + 2 = 3$
14	$1 + 4 = 5$
16	$1 + 6 = 7$
18	$1 + 8 = 9$
20	$2 + 0 = 2$

W 3 Mark 9 equally spaced points around a circle.
Number them 1 to 9.

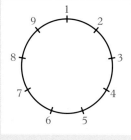

4 Join the points in the order of the red numbers.
Always use a ruler.

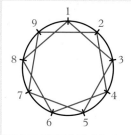

5 Investigate patterns made by other tables.
Are all the patterns different?
Can you group the patterns in some way?
Can you predict which pattern will come from each table?
What will you do with numbers like $7 \times 4 = 28$ where $2 + 8 = 10$?

6 Write a short report on what you have found out.
Explain any patterns that you have found.
Include your diagrams. You could colour them.
You could make a display for your classroom.

3 Rules and robots

Imagine that we have a robot to
help us with our patterns.

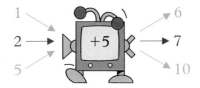

This robot adds 5 to any number.

Example   What answers will this robot give?

We only need to draw the robot's screen.

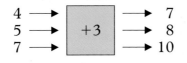

Exercise 3:8

Draw the screen for each robot.
Write down each robot's answers.

1 1 → +2 →
3 →   →
5 →   →

5 2 → ×2 →
3 →   →
4 →   →

2 2 → +7 →
4 →   →
5 →   →

6 2 → ×5 →
3 →   →
5 →   →

3 3 → +10 →
4 →   →
8 →   →

7 2 → ×10 →
5 →   →
8 →   →

4 3 → −1 →
5 →   →
10 →   →

8 4 → −3 →
6 →   →
9 →   →

One day, the robot's screen does not work.
What should the robot's screen show?

5 → Normal service will → 10
10 → be resumed as soon → 15
25 → as possible → 30

The robot's screen should show +5.

Exercise 3:9

Write down the rule that belongs on each screen.

1 3 → → 14
17 → → 28
19 → ? → 30
32 → → 43
40 → → 51

2 13 → → 8
18 → → 13
21 → ? → 16
28 → → 23
32 → → 27

3

6 →		→ 18
8 →	?	→ 24
11 →		→ 33
14 →		→ 42
17 →		→ 51

5

18 →		→ 9
24 →	?	→ 12
30 →		→ 15
60 →		→ 30
100 →		→ 50

4

100 →		→ 1
200 →	?	→ 2
300 →		→ 3
500 →		→ 5
700 →		→ 7

6

5 →		→ 5
11 →	?	→ 11
7 →		→ 7
101 →		→ 101
230 →		→ 230

We can use two robots.

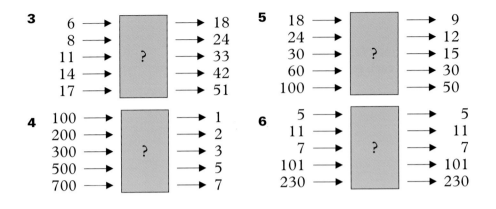

4 →		12 →		→ 13
7 →		21 →		→ 22
8 →	×3	24 →	+1	→ 25
9 →		27 →		→ 28
12 →		36 →		→ 37

Exercise 3:10

Copy these diagrams.
Write down the robots' answers.

1

1 →		?→		→ ?
3 →	×2	?→	+1	→ ?
5 →		?→		→ ?

2

3 →		→		→
7 →	×3	→	−1	→
8 →		→		→

3

2 →		→		→
9 →	×2	→	−1	→
12 →		→		→

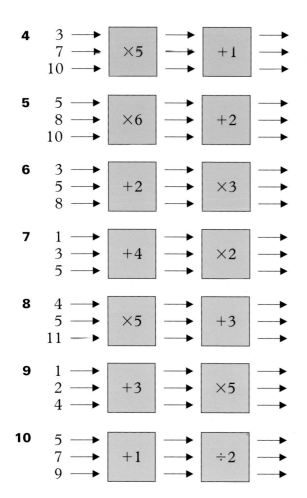

4 3 → ×5 → +1 →
7 →
10 →

5 5 → ×6 → +2 →
8 →
10 →

6 3 → +2 → ×3 →
5 →
8 →

7 1 → +4 → ×2 →
3 →
5 →

8 4 → ×5 → +3 →
5 →
11 →

9 1 → +3 → ×5 →
2 →
4 →

10 5 → +1 → ÷2 →
7 →
9 →

● **11** What should be written on these robot screens?

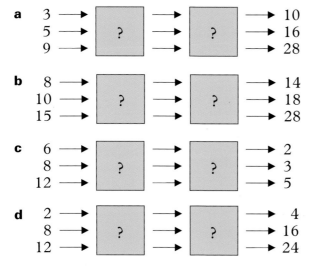

a 3 → ? → ? → 10
5 → 16
9 → 28

b 8 → ? → ? → 14
10 → 18
15 → 28

c 6 → ? → ? → 2
8 → 3
12 → 5

d 2 → ? → ? → 4
8 → 16
12 → 24

1   Write down the rule for each number pattern.
    a 15, 30, 60, 120, 240
    b 24, 32, 40, 48, 56
    c 45, 38, 31, 24, 17
    d 96, 48, 24, 12, 6

2   Copy and complete these patterns.
    Write down each rule.
    a 7, 14, 21, ..., 35, ..., ...
    b 64, 32, ..., ..., 4, ...
    c 1, 4, ..., 64, 256
    d 85, 73, ..., 49, ..., 25

3   Copy the diagrams.
    Write down each robot's answers.

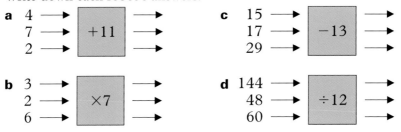

4   Copy the diagrams.
    Write down the robots' answers.

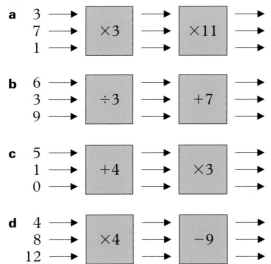

5 Look at these numbers:

      1 6 11 16 21 26 31 36

  a Write down the rule for this number pattern.

  b List the prime numbers in this pattern.

  c List the triangle numbers in this pattern.

  d List the square numbers.

  e List the multiples of 6.

  f Write down the number that has 7 as a factor.

6 A number that reads the same backwards as it does forwards is called a **palindromic** number.

323 is a palindromic number.

      33, 17, 88, 11, 29, 13, 22, 202

From this list of numbers write down:

  a the palindromic numbers.

  b the prime numbers.

  c the smallest palindromic prime number.

  d 1991 was a palindromic year.

    By writing down the years that follow 1991, find the next palindromic year.

7

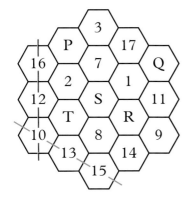

This hexagon puzzle contains the numbers 1 to 19.

Each number is used only once. Some of the numbers are missing.

  a Find the sum of the numbers in the red column.

  b Find the sum of the numbers in the blue diagonal.

The sum of the numbers in each column and diagonal is the same.

  c Write down the numbers that go in the spaces P, Q, R, S and T.

1 There is a rule which gives the number of diagonals from one vertex in a polygon.

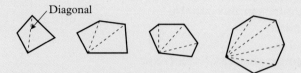

Diagonal

   a Copy and complete:

Number of sides	4	5	6	7	8	9
Number of diagonals						

   b Write down the number of diagonals from one vertex of a 20-sided polygon.
   c Write down the rule linking the number of sides to the number of diagonals from one vertex.
   d Investigate the rule linking the number of sides to the total number of diagonals.

2 **a** The factors of 6 are 1, 2, 3, 6.

   Add the factors 1, 2, 3 (but not the 6).
   What do you notice about your answer?
   Numbers like this are known as **perfect numbers**.

   b Copy the table below.
   Write down all the numbers from 2 to 30 and their factors.

   Find the sum of each set of factors, leaving out the number itself.
   Decide whether each number is a perfect number.

Number	Factors	Sum of factors (not including the number itself)	Is the number perfect?
2	1, 2̸	1	
3	1, 3̸	1	
4	1, 2, 4̸	3	

   c List the perfect numbers you have found.
   d What can you say about the numbers where 1 occurs in the third column?

- 1 2 3 4 5 6 7 8 9 10 11 12 ...
  The red numbers are **odd**.
  The blue numbers are **even**.
  Odd numbers always end in 1, 3, 5, 7 or 9.
  Even numbers always end in 0, 2, 4, 6 or 8.

- The **multiples** of 2 are 2, 4, 6, 8, 10, 12, ...
  The multiples of 3 are 3, 6, 9, 12, 15, ...
  The multiples of 4 are 4, 8, 12, 16, 20, ...
  All numbers are multiples of 1.

- Numbers which divide exactly into another number are called **factors**.
  1, 2, 5 and 10 are the factors of 10.
  The largest factor shared by two numbers is their **Highest Common Factor**.
  The highest common factor of 18 and 24 is 6.

- Prime numbers have only two factors, themselves and 1.
  Examples of prime numbers are 2, 3, 11, 19.
  1 is not a prime number.

  The factors of 12 are 1, 2, 3, 4, 6, 12.
  2 and 3 are **prime factors** of 12.
  24 as a **product** of **prime factors** is $2 \times 2 \times 2 \times 3$

- 1, 4, 9, 16, 25, ...
  are called **square numbers**.

- 1, 3, 6, 10, 15, ...
  are called **triangle numbers**.

- This robot adds 5 to any number

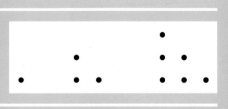

1   Copy and complete these number patterns.
    Write down the rule for each one.
    a   21, 28, ..., 42, ..., 56,
    b   100, ..., 80, ..., 60, 50
    c   3, 9, ..., 81, ...

2   List the first five multiples of 6.

3   **a**   List the factors of 30 and 42.
    b   Write down the highest common factor of 30 and 42.

4   Look at these numbers:
        1, 5, 9, 13, 17, 21, 25
    a   Write down the rule for this number pattern.
    b   List the prime numbers in this pattern.
    c   List the triangle numbers.
    d   List the square numbers.

5   Write down the prime factors of
    a   18   **b**   60

6   Express 54 as a product of its prime factors.

7   Write down the rule that belongs on this screen.

    2 ⟶ [?] ⟶ 10
    4 ⟶   ⟶ 20
    5 ⟶   ⟶ 25

8   Copy the diagram.
    Write down the robots' answers.

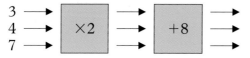

    3 ⟶
    4 ⟶ [×2] ⟶ [+8] ⟶
    7 ⟶

4 Arithmetic and the calculator

QUESTIONS

EXTENSION

SUMMARY

TEST YOURSELF

John Napier was born in Scotland in 1550. One of the calculating methods he invented is known as Napier's Bones or Napier's Rods.

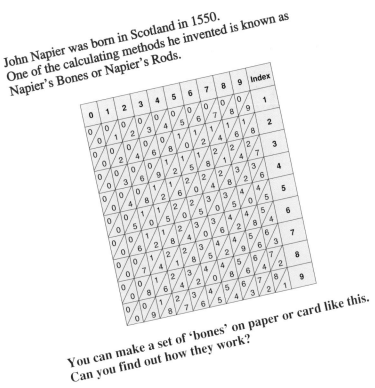

You can make a set of 'bones' on paper or card like this. Can you find out how they work?

1 Rounding up and rounding down

· ·

> **36 000 people attend rock concert**

Look at this newspaper headline.
It doesn't mean that exactly 36 000 people attended the concert.
The number who attended might be 35 987 or 36 245.
The exact number has been rounded to the nearest thousand.

Look at this number line. It shows the multiples of 10.

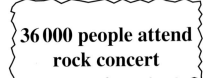

We can round numbers to the nearest 10.
Copy the number line and put a mark on it to represent 23.
The mark is nearer to the 20 than to the 30.
23 is rounded down to 20.

Put a mark on your line to represent 58.
This mark is nearer to the 60 than to the 50.
58 is rounded to 60 to the nearest 10.

Put a mark on your line to represent 35.
This mark is the same distance from 30 and 40.
When this happens we always round to the higher number.
35 is rounded up to 40.

Exercise 4:1

Do not draw a number line.
Round these numbers to the nearest 10.

1 49	**4** 65	**7** 124	**10** 672
2 81	**5** 34	**8** 346	**11** 535
3 27	**6** 8	**9** 285	**12** 198

Example

Sometimes we round numbers to the nearest 100.

Look at this number line. It shows the multiples of 100.

| 0 | 100 | 200 ↑ | 300 ↑ | 400 | 500 | 600 | 700 |

The mark that represents 236 is nearer to the 200 than to the 300.
So 236 is rounded to 200 to the nearest 100.

The mark that represents 350 is the same distance from 300 and 400.
It is rounded to the higher number.
350 is rounded to 400.

Exercise 4:2

Round these numbers to the nearest 100.
Do not draw a number line.

1 269   **4** 407   **7** 399   **10** 357

2 617   **5** 850   **8** 563   **11** 88

3 770   **6** 849   **9** 111   **12** 993

Exercise 4:3

Round these numbers to the nearest 1000. Look at the number line to help you.

| 0 | 1000 | 2000 | 3000 | 4000 | 5000 | 6000 | 7000 | 8000 |

1 2346   **4** 4500   **7** 2900   **10** 8050

2 6731   **5** 3499   **8** 5555   **11** 8500

3 6750   **6** 987   **9** 7097   **12** 9600

Exercise 4:4

Round these numbers to the nearest 10 000.

1 19 375	**4** 75 000	**7** 8395	**10** 92 673
2 64 987	**5** 39 275	**8** 56 847	**11** 13 869
3 10 473	**6** 34 251	**9** 45 029	**12** 97 241

A number has been rounded to the nearest 10. The answer is 30.
Look at this number line.

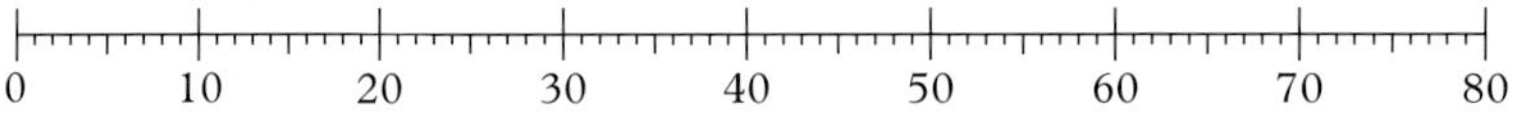

0   10   20   30   40   50   60   70   80

The smallest the number could be is 25. The largest the number could be is 34.

Now do the same for 60.
Use the number line to help you.

The smallest the number could be is 55. The largest the number could be is 64.

Exercise 4:5

1 Copy the table and fill it in.

Number to the nearest 10	Smallest number	Largest number
30	25	34
60	55	64
80		
20		
50		
10		
100		
380		
640		
700		

2 There is a label on a box of sweets. It says that there are 70 sweets in the box to the nearest 10.
Write down the smallest number of sweets that could be in the box.
Write down the largest number that could be in the box.

3 A box of matches is said to contain 300 matches to the nearest 100.
Write down the smallest number of matches that could be in the box.
Write down the largest number that could be in the box.

4 The attendance at a football match was 19 000. This figure is correct to the nearest thousand.
What is the largest number that could have attended the match?
What is the smallest number that could have attended?

● **5** The population of a town is 80 000. This number is correct to the nearest 10 000.
What is the smallest number the population could be?
What is the largest number the population could be?

● **6** The population of a village is 1400 to the nearest hundred.
What is the largest possible increase in population you could have without the number 1400 being changed?

Rounding in problems

We sometimes get a remainder when we divide.
Divide 9 by 2. The answer is 4 remainder 1.
Some questions must have a whole number as an answer.
You have to decide whether to round down or round up.

Examples   **1** Aniseed balls cost 2 p each.
How many can you buy for 9 p?

$9 \div 2 = 4$, remainder 1.
4 aniseed balls cost 8 p. You are left with 1 p.
You cannot buy half an aniseed ball.
You can only buy 4 aniseed balls.

2 The PE department needs 9 squash balls.
Squash balls are sold in packs of 2 balls.
How many packs will the PE department need to buy?

4 packs contain 8 balls.
The PE department needs 1 more ball.
They will need to buy 5 packs to get 9 balls.

Exercise 4:6

Work through these questions.
Think very carefully whether to round up or down.

1 Chocolate bars cost 20 p each.
How many bars can I buy for 75 p?

2 A lift carries eight people.
Seventeen people are waiting to
take the lift to the car park.
How many trips of the lift will it
take to get all the people to the
car park?

3 A farmer has 32 eggs to put into boxes.
Each box holds six eggs.
How many boxes can the farmer fill?

4 A small jar of coffee contains 53 spoonfuls of coffee.
A mug of coffee needs 2 spoonfuls of coffee.
How many mugs of coffee can be made from this jar?

5 A ferry-boat can carry 50 people at one time.
How many trips must the ferry-boat make to carry 110 people?

6 One tin of paint will cover 2 bikes.
How many tins of paint will be needed to cover 5 bikes?

7 One tin of tuna makes 20 sandwiches.
I need to make 50 sandwiches.
How many tins of tuna do I need to buy?

8 A packet of screws contains 12 screws.
I need 25 screws.
How many packets do I need to buy?

9 It takes 42 beads to make a necklace.
How many necklaces can I make with 150 beads?

10 A puppy eats 1 large tin of food
every two days.
How many tins of food must I
buy to feed the puppy for a week?

2 Mental arithmetic

How well do you know your times tables?

Exercise 4:7

1 Use a copy of the multiplication table.
Fill in as many answers as you can in 5 minutes.
Do not use a calculator.

2 Now use a calculator to check your answers.

3 Fill in any empty spaces in a different colour.
You may use a calculator.

Example

Can you multiply 23×6 in your head?
You can make it easier by doing two multiplication sums.

23×6 is the same as $\quad 20 \times 6 \quad$ and $\quad 3 \times 6$

This gives $\quad 120 \quad$ and $\quad 18$

The answer is $\quad 120 \quad + \quad 18 \quad = 138$

Exercise 4:8

Copy and complete:

1 $52 \times 2 =$ **4** $54 \times 6 =$ **7** $45 \times 7 =$

2 $42 \times 4 =$ **5** $65 \times 6 =$ **8** $55 \times 8 =$

3 $35 \times 5 =$ **6** $36 \times 7 =$ **9** $67 \times 8 =$

Example   Look at these number facts:

$$5 \times 4 = 20 \qquad 20 \div 5 = 4$$
$$20 \div 4 = 5$$

Exercise 4:9

1 Copy and complete these number facts:

    a $3 \times 7 = 21$ $21 \div 7 = \ldots$ **b** $3 \times 8 = 24$ $24 \div \ldots = \ldots$

                                $21 \div \ldots = 7$ $24 \div \ldots = \ldots$

Look at your multiplication table.
Find the number 24. It appears twice.
We can get 24 by using 4 and 6 as well as by using 3 and 8.

$4 \times 6 = 24$ $24 \div 6 = 4$ $3 \times 8 = 24$ $24 \div 8 = 3$

                $24 \div 4 = 6$ $24 \div 3 = 8$

We have four division facts for 24.

W **2** Look at your copy of the division table.
The division facts for 24 have been entered.
Complete the table on the worksheet.
Remember there may be four division facts for some numbers.
Use your multiplication table to help you.

Some spaces will still be empty. Try to fill these using your calculator.

3   Estimation

. . . .

Estimating

Wei Yen buys 1 chocolate bar and 1 packet of mints.
Harry adds 28 and 19 and asks for 83 p.
Wei Yen thinks that this is wrong.

Wei Yen can't add 28 p and 19 p in her head.
She does an easier sum. She rounds 28 to 30 and 19 to 20
    30 + 20 = 50
Wei Yen knows that Harry has made a mistake because 83 p is not close
to 50 p.

To make an estimate:

Step 1: Round the numbers to the nearest 10 or 100.
Step 2: Do the simple sum in your head.
Step 3: Write down your estimate.

___

Examples   **1**   Add together 119 and 56.
                Estimate: 100 + 60 = 160
                             160 is the estimate.
                Calculation: 119 + 56 = 175

          The answer 175 is close to the estimate of 160.
          It is probably correct.

2   Find $221 - 135$
        Estimate: $200 - 100 = 100$
                     100 is the estimate.

Scott does the calculation.

        Calculation: $221 - 135 = 26$

Scott's answer 26 is not close to the estimate. This tells him
the answer 26 is wrong.
Scott must do the calculation again.

$$221 - 135 = 86$$

The answer is close to the estimate.
It is probably correct.

Exercise 4:10

1 Copy the table and fill it in.
      The first problem has been done for you.

	Problem	Estimate	Correct answer
a	$69 + 34$	$70 + 30 = 100$	103
b	$73 + 19$		
c	$29 + 38$		
d	$269 + 132$		
e	$67 - 15$		
f	$491 - 187$		
g	$508 - 392$		

We can make estimates for multiplication sums.

2 Copy the table and fill it in.
      The first one has been done for you.

	Problem	Estimate	Correct answer
a	28×43	$30 \times 40 = 1200$	1204
b	31×49		
c	12×78		
d	19×59		

We can make an estimate for more difficult sums.

$22 \times 66 \div 12$ becomes $20 \times 70 \div 10$.
This gives 140 as the estimate.

Using a calculator $22 \times 66 \div 12 = 121$.
This is close to our estimate and so it is probably correct.
Notice that we cannot be sure it is correct.
An estimate can only tell us that we might be wrong.

3 Copy the table and fill it in.

Problem	Estimate	Correct answer
a $22 \times 66 \div 12$	$20 \times 70 \div 10 = 140$	121
b $69 \times 42 \div 21$		
c $69 \times 72 \div 18$		
d $36 \times 99 \div 44$		
e $54 \times 25 \div 45$		

Problem-solving with a calculator

When you are given a problem it is important to read it carefully.

Step 1: Imagine what is happening in the question.
Write down the facts given to you.

Step 2: Decide whether to add, subtract, multiply or divide.

Step 3: Work out an estimate for the answer.

Step 4: Work out and write down the answer.
Check this answer with the estimate.

Examples

1 Stanthorne High School cricket team scored 29 runs before lunch. After lunch they score another 37 runs.
What is their total score?

Step 1:

37 more runs.

Step 2: We need to add.

Step 3: 29 + 37
Estimate: 30 + 40 = 70   The estimate is 70.

Step 4: 29 + 37 = 66
66 is close to 70.

2 A box weighs 123 kg. There are 21 boxes.
How much do they weigh altogether?

Step 1: 21 boxes.   123 kg

Step 2: We need to multiply.

Step 3: 21 × 123
Estimate: 20 × 100 = 2000   The estimate is 2000.

Step 4: 21 × 123 = 2583
2583 is close to 2000.
It is probably correct.

Exercise 4:11

1 Lucy collected 32 empty cans for recycling.
Paul collected 59 cans.
How many cans did they collect altogether?

2 Theo is 152 cm tall. Michael is 139 cm tall.
What is the difference in their heights?

3 A student was training to run the marathon.
He ran 22 miles every day for 12 days.
How far did he run altogether?

4 A 117 cm length of string is cut into pieces of length 13 cm.
How many pieces are there?

5 Raaziya is 146 cm tall.
She climbs a tree that is seven times as tall as she is.
How tall is the tree?

6 Zeta had scored 249 000 on a pinball machine.
She scored 32 500 with her next ball.
What was her new total?

7 Jonathan has to buy cans of cola for a disco.
He needs 168 cans.
The cans are sold in packs of 12.
How many packs must he buy?

Exercise 4:12

Use your calculator to answer these questions.

1 How long would it take to count to one million at a rate of
one number per second?

2 For this question you will need to find out:
the width and the thickness of a 2 p coin,
the length of the equator.

   a One thousand 2 p coins are placed one on top of the other.
How high do they reach?

   b How many 2 p coins, laid edge to edge, would reach around the
equator?

Show all your working.

4   Priority of operations

Here are two calculators.

Scientific calculator   Simple calculator

These two calculators work differently.

If you do 2 + 5 × 3 on the scientific calculator you get 17.
If you do 2 + 5 × 3 on the simple calculator you get 21.

Can you see why?

The scientific calculator does **5 × 3** first then +2.

The simple calculator does **2 + 5** first then ×3.

We should only have one answer. The simple calculator is wrong.

The rule is:
Always do multiplication and division *before* addition and subtraction.

Examples   **1**   3 × 4 + 2   We do the multiplication first.

                12 + 2   Then we do the addition.

                   14   The answer is 14.

        2   7 − 12 ÷ 3   We do the division first.

                7 − 4   Then we do the subtraction.

                   3   The answer is 3.

Exercise 4:13

Copy and complete these questions.
Do the red part first.
The first question has been done for you.

1 $2 \times 3 + 4$
     $= \quad 6 \quad + 4$
     $= 10$

3 $6 + 4 \times 7$
     $=$
     $=$

5 $10 - 6 \div 2$

2 $5 + 2 \times 4$
     $= 5 +$
     $=$

4 $12 \div 6 + 2$

6 $25 - 16 \div 8$

Copy these questions. Underline the part to be done first. Then work out the answer.

7 $4 \times 3 + 2$

11 $8 \div 4 + 3 \times 5$

15 $14 \div 2 - 2 \times 3$

8 $5 + 4 \times 3$

12 $12 \times 3 - 8 \div 2$

16 $7 \times 7 + 18 \div 9$

9 $14 \div 2 - 5$

13 $20 \div 5 + 12 \div 2$

17 $24 \div 6 + 9 \div 3$

10 $17 - 15 \div 5$

14 $6 \times 2 - 10 \div 5$

18 $5 \times 7 - 20 \div 10 + 3 \times 4$

Sometimes we want the addition or subtraction done first.
We use brackets to show this.

The rule is:
Always do the brackets first.

Examples   **1** $6 \times (3 + 4)$ Do the bracket first.

                  $= 6 \times 7$ Then do the multiplication.

                  $= 42$ The answer is 42.

           2 $(6 + 8) \div (5 + 2) + 10$ Do the brackets first.

                $= \quad 14 \quad \div \quad 7 \quad + 10$ Then do the division

                $= \qquad\qquad 2 \qquad + 10$ Then do the addition.

                $= \qquad\quad 12$ The answer is 12.

Exercise 4:14

Copy and complete these calculations.

1 $(3 + 2) \times 4$
   $= \quad \ldots \quad \times 4$
   $=$

2 $(5 + 3) \div 2$
   $= \quad \ldots \quad \div 2$
   $=$

3 $(12 - 4) \times 6$
   $=$
   $=$

4 $(14 - 8) \times 2$

5 $(6 + 4) \div (5 - 3)$

6 $(7 - 4) \times (3 + 5)$

7 $6 + 3 \times 7 - (4 + 5)$

8 $(9 - 4) \times 3 - 10 \div 2$

9 $24 \div 6 + 5 \times (12 - 8)$

10 $20 - 3 \times (4 + 2) + 7$

11 $(10 - 7) \times (6 + 5) - 12$

12 $5 \times 2 + 4 \times (11 - 4) - 6$

Divide, multiply, add and subtract are called **operations**.
We use the codeword BODMAS to remind us which to do first.

We do	**B**rackets first
then powers	**O**f
Next we do	**D**ivision
and	**M**ultiplication
Then we do	**A**ddition
and	**S**ubtraction.

Powers of

You sometimes have to multiply a number by itself many times
   $2 \times 2 \times 2 \times 2 \times 2$

A quick way of writing this is 2^5
The small number 5 is called a **power**.
It tells you how many twos are multiplied together.

| **Power** | 4^3 The **power** '3' tells you how many fours are multiplied together. $4^3 = 4 \times 4 \times 4$ |

Exercise 4:15

1 Write these numbers using a power.

    a $2 \times 2 \times 2$ **b** 5×5 **c** $6 \times 6 \times 6 \times 6 \times 6$

    d $10 \times 10 \times 10 \times 10$ **e** $3 \times 3 \times 3 \times 3 \times 3 \times 3 \times 3$

Example   Find the value of: **a** 4^2 **b** 2^5

                    a $4^2 = 4 \times 4$ **b** $2^5 = 2 \times 2 \times 2 \times 2 \times 2$

                                  $= 16$ $= 32$

---

2 Find the value of:

    a 2^3 **c** 5^2 **e** 10^3 **g** 4^3

    b 8^2 **d** 3^4 **f** 7^3

Example   We can use the y^x key on a calculator to work out powers.

                    To find the value of 3^2

                    Key in   `3` `yˣ` `2` `=`   The answer is 9.

                    To find the value of 5^3

                    Key in   `5` `yˣ` `3` `=`   The answer is 125.

---

3 Use your calculator to find the value of:

    a 5^2 **c** 2^5 **e** 4^8 **g** $2^3 + 5$ **i** $3^4 + 2^5$

    b 6^4 **d** 3^6 **f** 1^6 **h** $20 - 2^4$ **j** $3^5 + 2^4$

Exercise 4:16

Do these calculations using the rules of BODMAS.

1 $3 \times 7 + 5$ **6** $110 - 7^2 + 22 \div 2$

2 $9 \times (3^2 - 2)$ **7** $5 \times 8 - (7 + 8) \div 3$

3 $3 + 6 \times 4^3$ **8** $6 + 2 \times 5 - 18 \div 6 + 6 \div 3$

4 $(9 - 6) \times (2^3 + 5)$ **9** $(24 - 20) \times 6 \div 3 + 7^2$

5 $25^2 - (8^3 - 3)$ **10** $16 - (5 + 1) \times (7 - 5) \div (4 + 2)$

Bracket keys

Example $20 - (3 + 4)$

We can use the bracket keys to do this

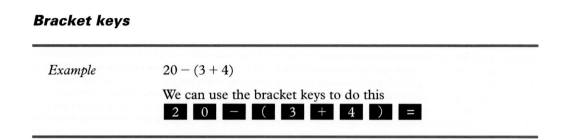

Exercise 4:17

1 Use the bracket keys for these calculations.

    a $10 \times (3 - 5)$ **d** $(6 + 5) - (12 - 8)$

    b $20 - (6 + 4)$ **e** $(14 - 3) + (21 - 16)$

    c $17 + (18 - 10)$ **f** $(24 - 19) \times (4 + 3)$

Memory keys

Switch on your calculator.

Press ON/C STO M+ . This clears the memory.

Press RCL M+ ; the calculator display shows 0.

To put the number 5 into the memory press 5 STO M+ .

Clear the calculator display by pressing ON/C .

Press RCL M+ . The calculator displays the number 5. It has stored the number 5 in its memory.

To clear the memory press ON/C STO M+ again.

2 Follow the key presses for the sum $30 - (3 \times 4)$ and answer the questions.

    a | 3 | × | 4 | = | What number is on the screen?

    b | STO | M+ | What number is on the screen?

    c | 3 | 0 | − | RCL | M+ | What number is on the screen?

    d | = | What is the answer?

3 Do these calculations using the memory keys.

    a $40 - (3 + 5)$ **f** $(16 - 11) \times (21 + 13)$

    b $14 \times (18 - 6)$ **g** $(26 \times 2 + 5) + (8 \times 5 - 2)$

    c $50 - (24 - 17)$ **h** $(24 \times 3 - 12) + (12 \times 13 + 10)$

    d $24 \div (13 - 7)$ **i** $(21^2 - 13 + 4) - (52 - 26 + 31)$

    e $56 - (15 - 9)$ **j** $(24 \times 3^2 - 16) - (13 \times 2^3 + 4)$

1 Copy the table and fill it in.
The first line is done for you.

Number	To the nearest ten	To the nearest hundred
369	370	400
814		
386		
855		
632		
208		
197		
709		
550		
961		

2 Jars of jam are packed in boxes of 36.
How many boxes are needed to pack 972 jars?

3 Eight people won a prize on the football pools.
The prize was worth £125 000.
How much did each person get?

4 Alison bought a second-hand car.
It had done 23 651 miles before she bought it.
After she had driven it for a year it had done 31 258 miles.
How many miles did she drive during that year?

5 The Smith family have just come back from holiday.
They take the films from their camera to the shop for developing.
The table shows how much the shop charges.

Number of exposures	12	24	36
Cost of processing	£3.99	£4.99	£5.99

They have 6 films. One is 36 exposures, three are 24 exposures and
two are 12 exposures.
a How much will it cost to have their films processed?
b Which size of film gives the cheapest price per photo?

6 This is a well-known saying:
'Thirty days has September, April, June and November.
All the rest have 31 except February alone.
It has 28 in a normal year and 29 in a leap year'.

How many days are there in:
a August?
b July?
c November and December?
d The first three months of a leap year?
e The third and fourth months?
f March, October and December?
g The last six months?
h The first and seventh months?

7 Do these calculations.

a $2 \times 7 - 5$

b $8 - 2 \times 3$

c $2 \times 12 \div 6$

d $9 \times (8^2 - 6^2)$

e $4 \times 5 - 6 \times 3$

f $18 \div 2 + 6 \times 7$

g $(16 - 7) \times (13 - 4)$

h $(215 - 45) \div (58 - 41)$

i $(316 - 214) \div (64 - 13)$

j $(32 + 14) \times (56 + 12)$

k $(86 + 32) \times (24 - 15)$

l $(6^3 - 2^5) \times (130 - 5^3)$

8 A supermarket sells two brands of cat food, Pussdins and Kittimeat.
Pussdins is 37 p per can and there is a special offer, 'Buy any 5 – get
the sixth free'.
Kittimeat is 36 p per can. A set of 12 cans is on offer for £4.20.
Which is the better buy?
Show your working.

9 A DIY shop sells nails at 44 p for 4 oz. A local hardware store sells the
same nails for 65 p for 6 oz.
a I want 12 oz of nails.
Which shop should I choose?
How much will the nails cost?
b I want 8 oz of nails.
Which shop should I choose?
How much will the nails cost?

1 A newspaper article said that 45 000 people took part in a fun run.
This figure was correct to the nearest thousand.
  a What is the smallest number of people that could have taken part?
  b What is the largest number of people that could have taken part?

2 The distance between Manchester and London is 200 miles to the
nearest 10 miles.
  a What is the largest value the distance can be?
  b What is the smallest value the distance can be?

3 The total number of pupils at Stanthorne High School in 1994 was
1200 to the nearest hundred,
  a What is the least the total number could be?
  b What is the most the total number could be?

4 A piece of string is measured to the nearest centimetre using a ruler.

The string is 4.7 cm long. This is nearer to 5 than 4.
4.7 is 5 cm to the nearest centimetre.

Round these lengths to the nearest centimetre:
  a 2.8 cm   **e** 9.35 cm
  b 5.3 cm   **f** 7.72 cm
  c 7.48 cm   **g** 6.08 cm
  d 6.8 cm   **h** 9.6 cm

5 A piece of string measure 5 cm to the nearest centimetre.
  a What is the smallest length it can be?
  b The longest length it can be is just up to 5.5 cm but not equal to
    5.5 cm.
    4.5 cm is called the lower bound.
    5.5 cm is called the upper bound.

  Copy the table and fill it in.
  The first row has been done for you.

Length to nearest cm	Lower bound	Upper bound
13 cm	12.5 cm	13.5 cm
2 cm		
9 cm		
4 cm		
16 cm		
23 cm		
45 cm		
138 cm		
40 cm		

6 A family drive from Leeds to Paris for a holiday.

a Use this table to find the distance from Leeds to Dover.

Distance between towns in miles.
e.g. Bristol to Oxford is 74 miles.

Aberdeen							
515	Bristol						
630	210	Dover					
146	380	496	Glasgow				
461	236	354	328	Holyhead			
336	220	265	222	167	Leeds		
500	74	150	365	222	171	Oxford	
630	125	292	497	352	334	196	Plymouth

They cross the channel to Calais. From Calais they drive to Paris.

b Use this table to find the distance from Calais to Paris.

Distance between towns in kilometres.

Bordeaux							
876	Calais						
679	740	Geneva					
544	758	151	Lyon				
646	1069	454	312	Marseille			
581	296	536	460	775	Paris		
713	275	471	483	792	143	Reims	
921	624	403	479	791	491	347	Strasbourg

c The distance from Calais to Paris is in kilometres.
To change kilometres to miles **divide by 8 and multiply by 5**.
e.g. 240 kilometres is $240 \div 8 \times 5 = 150$ miles

Change the distance from Calais to Paris into miles.

d What is the total distance in **miles** from Leeds to Paris and back to Leeds?

e Their car does 45 miles for each gallon of petrol.
How many gallons of petrol will they need?

f A gallon of petrol costs £2.55.
How much will they spend on petrol for the journey?

- **Rounding**

  To round a number to the nearest 10 we look at a number line. We decide which multiple of 10 it is closer to.

  If the number is half-way between two multiples of 10 we always choose the higher one.

  To the nearest 10:   24 becomes 20

                           25 becomes 30

                           28 becomes 30

  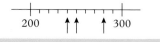

  To round a number to the nearest 100 we decide which multiple of 100 it is closer to.

  If it is half-way between two multiples of 100 we always choose the higher one.

  To the nearest 100: 240 becomes 200

                          250 becomes 300

                          280 becomes 300

- **Estimating**

  The calculator will show the wrong answer if you key in the wrong number by mistake.

  You should always make an estimate of the answer in your head.

  21×39 Estimate: $20 \times 40 = 800$

                Calculation: $21 \times 39 = 819$

- **Power**

  4^3 The **power** 3 tells you how many fours are multiplied together.

- **BODMAS**

  Divide, multiply, add and subtract are called operations. The word BODMAS reminds us which operation to do first:

  Brackets, **P**owers **O**f, **D**ivide, **M**ultiply, **A**dd, **S**ubtract

- **Memory key**

  The memory key stores numbers to use later.

  $30 \div (10 - 4)$

  We use these keys:

  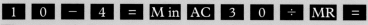

  The answer is 5.

- **key**

  We use this key to find powers.

  To calculate 3^4 we use the keys:

  The answer is 81.

1   Round these figures to the nearest 10:

    a   38   **b**   85   **c**   253

2   Round these figures to the nearest 100:

    a   449   **b**   681   **c**   250

3   Make an estimate of the following sums and then use your calculator to find the exact answer:

    a 79×31 **b** $59 \div 19 \times 38$

4   A piece of rope is 238 metres long.
It is cut into pieces 7 metres long.
How many pieces will there be?

5   Katy's three cats eat three large tins of cat food between them each day.
Each tin costs 36 p.
How much will it cost to feed the cats each week?

6   A company gives a mileage allowance to their car drivers. It is 28 p per mile for the first 50 miles and 17 p per mile after that.
How much will a driver get if she does 124 miles?

Do these calculations

7   **a** $3 + 2 \times 7$ **b** $20 \div 2 - 8$ **c** $24 \div 2 + 2 \times 4$

8   **a** $(5 + 4) \times 2$ **b** $(16 - 11) \times 3$ **c** $60 \div (7 + 5)$

9   **a** $32 - (20 + 2)$ **b** $(13 + 5) \div (14 - 8)$ **c** $(25 - 13) + (16 - 4)$

10   **a** $5^3 - 2^4$ **c** $(5^2 + 5 \times 7) \div (1^{10} + 2^2)$
      b $(6^4 - 4^2) \times (2^4 - 3^2)$

5 Shape and construction

QUESTIONS

EXTENSION

SUMMARY

TEST YOURSELF

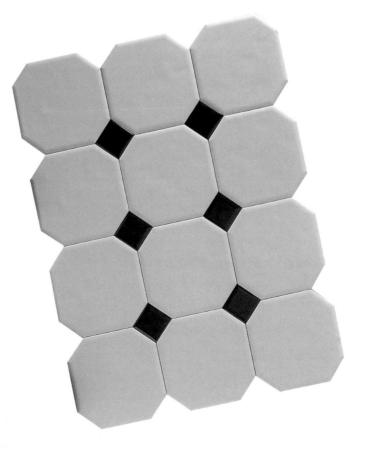

1   Names of polygons

Shapes can be seen everywhere. The design of this building uses shape for decoration.

A clock face has twelve points equally spaced around its edge.

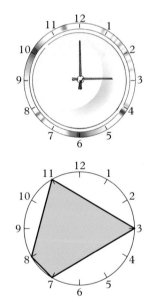

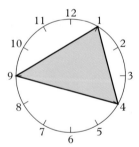

Join the points:
$1 \rightarrow 4 \rightarrow 9 \rightarrow 1$
to get a triangle.

Join the points:
$11 \rightarrow 3 \rightarrow 7 \rightarrow 8 \rightarrow 11$
to get a quadrilateral.

Exercise 5:1 Special triangles

W   You will need copies of a clock face for this exercise.

1   **a**   Join the points:
  (1) $12 \rightarrow 4 \rightarrow 8 \rightarrow 12$ (3) $3 \rightarrow 7 \rightarrow 11 \rightarrow 3$
  (2) $1 \rightarrow 5 \rightarrow 9 \rightarrow 1$

  b   What do you notice about the sides of the triangles in part **a**?
  c   Draw a triangle like those in part **a**. Start at 2.

2 a Join the points:

(1) $2 \rightarrow 4 \rightarrow 9 \rightarrow 2$ (3) $11 \rightarrow 1 \rightarrow 6 \rightarrow 11$

(2) $6 \rightarrow 12 \rightarrow 3 \rightarrow 6$ (4) $10 \rightarrow 4 \rightarrow 1 \rightarrow 10$

b What do you notice about the sides of the triangles in part **a**?

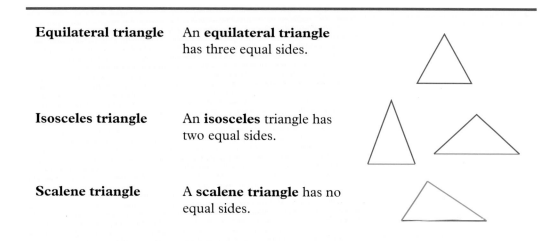

Equilateral triangle An **equilateral triangle** has three equal sides.

Isosceles triangle An **isosceles** triangle has two equal sides.

Scalene triangle A **scalene triangle** has no equal sides.

---

3 Measure the sides of these triangles.

Write the lengths down.

For each triangle write down whether it is equilateral, isosceles or scalene.

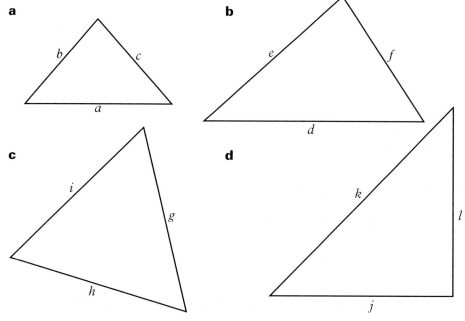

a

b

c

d

Quadrilateral   A **quadrilateral** has four sides.
Here are some special quadrilaterals.

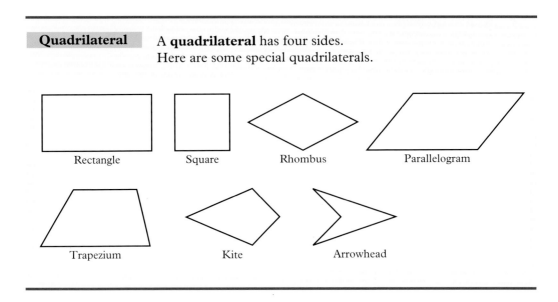

Rectangle   Square   Rhombus   Parallelogram

Trapezium   Kite   Arrowhead

Exercise 5:2 Special quadrilaterals

W **1**   You will need copies of a clock face for this question.

    a   Join the points:

       (1) $2 \rightarrow 4 \rightarrow 8 \rightarrow 10 \rightarrow 2$ (4) $12 \rightarrow 3 \rightarrow 6 \rightarrow 9 \rightarrow 12$

       (2) $1 \rightarrow 3 \rightarrow 5 \rightarrow 11 \rightarrow 1$ (5) $4 \rightarrow$ Centre $\rightarrow 8 \rightarrow 12 \rightarrow 4$

       (3) $2 \rightarrow 6 \rightarrow 10 \rightarrow 12 \rightarrow 2$ (6) $11 \rightarrow 1 \rightarrow$ Centre $\rightarrow 9 \rightarrow 11$

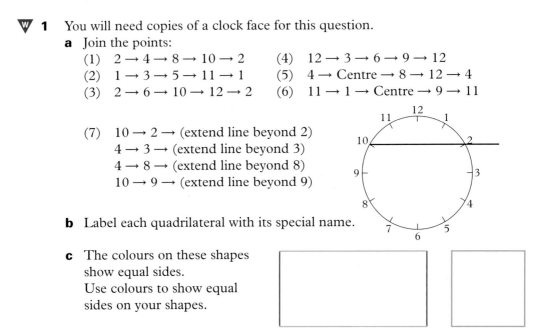

       (7) $10 \rightarrow 2 \rightarrow$ (extend line beyond 2)
            $4 \rightarrow 3 \rightarrow$ (extend line beyond 3)
            $4 \rightarrow 8 \rightarrow$ (extend line beyond 8)
            $10 \rightarrow 9 \rightarrow$ (extend line beyond 9)

    b   Label each quadrilateral with its special name.

    c   The colours on these shapes
       show equal sides.
       Use colours to show equal
       sides on your shapes.

2 Which, if any, quadrilaterals have:
  a four equal sides?
  b three equal sides?
  c two pairs of equal sides?
  d two equal sides?
  e no equal sides?

Some special quadrilaterals have parallel sides.

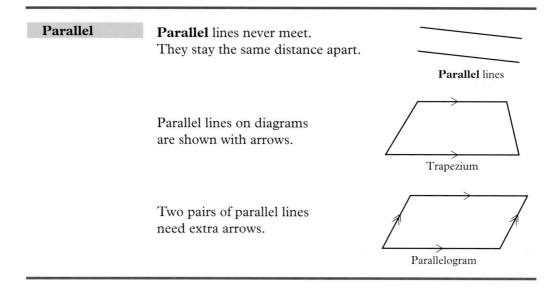

Parallel

Parallel lines never meet.
They stay the same distance apart.

Parallel lines

Parallel lines on diagrams
are shown with arrows.

Trapezium

Two pairs of parallel lines
need extra arrows.

Parallelogram

3 You need your answers to question **1** for this question.
  a Look at your trapezium and your parallelogram.
     Mark their sides with arrows like the examples.
  b Find the pairs of parallel lines on other special quadrilaterals.
     Mark them with arrows.
  c Write down the quadrilaterals that have:
     (1) two pairs of parallel sides
     (2) one pair of parallel sides
     (3) no parallel sides.

4 Can a triangle have parallel sides?
   Explain your answer.

Shapes can have more than four sides.

Polygon

A **polygon** is a shape with straight sides.
Triangles and quadrilaterals are polygons.
Some other polygons have special names.

The polygons we see most often
are in red type in this table.

6 sides: hexagon

Number of sides	Name of polygon
3	Triangle
4	Quadrilateral
5	Pentagon
6	Hexagon
7	Heptagon
8	Octagon
9	Nonagon
10	Decagon
11	Hendecagon
12	Dodecagon

8 sides: octagon

Exercise 5:3

1 This shape is not a polygon.
Explain why.

2 Penny and Paul on the next page are made from polygons.
Copy the tables and fill them in.
Give the special names of the quadrilaterals.

a Penny

Description	Number of sides	Name of polygon
(1) Neck		
(2) Head		
(3) T-shirt		
(4) Name badge		
(5) Skirt		
(6) Shoes		

b Paul

Description	Number of sides	Name of polygon
(7) Head		
(8) T-shirt		
(9) Name badge		
(10) Trousers		
(11) Legs		
(12) Shoes		

3 a Draw a square of side 8 cm on plain paper.
Cut out the square.

b Divide the square into four by folding.
Cut out the four triangles.

c Use two triangles to make these:
(1) a small square
(2) an isosceles triangle
(3) a parallelogram.
Sketch them in your book.

d Use three triangles to make a trapezium.
Sketch the trapezium.

e Use four triangles to make these:
(1) a rectangle
(2) a large isosceles triangle
(3) a trapezium
(4) a hexagon.
Sketch them in your book.

f Can you make an octagon?

g Can you make a pentagon?

2 More about polygons

In front of Stanthorne High School is a rectangle of grass.
The pupils should go round the edge.
They like to take a short-cut from one corner to another.

Vertex

Vertices

A point or corner of a shape is called a **vertex**. For more than one point we say **vertices**.

A triangle has three vertices.

Diagonal

A line joining two vertices is a **diagonal**.

One diagonal is drawn in this pentagon.

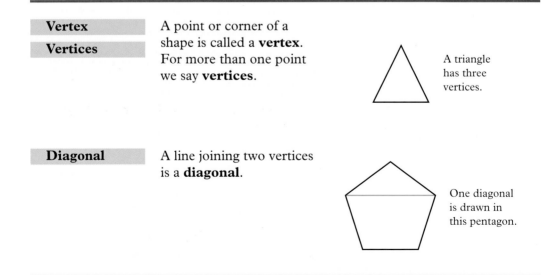

Exercise 5:4

1 Trace these shapes:

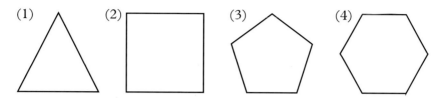

(1)   (2)   (3)   (4)

  a Draw all the diagonals in each shape.
Make sure each vertex is joined to every other vertex.

  b Copy this table and fill it in for each shape.

Name of shape	Number of sides	Number of vertices	Number of diagonals
(1)			

2 The number pattern of the diagonals in question **1** is:

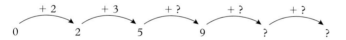

   + 2   + 3   + ?   + ?   + ?

0   2   5   9   ?   ?

  a Copy and complete the number pattern.
  b Describe the rule in words.
  c Use the rule to find the maximum number of diagonals in a
dodecagon (12 sides).

The shapes in question **1** are all regular polygons.

Regular   **Regular** polygons have all their sides the same length.
Also all their vertices look the same.

An equilateral triangle and a square are special regular polygons.

---

3 Which of these shapes are regular polygons?

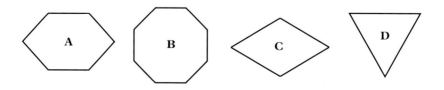

A   B   C   D

The arrowhead has one of its diagonals outside its shape.
It is concave.

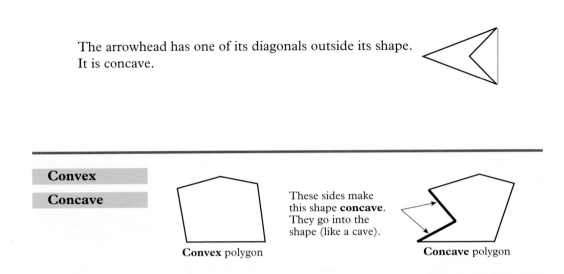

Convex

Concave

These sides make this shape **concave**. They go into the shape (like a cave).

Convex polygon   **Concave** polygon

4 Sketch these polygons and label them **concave** or **convex**.

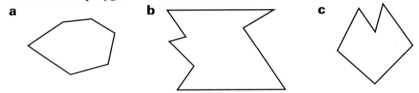

a   b   c

5 The red diagonal is wholly outside the concave pentagon. The green diagonal is partly inside and does not count.

a Draw a pentagon with two outside diagonals.

b Draw a hexagon with:
  (1) one outside diagonal
  (2) two outside diagonals
  (3) three outside diagonals.

c Draw an octagon with four outside diagonals.

Exercise 5:5 Symmetry in polygons

1 Trace these triangles:

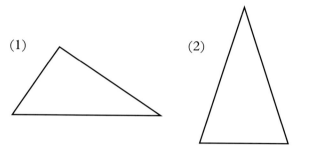

a Draw all the lines of symmetry on the triangles.
b Copy this table and fill it in.

Name of triangle	Number of lines of symmetry
(1)	
(2)	
(3)	

c Is there a triangle with two lines of symmetry?

2 Trace these special quadrilaterals:

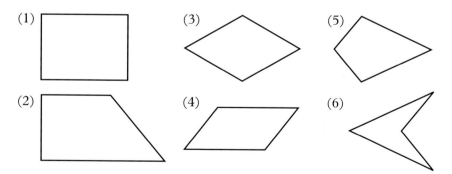

a Draw the diagonals of each shape.
b Which of the diagonals are lines of symmetry?
Go over these lines in red.
c Write down the quadrilateral that has equal diagonals.
d The rectangle has lines of symmetry which are not diagonals.
Draw these lines of symmetry.

3 Trace the regular polygons in Exercise 5:4 question **1**.
   a Draw **all** the lines of symmetry on the polygons.
   b Polygons can have three kinds of lines of symmetry.

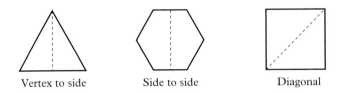

Vertex to side   Side to side   Diagonal

Copy this table and fill it in for your regular polygons.

		Lines of symmetry			
Number of sides	Name of regular polygon	Vertex to side	Side to side	Diagonal	Total
3	Equilateral triangle	3	0	0	3
4					

   c Write down the total number of lines of symmetry for a regular octagon.

4 **a** Use tracing paper and the regular polygons in Exercise 5:4 question **1**.
      Write down the order of rotational symmetry of:
      (1) an equilateral triangle   (3) a regular pentagon
      (2) a square   (4) a regular hexagon.
   b Write down the order of rotational symmetry of a regular octagon.

5 **a** Draw a new table or extend the table for question **3** to go up to polygons with 10 sides.
   b Without drawing the polygons, complete your table.
      Use the results of question **3** to help you.
   c Describe in words the rules for completing the table.

6 Write down the quadrilaterals in question **2** that have:
   a rotational symmetry of order 2.
   b rotational symmetry but not line symmetry.
   c line symmetry but not rotational symmetry.

This rectangle has its vertices labelled ABCD.

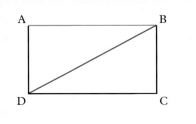

The green side is AB.
The red diagonal is DB.

Exercise 5:6

1 Write down the letter name of:
   a the green side
   b the blue side
   c the red diagonal.

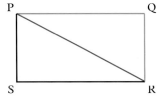

2 a Write down the colour of:
   (1) ZW
   (2) YZ
   b Write down the letter names of:
   (1) the red diagonal
   (2) the green diagonal.

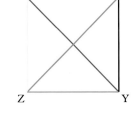

3 Write down:
   a the special name of this triangle.
   b the letter names of the two equal sides.

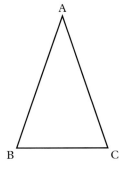

● **4 a** Draw accurately rectangle ABCD.
   AB = 4 cm, BC = 3 cm
   b Join the diagonal BD.
   Write down its length.

3　Using compasses

There is a legend about King Arthur.
He and his knights lived in Britain long ago.
They all sat at a round table.
The table top was a **circle**.

Parts of a circle have special names.

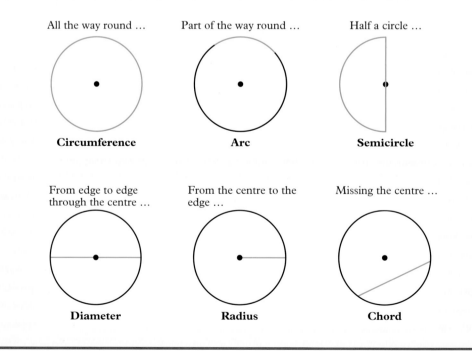

All the way round …	Part of the way round …	Half a circle …
Circumference	**Arc**	**Semicircle**

From edge to edge through the centre …	From the centre to the edge …	Missing the centre …
Diameter	**Radius**	**Chord**

Exercise 5:7

Use compasses to draw your circles.

1 **a** Draw a circle of radius 4 cm.
  b Draw in your circle:
     (1) a diameter
     (2) a radius
     (3) a chord.
  c Label these lines with their names.

2 **a** Draw a circle of radius 3 cm.
  b Draw a diameter in your circle.
     The diameter divides the circle into two semicircles.
  c Colour the two semicircles in different colours.
     Label one of them 'semicircle'.

3 **a** Draw two circles of radius 2.5 cm.
  b Go over the whole edge of the first circle in colour.
     Label your coloured edge 'circumference'.
  c Go over part of the edge of the second circle in colour.
     Label the coloured part 'arc'.

4 A circle has a diameter of 5 cm.
  a Write down the length of the radius of the circle.
  b Draw the circle.
  c Draw a chord in the circle. Use a ruler to join each end of the
     chord to the centre of the circle.
  d What special triangle is drawn in your circle?
  e Repeat **c** for another chord.
  f Explain why every time you repeat **c**, you get the same sort of
     special triangle.

You can use compasses to draw triangles accurately.

Example   Draw triangle ABC.
       AB = 7 cm, AC = 5 cm,
       BC = 4 cm

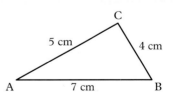

A sketch of the triangle.

1 Draw a line AB, 7 cm long.

A ─────────────────────────── B

2 Open your compasses to 5 cm.
Put the point on A. Draw an arc.

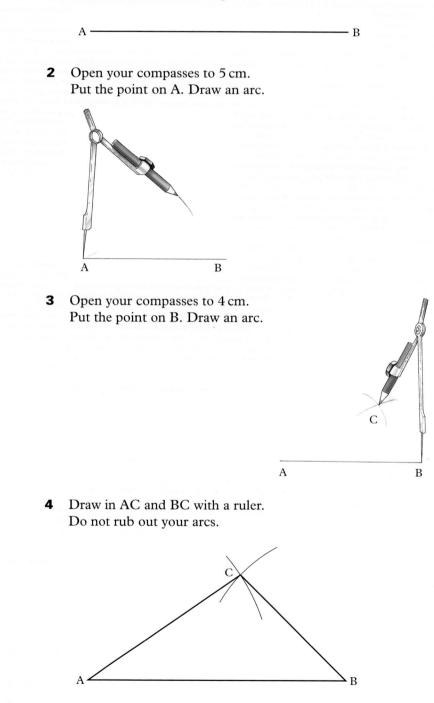

3 Open your compasses to 4 cm.
Put the point on B. Draw an arc.

4 Draw in AC and BC with a ruler.
Do not rub out your arcs.

Exercise 5:8

1 Draw the triangle ABC as shown in the example.

2 Triangle PQR has
PQ = 7 cm, QR = 6 cm, RP = 4 cm.

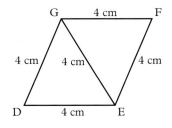

Draw triangle PQR accurately.

3 Triangle XYZ has
XY = 6 cm, YZ = 4 cm, ZX = 4 cm.
  a Draw a labelled sketch of triangle XYZ.
  b Draw triangle XYZ accurately.
  c Write down the special name of triangle XYZ.

4 Make an accurate drawing of an equilateral triangle of side 5 cm.

5 **a** Use compasses to make an
      accurate drawing of the
      rhombus DEFG.
   b Draw the diagonal DF.
      Measure and record its length.

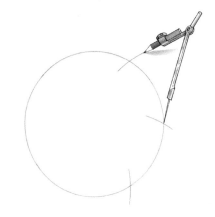

Exercise 5:9 Constructing regular polygons

1 **a** Draw a circle of radius 3 cm.
   b Keep your compasses open to 3 cm.
      Go round the circle making
      arcs 3 cm apart.

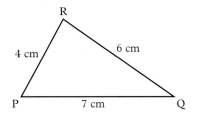

c Join the points where the arcs cross the circle.

d Label your polygon 'a regular ....'.

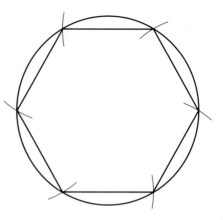

2 a Draw a circle of radius 4 cm on plain paper. Cut out the circle.

    (1) Fold the circle in half.

    (2) Then fold it in half again.

    (3) Then fold once again.

    (4) Unfold your circle.

(1)   (2)   (3)   (4)

b Join the points where the folds reach the circumference.

c Label your polygon 'a regular ....'.

3

a Cut out a strip of paper 3 cm wide and about 25 cm long. Tie a knot in this strip.

b Gently pull the knot tight. Press down until the knot is flat.

c Fold back the spare ends. Label your polygon 'a regular ....'.

4 Tessellations and congruence

Many patterns are made by repeating the same shape. Such patterns are often found on floors and walls.

Tessellation

A **tessellation** is a pattern made by repeating the same shape over and over again.
There are no gaps in a tessellation.

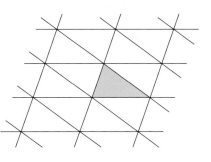

The triangle shape has been repeated over and over again.

Exercise 5:10

Use squared paper for drawing these tessellations.

1 Rectangles tessellate.

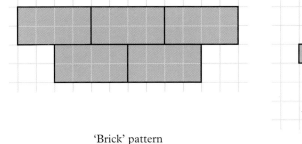

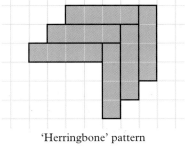

'Brick' pattern   'Herringbone' pattern

Draw a tessellation of rectangles.
Copy one of these tessellations or make up your own.

2 All quadrilaterals tessellate.
Copy one of these tessellations or make up your own.
Use a special quadrilateral.

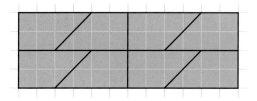 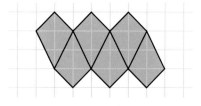

3 All triangles tessellate.
Draw a tessellation of triangles.

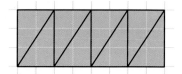

4 Lots of other shapes tessellate.
Experiment with some shapes of
your own.

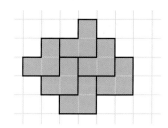

5 **a** (1) Look for tessellations in your school.
Look at the floor, the walls and the ceiling.
(2) Make sketches of the tessellations you find.
Write down where you find them.
b Repeat **a** for tessellations outside school.

· ·

A tessellation is made up of many identical shapes.
Identical shapes in maths are called congruent shapes.

Congruent   When shapes are identical we
say they are **congruent**.

Congruent shapes can be
reflections of each other.

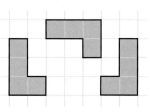

These shapes are congruent.

Exercise 5:11

1 In each of these write down the shape that is not congruent to the others.

a

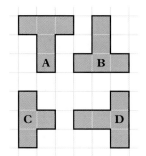

c

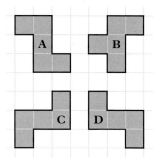

b

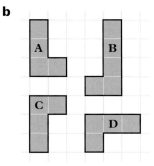

d

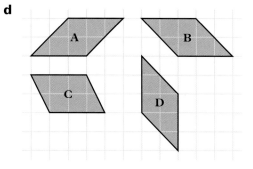

2 **a** Draw a square of side 3 cm.
   b Join one diagonal to give two triangles.
   c Are the two triangles congruent?
   d Join the other diagonal to give four triangles.
   d Are the four triangles congruent?

3 Trace the special quadrilaterals in Exercise 5:5, question **2**.
   Divide each shape into two congruent triangles.

   You cannot do this for one shape.
   Which is it?

● **4** In a square it does not matter
   which diagonal you draw.
   You always get two congruent triangles.

   Which other special quadrilaterals
   have this property?

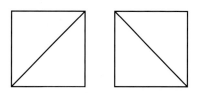

1   Make a copy of this 9-point grid on squared paper for each part of this question.

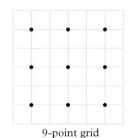

9-point grid

Join dots on your grid to make these.
Label each shape with its name.
a   isosceles triangle
b   scalene triangle
c   square
d   parallelogram
e   trapezium
f   rectangle
g   arrowhead
h   convex pentagon
i   convex hexagon
j   concave hexagon

2   **a**   Write down the letter names of:
     (1) two diameters
     (2) two chords
     (3) four radiuses
     (4) a pair of parallel lines.
   b   Copy and complete:

     Triangle AOB is

     ....

     It is .... to triangle

     COD.

     Triangle COD is also ....

     (choose from: isosceles, congruent)

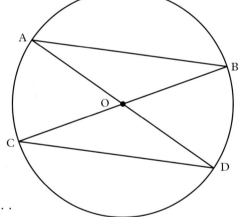

3   **a**   Triangle ABC has
     AB = 7 cm, AC = 7 cm and BC = 6 cm.
     (1) Draw a sketch of triangle ABC.
     (2) Use a compass to make an accurate drawing of triangle ABC.
     (3) Write down the name of triangle ABC.
   b   Make an accurate drawing of equilateral triangle PQR with sides 6 cm.

4 a Draw a circle of radius 4 cm.
  b Draw a diameter.
   Mark points (1) and (2) 2 cm
   from the centre.
  c With a radius of 2 cm, draw
   semicircles centre (1) and (2).
  d Rub out your diameter to get
   the pattern shown.
  e Describe the symmetry of your
   pattern.

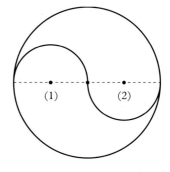

5 a Draw round a circular coin.
   Shade this circle.
  b Use the same coin.
   Place it around your shaded circle
   Draw round your coin each time.
  c Write down the number of
   coins you needed to go round
   the shaded circle.
  d Join the centres of the
   unshaded circles.
   Write down the name of the
   polygon you get.
  e Write down the British coins
   that are not circular.
   Are these coins polygons?
  f Explain why circles do not
   tessellate.

6 Using triangular grid paper make a tessellation of:
  a rhombuses   **b** trapeziums   **c** hexagons.

7 a Write down the shapes of the rooms in your school.
  b Give a reason for the shape of the rooms.

1   **a**   Copy the special quadrilaterals in Exercise 5:5 question **2**.
Leave out the arrowhead but draw a square.

    b   Draw the two diagonals in each shape.
Each shape will now be divided into four triangles.

    c   Write down the quadrilaterals that contain:
(1) four congruent triangles.
(2) two pairs of congruent triangles.
(3) no congruent triangles.

2   Draw a large circle.

    a   Draw two chords that
intersect (cross each other).

    b   Measure AE and EB.
Find their product.

    c   Measure CE and ED.
Find their product.

    d   Compare the two products.

    e   Repeat steps **b**, **c** and **d** twice
more with different pairs of
intersecting chords.

    f   Write about what you notice.

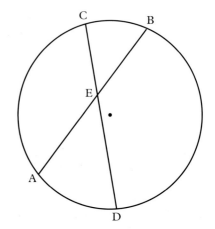

3   Any quadrilateral will tessellate.
Test this with any irregular
quadrilateral tile cut from paper
or card.
Draw round your tile to show the
tessellation.

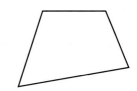

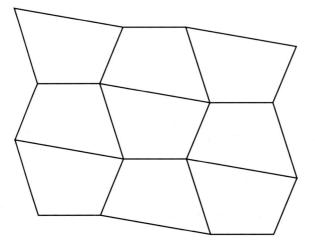

- A **polygon** is a shape with straight sides.
  Triangles and quadrilaterals are polygons.
  A polygon can be **convex** or **concave**.

Number of sides	Name of polygon
5	Pentagon
6	Hexagon
8	Octagon

- An **equilateral triangle** has three equal sides.
  An **isosceles triangle** has two equal sides.
  A **scalene triangle** has no equal sides.

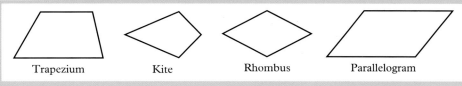

Trapezium   Kite   Rhombus   Parallelogram

- A point at the corner of a shape is called a **vertex**.
  A line joining two verticcs is a **diagonal**.

- **Parallel** lines never meet.
  Parallel lines on diagrams are shown with arrows.
  Two pairs of parallel lines need extra arrows.

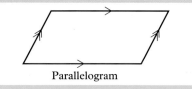

Parallelogram

- **Regular polygons** have all their sides the same length.
  Also all their vertices look the same.
  An equilateral triangle and a square are special regular polygons.

-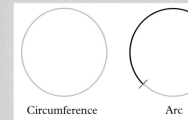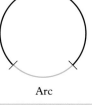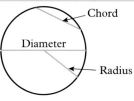

  Chord

  Diameter

  Radius

  Circumference   Arc   Semicircle

- A **tessellation** is a pattern made by repeating the same shape over and over again. There are no gaps in a tessellation.

  When shapes are identical we say they are **congruent**.
  Congruent shapes can be reflections of each other.

  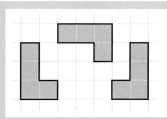

1 **a** Sketch these quadrilaterals:
   (1) square   (4) parallelogram   (7) arrowhead
   (2) rectangle   (5) trapezium
   (3) rhombus   (6) kite
   b Use arrows to show the parallel sides.
   c Which quadrilateral is concave?
   d Which quadrilateral is regular?

2 **a** Write down the names of triangles with:
   (1) no equal sides   (2) two equal sides   (3) three equal sides.
   b Write down the names of polygons with:
   (1) five sides   (2) six vertices   (3) eight sides.

3 Sketch this regular pentagon.
   a Write down the order of
   rotational symmetry of the
   pentagon.
   b Draw the lines of symmetry of
   the pentagon on your sketch.

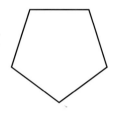

4 The diagram shows a trapezium.
   Write down the letter names for:
   a the pair of parallel sides
   b the diagonal.

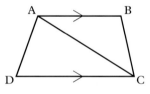

5 Draw a circle of radius 3 cm.
   In your circle draw and label:
   a an arc   **c** a chord   **e** a radius
   b a semicircle   **d** a diameter   **f** the circumference.

6 Use compasses to draw triangle ABC accurately.
   AB = 6 cm, BC = 5 cm, CA = 4 cm

7 Sally has tried to draw a tessellation.
   a Explain what is wrong with Sally's drawing.
   b Draw a tessellation using the same shape.
   Use squared paper.

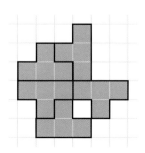

6 | Decimals: what's the point?

QUESTIONS

EXTENSION

SUMMARY

TEST YOURSELF

WHO INVENTED THE DECIMAL POINT?

In different countries mathematicians tried different ways. **Jemshid Al-Kashi**, a Persian who died about 1436, wrote 3 142 (the space is for the end of the whole numbers).
Christoff Rudolf, a German, published a book in 1530. He calculated interest on money and wrote 413|4347 (the line is used like our decimal point).
In about 1585 a Flemish mathematician, **Simon Stevin,** published the rules for using decimal fractions. He wrote numbers like this 27(0)8(1)4(2)7(3), meaning 27.847.
Even today people do not agree. The United Kingdom and the United States use a decimal point. In Europe a comma is used.

1 Place value in whole numbers

We can write five hundred and seventy-four as 574 using the figures or
digits 5, 7 and 4.
457 and 745, can be made from the same digits.
The 7 is in different places in 574, 457 and 745. The 7 has a different
value each time.
Numbers can be written in columns. The columns have names
according to their value.

thousands 1 000s	hundreds 100s	tens 10s	units 1s	
	4	5	7	7 units .... value 7
	5	7	4	7 tens .... value 70
	7	4	5	7 hundreds .. value 700

Exercise 6:1

1 What is the **value** of the red digit in these numbers?

	thousands	hundreds	tens	units
a	3	4	2	1
b		2	4	3
c	4	8	0	4
d	1	9	7	1
e		6	0	5

2 What is the value of the red digit in these numbers?

    a 365   **b** 491   **c** 824   **d** 395   **e** 677   **f** 3249

3 **a** Make as many numbers as you can from 5, 3 and 6. 536, 653, ...
    Use all the digits.

    b Which is the largest of these numbers?

    c Which number is the smallest?

4 **a** Choose any 3-digit number and write it down.

    b Write the number backwards.

    c Decide which number is larger.

    d Subtract the smaller number from the larger number.

    e Write the answer to **d** backwards.

    f Add your answers to **d** and **e**.

    g Choose another 3-digit number and work through this question
    again. What do you notice?
    Compare your answers with other pupils' answers.

· ·

When we write large numbers we group the digits in 3s.
We write forty-three thousand six hundred and seventeen as 43 617
                                                  ↑

                                       We leave a small gap

We write five million eight hundred and seventy-four thousand three
hundred and nineteen as 5 874 319.
                             ↑ ↑

                      We leave small gaps

In old books you may see numbers grouped with commas: 43,617
We no longer use a comma.

Exercise 6:2

1 Write these numbers in figures.

    a seven hundred and fifty six

    b two thousand four hundred and eighty two

    c nine hundred and three

    d one thousand six hundred and twenty-nine

    e thirteen thousand five hundred and twenty

    f two million five hundred and ninety-eight thousand two hundred
    and thirty-one

    g six million four hundred and six thousand and four

2 Write these numbers in words.

   a 617

   b 5 259

   c 12 406

   d 107 529

   e 5 231 825

· ·

Start at the 'units' column. We can add extra columns to the left.

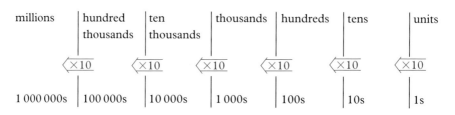

millions	hundred thousands	ten thousands	thousands	hundreds	tens	units
1 000 000s	100 000s	10 000s	1 000s	100s	10s	1s

Each column is 10 times the one on its right.

Look at the numbers 25, 250, 2500.

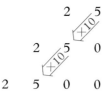

The 5 in 250 is 10 times the value of the 5 in 25.
The 5 in 2500 is 10 × 10 or 100 times the value of the 5 in 25.
When we multiply by **10** the digits change by **one** column.
When we multiply by **10 × 10** or **100** the digits change by **two** columns.

Exercise 6:3

1 How many times greater is the value of the 3 in 300 than the 3 in 30?

2 How many times greater is the value of the 5 in 5000 than the 5 in 500?

3 How many times greater is the value of the 7 in 7000 than the 7 in 70?

4 **a** What is the value of the 3 in 2 316?

    b What is the value of the 3 in 3 419?

    c How many times greater is the value of the 3 in 3 419 than
      the 3 in 2 316?

5   What would you multiply the 5 in 205 by to give it the same value as the 5 in 2 500?

6   What would you multiply the 6 in 216 by to give it the same value as the 6 in 3 694?

7   What would you multiply the 4 in 3 941 by to give it the same value as the 4 in 4 872?

8   What would you multiply the 8 in 248 by to give it the same value as the 8 in 834 921?

9   What is 6 multiplied by to give it the correct value in 60 000?

10   What is 3 multiplied by to give it the correct value in 3 000 000?

11   *Remember*: $10 \times 10 = 10^2$
$$10 \times 10 \times 10 = 10^3$$
The 5 in 500 is 100 or 10×10 times greater than 5.
We write $500 = 5 \times 10^2$
Write these in the same way:
a $400 = 4 \times 10^?$
b $8\,000 = 8 \times 10^?$
c $900 = ? \times 10^2$
d $60\,000 = ? \times ?$
e $2\,000 =$

● 12   **a** $5 \times 10^2 =$
  b $3 \times 10^4 =$
  c $8 \times 10^3 =$
  d $4 \times 10^2 =$
  e $7 \times 10^3 =$

2 The decimal point

A scientist needs to measure a special screw very accurately.

```
  1   2   3   4   5   6   7   8   9   10   11
                                       centimetres
```

This is part of a simple ruler. The screw measures between 2 and 3 centimetres. This is no good to the scientist.

```
  1   2   3   4   5   6   7   8   9   10   11
                                       centimetres
```

This ruler is better. Each whole centimetre has been divided into **10** equal parts or **tenths**.
The screw looks a little more than 2.8 cm long.

The dot between the 2 and 8 is called a **decimal point**.

Decimal point | The word **decimal** comes from the Romans' word for 10.
Our number system is based on ten.
The **point** marks where whole numbers end and fractions or parts of numbers begin.
Examples of numbers with decimal points are 2.8 3.145 14.08

1.9 **2** 2.1 2.2 2.3 2.4 2.5 2.6 2.7 2.8 2.9 **3** 3.1

Here is an enlargement of part of the screw and ruler. There are now
100 tiny spaces or **hundredths** between 2 and 3.
The screw is a little more than 2.85 (two point eight five) cm.

2.79 **2.8** 2.81 2.82 2.83 2.84 2.85 2.86 2.87 2.88 2.89 **2.9** 2.91

We can enlarge the ruler again. There are now **1000** very small spaces
or **thousandths** between 2 and 3.
The screw is now too large to be shown. It would end at 2.856 (two
point eight five six).
To measure this accurately, we would need a special measuring device.

If we used accurate enough ways of measuring, we could add more
and more numbers: 2.856 18 …   and so on.

Decimals in words	2.35 in words is two point **three five**.

£4.76 in words is four pounds seventy-six. We really mean
four pounds and seventy-six pence.

Exercise 6:4

1 Write these decimal numbers in words.
   a 3.29   **b** 4.125   **c** 0.06   **d** 7.302   **e** 5.19

2 Write these numbers in figures.
   a Seven point eight   **d** Five point nought five three
   b Nought point three nought four   **e** One point two three five
   c Six point nine six

W 3 Ask your teacher for a copy of 'Labelling number lines' worksheet.

thousands	hundreds	tens	units	.	tenths	hundredths	thousandths
		2	4	.	3	0	6

For the number 24.306 the three is in the tenths column.
The value of the red digit in words is **three tenths**.

Exercise 6:5

Write the value of each red digit in words.

1 35.643   **6** 253.05   **11** 125

2 114.705   **7** 4.563   **12** 13

3 61.65   **8** 0.601   **13** 5.123

4 230.92   **9** 12.03   **14** 4210

5 1032.6   **10** 4.191   **15** 1305.19

Multiplying by powers of 10

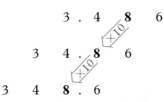

When we multiply by **10**, the digits change by **one** column.
When we multiply by **10 × 10** or **100**, the digits change by **two** columns.

Exercise 6:6

You may need to use a calculator to start.

1 Multiply each of these numbers by 10.

a 4	**e** 2.4	**i** 5.78	**m** 0.3
b 7	**f** 7.1	**j** 6.125	**n** 0.9
c 1.4	**g** 27.3	**k** 4.708	**o** 0.75
d 8.6	**h** 56.9	**l** 12.61	**p** 0.54

2 Multiply each of these numbers by 100.

a	6	**d**	5.4	**g**	17.34	**j**	0.613
b	13	**e**	17.9	**h**	12.54	**k**	0.97
c	7.4	**f**	34.3	**i**	3.245	**l**	0.075

3

a 2.6×10	**e** 80×10	**i** 0.56×100
b 65×10	**f** 6.3×10	**j** 4.1×100
c 0.5×10	**g** 0.04×100	**k** 2.3×100
d 15.6×100	**h** 0.9×100	**l** 0.004×100

Example   The column change in division is the opposite way.
a $42 \div 10 = 4.2$
b $36.5 \div 100 = 0.365$

4

a $36 \div 10$	**e** $5060 \div 100$	**i** $5.41 \div 10$
b $7.8 \div 10$	**f** $76.54 \div 10$	**j** $0.762 \div 10$
c $760 \div 100$	**g** $8.9 \div 100$	**k** $1.62 \div 100$
d $4500 \div 100$	**h** $90 \div 100$	**l** $67.125 \div 100$

5 What number does 14.5 have to be multiplied by to get 1450?

6 What number does 17.2 have to be divided by to get 0.172?

7 A number is multiplied by 10 to give 3.5. What is the number?

8 What number divided by 100 gives 0.25?

9 A number is divided by 10 to give 0.042. What is the number?

10 A number is multiplied by 100 to give 78.5. What is the number?

11 What number divided by 100 gives 7.4?

12 Check your answers to questions **5** to **11** using a calculator.

The 8 in 938.1 is two columns away from the 8 in 9.381.
It is 10×10 or 100 times greater.

The 8 in 35.68 is two columns away from the 8 in 3568
It is 100 times smaller.

Exercise 6:7

1 What would you multiply the 8 in 28.3 by, to give it the same value as the 8 in 283?

2 What would you multiply the 5 in 36.5 by, to give it the same value as the 5 in 365?

3 What would you divide the 4 in 417.5 by, to give it the same value as the 4 in 41.75?

4 What would you divide the 6 in 467.5 by, to give it the same value as the 6 in 46.75?

5 How many times greater is the 5 in 56.12 than the 5 in 0.5612?

6 How many times greater is the 1 in 21.75 than the 1 in 0.2175?

7 What would you divide the 8 in 58.6 by, to give it the same value as the 8 in 5.86?

8 What would you multiply the 8 in 31.58 by, to give it the same value as the 8 in 3158?

9 How many times smaller is the 3 in 13.9 than the 3 in 1390?

10 What would you divide the 2 in 32.18 by, to give it the same value as the 2 in 0.3218?

3 Working with decimals

Robin, Rachel and Mark have to line up in alphabetical order.
M for **M**ark comes before **R** for **R**obin and **R** for **R**achel.

As Robin and Rachel both start with R, they will have to look at the next letters.
Robin, Rachel: **a** comes before **o** so Rachel is before Robin.
The order is: Mark, Rachel, Robin.

Decimals are put in order in the same way.

Example

Put 4.615, 3.842 and 4.67 in order of size, smallest first.
a 4.615   3.842   4.67
3 is smaller than 4.
3.842 is the smallest number.
b 4.615   4.67
The first figure after the decimal point is the same.
c 4.615   4.67
1 is smaller than 7, so 4.615 is smaller than 4.67.
The numbers in order are: 3.842, 4.615, 4.67.

Exercise 6:8

In questions 1 to 13, put the numbers in order of size, smallest first.

1 2.53, 4.68

2 7.61, 3.2

3 4.57, 4.21

4 7.63, 7.8

5 1.24, 1.27

6 2.54, 3.812, 3.65

7 1.234, 2.34, 1.34

8 7.643, 6.41, 7.65

9 6.4, 6.41

10 5.704, 5.71

11 16.3, 16.29

12 8.094, 8.049

● **13** 2.60, 2.06, 2.161

14 These are the longest throws of each person entered in a javelin competition.
Pick out the first, second and third places.

M. Bland	40.66 m	D. Smith	47.91 m
T. Jones	48.05 m	L. George	47.63 m
P. Grant	47.95 m	C. Peters	43.80 m

14 Replace ? with < (less than) or > (more than)
  a 12.75 ? 12.705   **c** 8.424 ? 8.42   **e** 0.607 ? 0.67
  b 6.091 ? 6.19   **d** 3.012 ? 3.102

• •

Exercise 6:9

Write down the next four terms in these patterns.

1
  a 0.2, 0.4, ... (Adding 0.2)   **f** 0.05, 0.10, ... (Adding 0.05)
  b 0.3, 0.6, ... (Adding 0.3)   **g** 0.25, 0.50, ... (Adding 0.25)
  c 0.4, 0.8, ... (Adding 0.4)   **h** 1.5, 3.0, ... (Adding 1.5)
  d 0.5, 1.0, ... (Adding 0.5)   **i** 12.0, 11.5, ... (Subtracting 0.5)
  e 0.02, 0.04, ... (Adding 0.02) **j** 6.0, 5.8, ... (Subtracting 0.2)

2 Check your answers.
The *ans function* on your calculator would be very useful.

Calculators are different but most can do patterns.

To get 5, 7, 9, 11, 13, 15, ... (adding 2) try:

On some calculators you could use:

or

3 Complete these patterns.
Write down the rule for each one.
  a 4.8, 5.0, ..., 5.4, 5.6, 5.8, ...   **d** 1.05, 1.15, 1.25, ..., 1.45, ...
  b 7.0, ..., 6.0, 5.5, 5.0, ..., 4.0   **e** 0.5, ..., 2.5, 3.5, 4.5, ...
  c 12.0, 10.5, 9.0, 7.5, ..., ...   **f** 16, 8, 4, 2, 1, ..., ...

4 Complete these patterns.
Write down the rule for each one.
    a   0.1, 1.0, ..., 2.8, 3.7, ...   **d**   0.05, 0.09, 0.13, ..., 0.21, ...
    b   ..., 0.25, 0.375, ..., 0.625, 0.75   **e**   10, 2, ..., 0.08, 0.016, ...
    c   125, 25, 5, 1, ..., ...   **f**   9.36, 9.27, 9.18, ..., 9, ...

Addition and subtraction of decimals

Examples   **1** $4.52 + 6.851$

The decimal points go underneath each other.
Some people find it helps to put in 0s.

$$\begin{array}{r} 4.520 \\ +6.851 \\ \hline 11.371 \end{array}$$

The extra 0s are important when doing subtraction.

   2 $19.6 - 7.53$

$$\begin{array}{r} 19.\overset{5}{6}0 \\ -7.53 \\ \hline 12.07 \end{array}$$

Here is a mixture of whole numbers and decimals.

   3 $4 - 1.58$

$$\begin{array}{r} 4.00 \\ -1.58 \\ \hline 2.42 \end{array}$$

Exercise 6:10

1   **a** $4.81 + 2.34$ **b** $141.6 + 82.71$ **c** $15.25 + 0.675$

2   **a** $5.38 - 2.16$ **c** $3.68 - 0.79$ **e** $9.3 - 5.67$
     b $12.47 - 6.29$ **d** $6.4 - 3.172$ **f** $7 - 4.2$

3 **a** $14 + 35.9$
   b $15.7 + 39$
   c $7 + 4.97$
   d $178 + 0.56$
   e $5 - 1.8$

   f $23 - 6.75$
   g $17 + 0.04 + 0.57$
   h $125 + 5.6 + 17.63$
   i $900 - 56.41$
   j $3015 + 12.1 + 8.0003$

Multiplication of a decimal by a whole number

Examples **1** 16.2×3

$$\begin{array}{r} 16.2 \\ \times\quad 3 \\ \hline 48.6 \\ \hline \scriptstyle 1 \end{array}$$

2 23.6 by 5

$$\begin{array}{r} 23.6 \\ \times\quad 5 \\ \hline 118.0 \\ \hline \scriptstyle 1\ 3 \end{array}$$

Exercise 6:11

1 12.5×5 **4** 20.2×7 **7** 3.42×6

2 6.8×4 **5** 5.74×9 **8** 408.5×2

3 5.72×3 **6** 15.06×8 **9** 0.0056×5

Division of a decimal by a whole number

Examples **1** $23.6 \div 4 =$

$$\begin{array}{r} 5.9 \\ 4\overline{)2\,3\,.\,{}^3 6} \end{array}$$

2 $23.5 \div 4 =$

$$\begin{array}{r} 5.875 \\ 4\overline{)2\,3\,.\,{}^3 5\,{}^3 0\,{}^2 0} \end{array}$$

0s are added until there is no remainder.

3 $51.5 \div 3 =$

$$\begin{array}{r} 17.1666\ \dots \\ 3\overline{)5\,{}^2 1\,.\,5\,{}^2 0\,{}^2 0\,{}^2 0}\ \dots \end{array}$$

This can be written $17.1\dot{6}$
We say 'seventeen point one six **recurring**.'

Exercise 6:12

1 $72.6 \div 3$ **5** $93.72 \div 3$ **9** $13.7 \div 5$

2 $12.1 \div 5$ **6** $296.46 \div 6$ **10** $4.6 \div 8$

3 $41.5 \div 5$ **7** $17.4 \div 4$ **11** $41.2 \div 3$

4 $160.2 \div 9$ **8** $31.5 \div 6$ **12** $23.5 \div 6$

4 Problems involving decimals

Sometimes we get more numbers after the decimal point than we need.

Aisha has enough beads to make seven necklaces.
She has 290 cm of cord.

She needs to cut the cord into seven equal pieces.

Aisha uses a calculator to work out 290 ÷ 7.
The display gives 41.428571

To use this tape-measure Aisha needs only one number after the decimal point.

Aisha looks at the next number as well.

41.428571

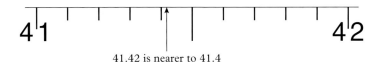

41.42 is nearer to 41.4

The number is **corrected to one decimal place**.

Exercise 6:13

Example	Round (a) 5.6179 and (b) 5.6879 correct to one decimal place. 5.6179 5.61 is nearer to 5.6 5.6879 5.68 is nearer to 5.7

1 Write these numbers correct to one decimal place.

a	56.91	**d**	6.219	**g**	14.098
b	62.97	**e**	3.439	**h**	1 306.107
c	12.678	**f**	43.6712	**i**	5.7284

Examples **1** Round the number 4.6 correct to the nearest whole number.

↑4.6

4.6 is closer to 5. It is rounded to 5.

2 3.5 is halfway between 3 and 4.
It is rounded to 4.

---

2 Round these decimals to the nearest whole number.

a	5.6	**f**	10.9	**k**	13.5
b	2.8	**g**	4.7	**l**	8.62
c	3.1	**h**	15.3	**m**	5.91
d	6.2	**i**	8.5	**n**	14.79
e	7.4	**j**	20.1	**o**	13.04

A rule to correct to any number of decimal places is:
look at the first unwanted figure.
if it is 1, 2, 3 or 4 miss off the unwanted figures.
if it is 5, 6, 7, 8 or 9, add one to the last figure you keep.

Example **a** 85.3296 correct to 2 decimal places is 85.33
b 1.7382 correct to 3 decimal places is 1.738

---

3 Write these numbers correct to two decimal places.

a	23.561	**d**	6.0048	**g**	4.0097
b	74.9873	**e**	58.9897	**h**	149.2048
c	102.5564	**f**	38.254	**i**	9.99743

4 Write these numbers correct to the number of decimal places (d.p.) given.

a	5.6715 (3 d.p.)	**f**	61.7509 (2 d.p.)
b	12.9164 (2 d.p.)	**g**	74.6891 (3 d.p.)
c	3.009 15 (2 d.p.)	**h**	46.137 91 (3 d.p.)
d	15.8478 (3 d.p.)	**i**	0.0039 (2 d.p.)
e	92.6149 (1 d.p.)	**j**	174.998 (2 d.p.)

Exercise 6:14

1 A wooden gate has the measurements:

height: 0.82 m
width: 1.05 m
diagonal: 1.3 m

What length of wood is needed to make the gate?

2 Lucy wants to invite twelve friends to a party. She buys two packets of invitation cards. The total cost is £4.70.

  a What is the cost of one pack of invitations?
  b One packet contains 8 invitations.
    How much does one invitation cost?

In another shop Lucy sees the invitations sold singly for 32p each.
  c How much would 12 have cost?
  d How much would Lucy have saved?

3 A machine makes screws 2.55 cm long. If the screws are 0.15 cm larger or smaller than 2.55 cm they are rejected.
Here are the sizes of some screws:

2.58 cm	2.39 cm	2.485 cm	2.70 cm
2.695 cm	2.655 cm	2.605 cm	2.68 cm

Miss Brown is the quality inspector. Which screws will she reject?

4 There are 143 children for the new year 7. There are five classes.
143 ÷ 5 = 28.6 children.
Suggest how many children should be in each class.

5 a What is the height of
Mr Khan's plant?

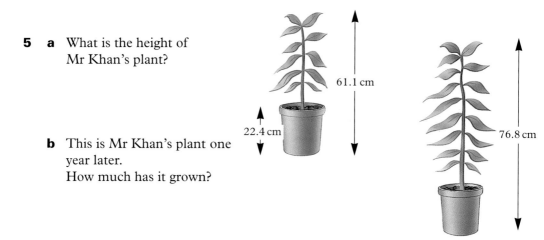

b This is Mr Khan's plant one
year later.
How much has it grown?

61.1 cm

22.4 cm

76.8 cm

6 Jolene saves for four weeks. She wants a book which costs £5.50.
Jolene saves: £1.50, £1.10, £2, £1.25.
Jolene adds like this:

```
      1.50
      1.10
         2
  +   1.25
      3.87
```

Jolene is sad that this is not £5.50.
Jolene can buy her book.
Explain why.

7 Kevin has a job in a sweet shop. Mrs Patel buys a box of chocolates
costing £2.29.
She pays with three pound coins.
Kevin works out the change

```
      3.00
  -   2.29
      1.29
```

What has Kevin done wrong?
What should the answer be?

8 Baldeep's mother gives him £6 to buy five meat pies.
They cost £1.16 each.
Baldeep works out the cost of the pies on his calculator

$5 \times 1.16 = 5.8$

Six pounds less five pounds and eight pence is 92p, thinks Baldeep.
What has Baldeep done wrong?
How much is the change?

1

Country	Population
Austria	7 526 000
Belgium	9 940 000
Denmark	5 175 000
France	54 414 000
Greece	9 665 000
Italy	56 189 000

This is the information that Craig has been given for homework.
a Which country has the largest population?
b Write the population of Italy in words.

2 Write the value of each red digit in words.
    a 123.45   **c** 1457   **e** 140.05
    b 61.004   **d** 9.152   **f** 0.607

3 Give the number between each of these pairs on a number line.
    Example 4.55, **4.56**, 4.57.
    a 3.51, ..., 3.53   **c** 1.58, ..., 1.6   **e** 0.3, ..., 0.32
    b 6.9, ..., 7.1   **d** 5.6, ..., 5.62

4 **a** Put these numbers in order of size, smallest first.
        (1) 5.417, 5.42, 5.4   (3) 0.504, 0.541, 0.514
        (2) 17.304, 17.34, 17.3   (4) 0.732, 0.7302, 0.73
    b These are times of six athletes for a 200 metre race. List the gold,
       silver, and bronze medal winners.
       R. Green   23.67 s   S. Newton   24.43 s
       W. Collins   24.90 s   L. Small   24.09 s
       T. James   25.01 s   P. Williams   23.85 s

5 **a** Complete these patterns by finding the next four terms in each case.
        (1) 0.7, 1.8, ... (Adding 1.1)
        (2) 3.86, 3.88, ... (Adding 0.02)
        (3) 10.0, 9.7, ... (Subtracting 0.3)
        (4) 0.60, 0.54, ... (Subtracting 0.06)
    b Complete these patterns.
       Write down the rule in each case.
       (1) 0.08, ..., 0.24, 0.32, ..., 0.48, 0.56, 0.64
       (2) 0.4, 0.7, ..., 1.3, 1.6, 1.9, ...
       (3) 40, 20, 10, 5, ..., 1.25, ..., 0.3125
       (4) 7.5, 7.25, ..., ..., 6.5, 6.25, 6

6 In each of these, add noughts until the division
    is finished or you get a pattern.
    a 7.31 ÷ 2   **c** 7.37 ÷ 4
    b 5.62 ÷ 3   **d** 13.6 ÷ 6

7 Sally has rounded 5.649 correct to one decimal place.
Sally's answer is 5.7.
Here is Sally's working:
5.649 rounds to 5.65
5.65 rounds to 5.7
  a Give the correct answer.
  b Explain where Sally went wrong.

8 These calculator displays show amounts of money in pounds. Write
them correctly using £. Round correct to the nearest penny if
necessary.
  a 6.4
  b 4.3 17
  c 17.3
  d 53
  e 4.752
  f 16.008

9 Mr. Truman has a shelf 110 cm wide.
Each of his video cases is 3 cm wide.
  a How many can he fit on to his shelf?
  b What size gap is left?

10 A child walks around the edge of
a rectangular lawn. He arrives
back at his starting point.
How far has the child walked?

6.2 m

3 m

11 Mr Jones bought three packets of
sandwiches and two beefburgers. He also
bought one tea, one coffee and three colas.
How much was his total bill?

Menu	
Tea	60p
Coffee	80p
Cola	60p
Packet of sandwiches	£1.80
Beefburger	£2.90

12 Kylie was asked to make up a problem for the sum 2.5 + 4.3 = 6.8.
Here is Kylie's answer.
'Andrew had 2.5 sweets. His friend gave him 4.3 sweets. Andrew now
has 6.8 sweets.'

What do you think of Kylie's answer?
Make up a better problem for the same sum.

1 Four pupils are asked to choose a number less than ten.
The numbers chosen are 9, 6, 3 and 9.
The digits are arranged to form **a** the largest number possible and
b the smallest number possible.
The numbers are: **a** 9963 and **b** 3699
The smallest number is subtracted from the largest number.

$$
\begin{array}{r}
9963 \\
-\ 3699 \\
\hline
6264
\end{array}
$$

6264 gives the next set of numbers. 6642 is the largest, 2466 is the smallest.
The method continues:

$$
\begin{array}{r}
6642 \\
-\ 2466 \\
\hline
4176
\end{array}
\qquad
\begin{array}{r}
7641 \\
-\ 1467 \\
\hline
6174
\end{array}
$$

this answer has not generated any new digits.
This stops the method.

(1) Choose your own four digits to work with and follow the same method.
(2) The example has three steps before it stops.
What is the largest number of steps that you can make before no new numbers appear?

2 Write down six different digits. Use your digits to make two 3-digit numbers. (You may only use a digit once.)
Working with your 3-digit numbers
  a find their sum
  b find their product.
  c Make two different 3-digit numbers from the same six digits.
  d find their sum
  e find their product.
  f Your aim is to find the 3-digit numbers which give the greatest sum and those which give the greatest product.
  g Describe any strategy that you have used in reaching your answers.

3 a In each of the following, write down any number which comes in between the given pair of numbers in value.
Example: 3.4 is between 3.1 and 3.5.
  (1) 7.4, 7.8   (7) 1.3, 1.4
  (2) 4, 4.2   (8) 0.41, 0.42
  (3) 2.8, 3   (9) 7, 7.1
  (4) 4.6, 4.62   (10) 0, 0.1
  (5) 1.78, 1.8   (11) 0.03, 0.031
  (6) 6, 7   (12) 0.8, 0.801
  b How many different numbers are there altogether between 1.7 and 1.9?

4 Complete these sequences by finding the missing terms. Write down the rule in each case.

a 0.01, 0.04, 0.09, ..., 0.25, ..., 0.49

b ..., 7.5, 3, 1.2, ..., 0.192, 0.0768

c ..., 1.1, 1.21, 1.331, 1.4641, ...

d 0.33, 0.5, 0.67, ..., ..., 1.18

e 1.21, 1.44, 1.69, 1.96, ..., ...

5 Dolores is wrapping a present in a box and wants to decorate it with ribbon in the way shown.

a How much ribbon is needed to finish the parcel?

b To make a bow takes an extra 50 cm.
What is the total length for the ribbon to include a bow?

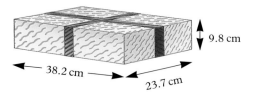

6 **a** Do the calculation 2 ÷ 3 on a scientific calculator.
Write down all the figures in the display.
You have probably written down something like 0.6666666.
Cancel the display.

b Enter exactly the same figures that you wrote down in part **a**.
Multiply by 3.
Write down all the figures in the display.

c Repeat part **a** but *do not* cancel the display.

d Multiply by 3. Compare the answer with that obtained in part **b**.
Write down what you notice.

e Repeat part **a**. Store the answer to 2 ÷ 3 in the memory.
Cancel the display. Do not cancel the memory.

f Press memory recall and multiply by 3.
Write down what you notice.

g Repeat parts **a** to **f** but use the calculation 20 ÷ 3.
Write down anything you think is interesting about your answers.

h If you noticed anything surprising in part **g**, try these
200 ÷ 3 and 0.2 ÷ 3.

i Different calculators are programmed differently. If possible, repeat parts **a** to **f** on a basic calculator. Also try a different make of scientific calculator.

j Try to explain the things you have noticed in carrying out this investigation.

- Five million eight hundred and seventy-four thousand three hundred and nineteen   5 874 319

- **Decimals in words**   *Example*: 2.35 is **'two point three five'**

- **Decimal point**   The **point** marks where whole numbers end and fractions or parts of numbers begin.
  Examples of numbers with decimal points are:
  2.4 3.145 14.08

-

thousands	hundreds	tens	units	.	tenths	hundredths	thousandths
		2	4	.	3	0	6

The red digit is **three tenths**

- **Place value**   The position of a digit in a number affects its **value**.
  Each column has a value **ten times** the one to the **right** of it.

-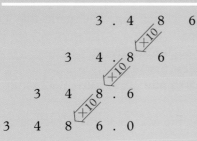

  When multiplying by **10**, the digits change by **one** column.
  When multiplying by **10 × 10** or **100**, the digits change by **two** columns.

- Putting 4.615 and 4.67 in order of size.
  4.615   4.67   The first figure after the decimal point is the same.
  4.615   4.67   1 is smaller than 7 so 4.615 is smaller than 4.67

-       4.520   19.⁶0́0   16.2   5.875
    +   6.851   −   7.53   ×   3   4)23.500
      11.371   12.07   48.6
                                       ₁

- 17.1666...   17.1̇6̇   'seventeen point one six recurring'

- A rule to correct to any number of decimal places is:
  Look at the first unwanted figure.
  If it is 1, 2, 3 or 4, miss off the unwanted figures.
  If it is 5, 6, 7, 8 or 9, add one to the last figure you keep.

1   What is the 3 in 4.312 multiplied by to give it the same value as the 3 in 431.2?

2   Add 10 to 895. Write your answer in words.

3   Multiply 2070 by 100. Write your answers in words.

4   Give the value of each red digit in words.
    a   763.42   **b**   0.608   **c**   7.004   **d**   108.43   **e**   9001.432

5   Give the number between each of these pairs on a number line.
    a   12.9, ..., 13.1   **c**   2.88, ..., 2.9   **e**   0.5, ..., 0.52
    b   7.04, ..., 7.06   **d**   6.7, ..., 6.72

6   **a** 5.637×100 **b** $20.79 \div 10$

7   **a**   Put these numbers in order of size, smallest first.
        (1)   4.053, 4.53, 4.5   (2)   0.158, 0.18, 0.58
    b   Spark plugs in car engines each have a small gap. The sparks that
        fire the petrol are made in these gaps.
        The gaps of the six plugs from one engine are given.
        Arrange them in order of size, smallest first.
        0.52 mm   0.505 mm   0.5 mm   0.575 mm   0.55 mm   0.525 mm

8   **a**   Complete these sequences by finding the next six terms in each case.
        (1)   4.4, 5.6, ... (Adding 1.2)
        (2)   0.96, 0.93, ... (Subtracting 0.03)
    b   Complete these sequences by finding the missing terms. Write
        down the rule in each case.
        (1)   ..., 0.3, 0.09, 0.027, 0.0081, ...
        (2)   7.9, ..., 6.9, 6.4, 5.9, 5.4, ...

Answer these questions without a calculator.

9   **a** $23.8 + 5.91$ **c** $53.2 - 6.8$
    b $62.9 + 7$ **d** $17 - 4.86$

10   **a** 12.8×5 **c** $17.04 \div 4$
     b $0.000\,46 \times 6$ **d** $10.2 \div 8$

11   Write these numbers correct to the given number of decimal places.
     a   2.543 (1 d.p.)   **c**   31.975 (2 d.p.)
     b   14.8761 (2 d.p.)   **d**   5.998 (1 d.p.)

7 3-D work: the extra dimension

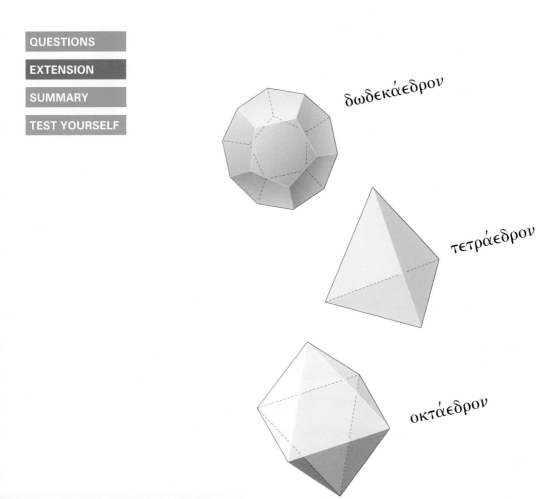

δωδεκάεδρον

τετράεδρον

οκτάεδρον

1 Identifying solids

A line has one dimension. We
need one number to give a
position in one dimension.
A is at the point 4.

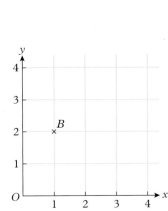

This page has two dimensions.
So does a pair of axes for a graph.
B is at (1, 2).
Its position is given by two
numbers.

Hold a pencil point about 4 cm
above *B*.

We need a third number for the
distance upwards. We can then
describe where the pencil point is.
We have three dimensions or 3-D for short.

Some books work in 3-D by
having 'pop-up' pages.

Most books rely on special methods of drawing 3-D solids on their
2-D pages.
They may also use photographs of actual solid objects.

| A jigsaw cat | An ornament cat | A real cat |

In mathematics 3-D shapes are drawn in special ways.
Hidden edges are shown by dashed lines.

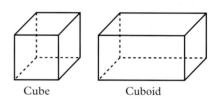

Cube Cuboid

Note: The horizontal and vertical edges can be drawn to scale.
The slanting edges give the solid effect.
They are not drawn to scale.

Exercise 7:1

1 Use this method to draw a cube on squared paper.
Use a pencil. Press lightly.

    a Start with a square.

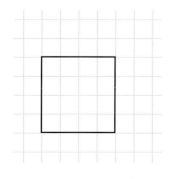

    b Draw a second square the same size.

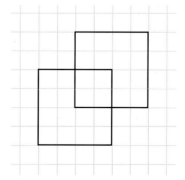

c Join the corners of the squares.

d Rub gaps in three lines. This makes the hidden edges appear dashed.

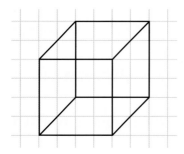 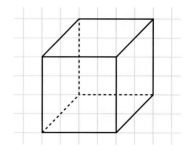

2 Draw two more cubes.
Make your cubes different sizes.

3 Copy these cuboids on to squared paper.

a

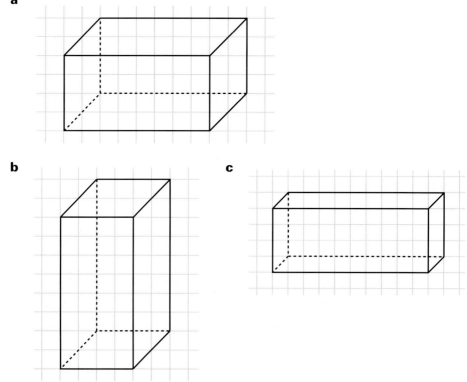

b

c

4 Two of the cuboids in Question **3** are the same.
Which two are they?
Why do you think different looking diagrams can show the same solid?

Prism

A **prism** has the same shape all the way through.
Its sides are parallel. So are its ends.

| Cube |
| Cuboid |

A prism takes its name from the shape of its ends.
Some prisms have special names. A **cube** and a **cuboid** are prisms.

The diagram shows a prism with a triangle at its ends.

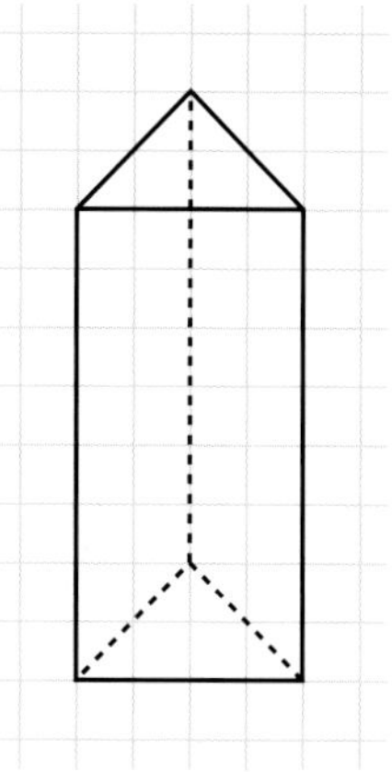

A triangular prism

5 Copy the triangular prism and label it.

Pyramid

A **pyramid** is a solid whose side edges meet in a point. All its side faces are triangles.

A pyramid takes its name from the shape of its base.

The diagram shows a pyramid with a square base.

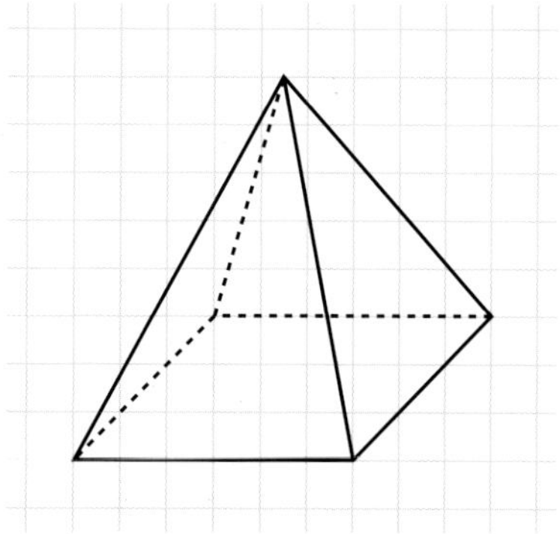

A square pyramid

Tetrahedron

A pyramid with a triangular base has a special name.
It is called a **tetrahedron**.

6 Copy the square pyramid.

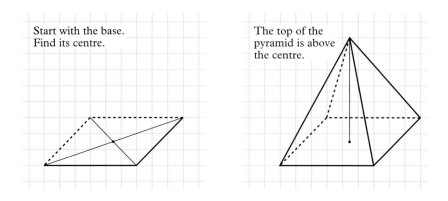

Start with the base.
Find its centre.

The top of the
pyramid is above
the centre.

Label it 'square pyramid'.

● **7** Make a list of the names of these shapes. You do not have to draw them.
Choose from: hexagonal pyramid, triangular prism, tetrahedron, pentagonal pyramid, hexagonal prism, square pyramid, pentagonal prism.

a **c** **e**

b **d**

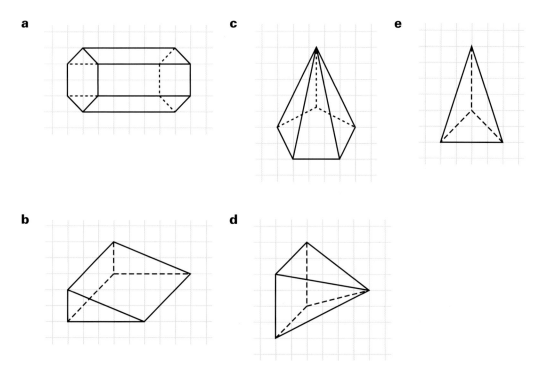

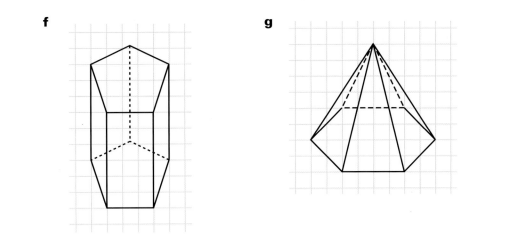

f

g

| **Polyhedron** | A **polyhedron** is a solid whose faces are all plane (flat). |

Exercise 7:2 Euler's formula

1 Copy the table leaving room for an extra column.

Polyhedron	F	V	E
(1) Cube			
(2) Cuboid			
(3) Triangular prism			
(4) Square pyramid			
(5) Tetrahedron			

2 Complete the table.
F is the number of faces. V is the number of vertices (corners).
E is the number of edges.

3 Look at the numbers.
Can you see a pattern?
Hint: If you are stuck, add an extra column, $F + V$.

4 Write about what you notice.

5 These three solids each have a curved face. They are not polyhedrons.
Do these solids fit your pattern?

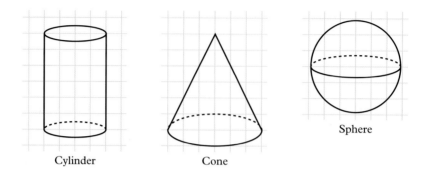

Cylinder   Cone   Sphere

Exercise 7:3

1 Copy the three solids from Exercise 7:2, Question 5.
Label each shape with its name.

2 The cylinder, cone and sphere are
common in everyday life.
Make a list or draw some of their
uses.

3 Cuboids are very common in
everyday life.
Do you know any uses for other
prisms or pyramids?

Look for all these shapes outside school.

2 Using isometric paper

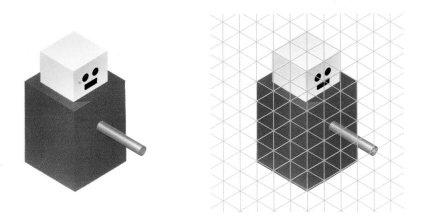

Paper with the pattern printed in triangles is called **isometric** paper.
Isometric means equal measure.
How do you think the paper got its name?

Isometric paper has a right way up.

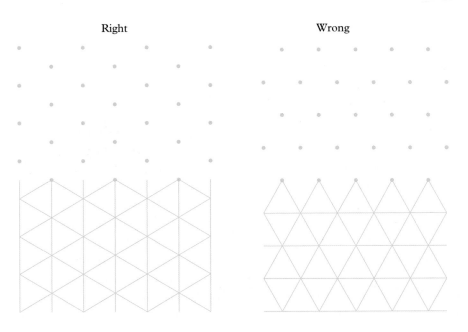

A cube or cuboid can be drawn on isometric paper with its edges shown their correct lengths. The dashed lines for the hidden edges are often missed out.

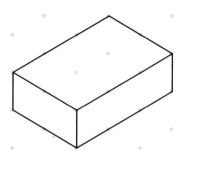

This cuboid has length 3 cm, width 2 cm and height 1 cm.

Exercise 7:4

Here are a cube and some cuboids.

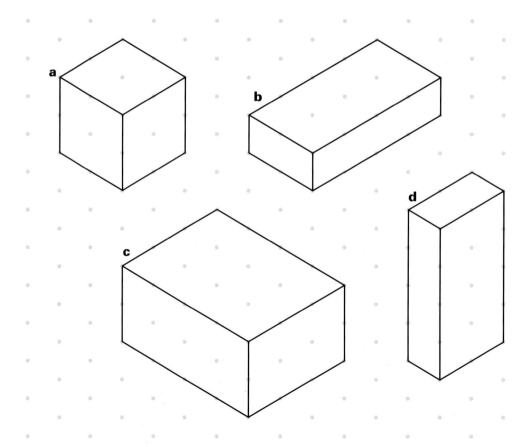

You will need 1 cm isometric paper for this exercise.

1 Copy the cube and cuboids.
For each one, write down the length, the width and the height.

2 Which two drawings show the same cuboid?

3 Draw a cube of side 3 cm.

4 Draw a cube of side 1 cm.

5 Draw a cuboid 5 cm by 2 cm by 2 cm.

6 Draw a cuboid 3 cm by 3 cm by 2 cm.

Exercise 7:5

You will need some cubes and some dotty isometric paper.

1 **a** Join two cubes as shown.
Two cubes can be joined in
only one way.
b Draw the two cubes on
isometric paper.

2 Three cubes can be
arranged in two ways.
Make the two
arrangements and draw
them.

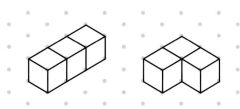

3 Take a fourth cube. Add the extra cube to each of the green faces in turn.

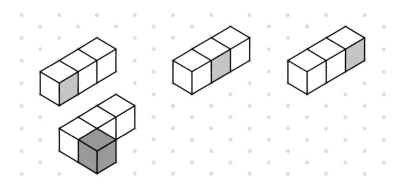

   a Are any of the arrangements the same?
   b The first arrangement has been drawn for you.
      Draw the arrangements with the cube added to each of the other two faces.

4 Repeat Question **3** with the other arrangement of three cubes.

   a Are any of the new arrangements the same?
   b Draw all the arrangements that you think are different.

5 Find other ways of joining four cubes.
Draw your results.

6 How many different ways of joining four cubes did you find altogether?

3 Nets of cubes and cuboids

Most boxes are cubes or cuboids.
They are cut from flat pieces of card and folded into box shapes.

| **Net** | A **net** is a pattern of shapes on a piece of paper or card. The shapes are arranged so that the net can be folded to make a hollow solid. |

Example

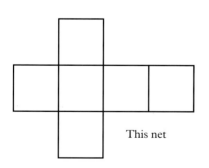 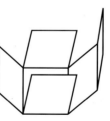

This net   would make   this cube

Exercise 7:6

1 **a** Copy the net of the cube. Make the sides 3 cm.
   b Cut out the net.
         Fold it into a cube.
   c Stick the net into your exercise book.

2 Here are more patterns. Some are nets of cubes.
  a Draw the patterns on squared paper.
  b Cut the patterns out.
     Fold them up. See which make cubes.
  c Stick the patterns into your book.
     Arrange them in two groups: those that are nets of cubes and those that are not.

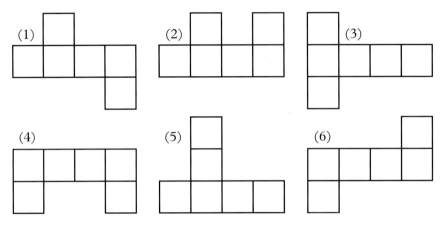

3 Six squares joined together as in Question **2** are called **hexominoes**.
  a Draw three more patterns of six squares.
  b Are your hexominoes nets of cubes?
     Cut them out and test them.
  c Stick your hexominoes in your book. Put them with the ones from Question **2**. Make sure each one goes in the correct group.

A cuboid also has six faces but they are not all the same size.

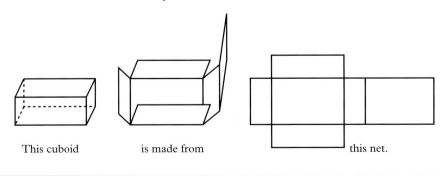

This cuboid   is made from   this net.

4 This net makes a cuboid 4 cm by 3 cm by 2 cm.

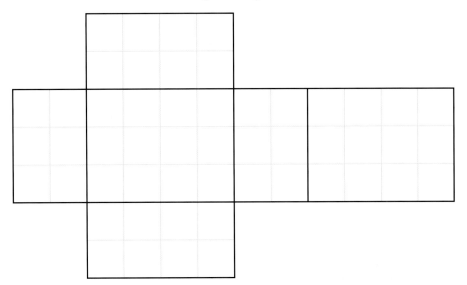

    a Make a copy of the net
    b Cut out the net. Fold it into a cuboid.
    c Stick the cuboid net into your book.

5 Here is a net. It makes a cuboid.
    a What is the length of the cuboid?
    b What is the width of the cuboid?
    c What is the height of the cuboid?
    d Make a copy of the net. Fold it to make the cuboid.

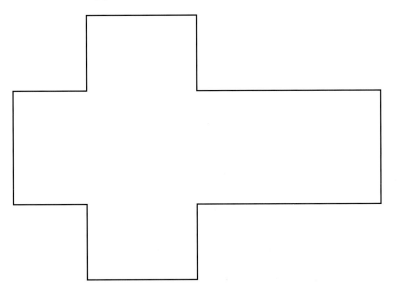

4 More about nets and solids

Exercise 7:7

Different shapes have different nets.

1 You will need some large, lined isometric paper for this question.

  a The diagram shows a pattern made by four triangles. Copy the pattern.

  b Find two other patterns of four triangles.

  c Look at the patterns.
Which of them are nets of tetrahedrons?
Cut out the patterns to see if you are right.

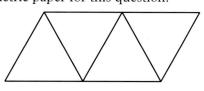

2 The diagram on the next page shows the net of a solid.

  a What is the name of the solid?

  b Measure the net.
Use compasses and a ruler to draw the net on plain paper.

  c Cut out the net.
Fold it to make a solid.

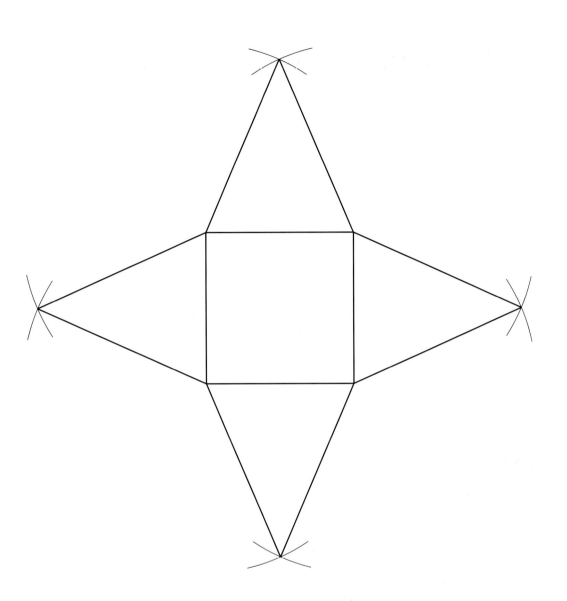

- **3** The diagram shows a triangular prism.
  - **a** Use compasses and a ruler to construct a net of the solid on plain paper.
  - **b** Cut out the net and fold it to make the solid.

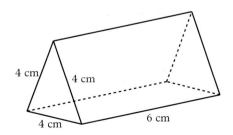

Exercise 7:8

1 A cube has each face painted a different colour.
   a How many colours will be needed?
   b How many colours will meet at any one edge?
   c How many colours will meet at any one vertex?

2 Name solids with the following numbers of faces.
   a 4   **b** 5   **c** 6   **d** 7   **e** 8

3 The rule for putting spots on the faces of dice is that opposite faces add up to seven.
This is the net of a dice.
How many spots would go on faces *A*, *B* and *C*?

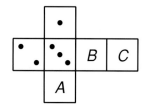

4 Which of the following are nets of cuboids?

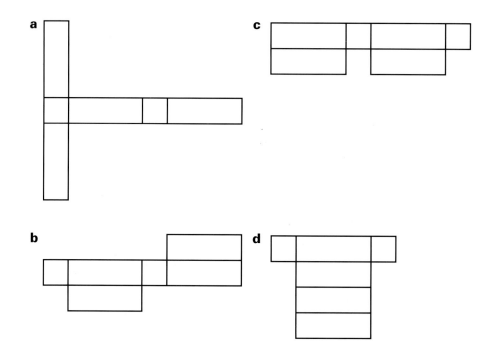

5 This cuboid is drawn on
1 cm isometric paper.
Draw a net for this cuboid.

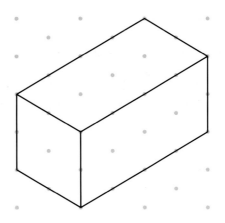

Extra things to do

1 Collect some boxes of different sizes. Open a box out flat.
You will see the net of the box. The net will have extra card.
The extra card is used as **flaps** to stick the box together. It will also
make the box stronger.
Open out some of the other boxes. The nets will not all be the same.

2 Copy the net of one of the boxes
that you have opened out on to
thin card.
Score along the fold lines.
Fold your net and glue it using
the flaps.

3 Make a cube with flaps like the
diagram.
Half the edges of this net have
flaps.

4 Make a model from different solids.
Use sellotape instead of flaps and glue.
Here are some ideas.

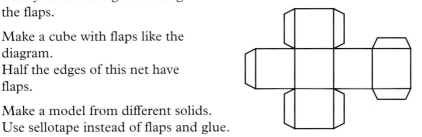

Tower

Church

Robot

House

5 Your mathematics room may have a book with nets of solids. You
could also look in the school library.

1 Sapna has stuck two solids together to get this shape.

  a What two solids has Sapna used?

  b Which of the solids is a prism?

  c How many faces, vertices and edges has Sapna's new solid?

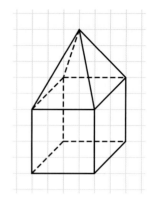

2 Draw these cuboids on 1 cm isometric paper.

  a

  b

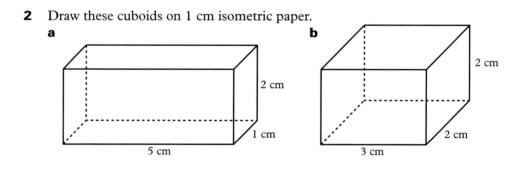

3 Draw nets of the two cuboids in Question 2.

4 The diagrams show four cubes joined together. A fifth cube is joined to each of the green faces in turn.

On isometric paper, draw sketches to show the three different solids.

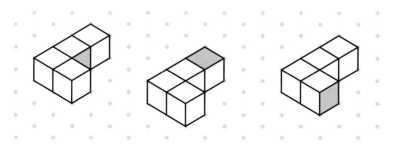

5   Here is a net. It makes a cuboid.
    a   What is the length of this cuboid?
    b   What is the width of this cuboid?
    c   What is the height of this cuboid?

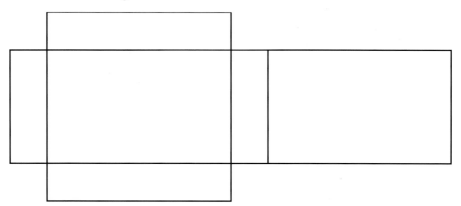

6   Copy the diagram in Question **5** on to paper.
    Cut it out and fold it to make a cuboid.

7   Write down the names of the solids that can be made from these nets.
    a   **b**   **c**

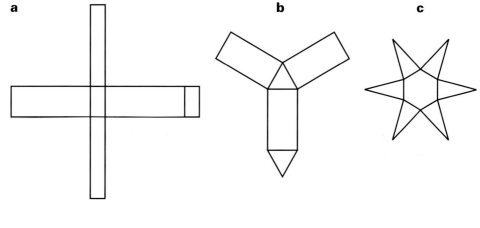

8   This cube is made of wire.
    Each edge is 5 cm long.
    What is the total length of wire
    needed?

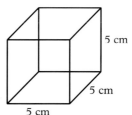

1 **a** What are the names of these solids?

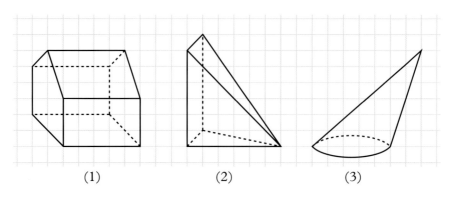

(1)   (2)   (3)

b Two identical square pyramids have their square faces stuck together.
(1) Draw a sketch of the new solid.
(2) How many faces, edges and vertices does the solid have?
(3) Can you suggest a name for the solid?
c Which of the solids in **a** and **b** is not a polyhedron?
Give a reason for your answer.

2 A regular polyhedron has identical regular polygons for its faces. This makes all the edges the same length and all the vertices look the same. There are five regular polyhedrons altogether.
a Which solids do you already know that are regular polyhedrons?
b Find out the names of the others.
c The regular polyhedrons used to be known as the Platonic solids. They were thought to have magical properties.
Find out all you can about them. You could make them.
Find their nets in a book in your school library or mathematics room.

3 Here is a solid made from four cubes.
On isometric dotty paper, draw three more views of the same solid, looked at from different angles.

You could repeat this question starting with different shapes made from cubes.

4 Six squares joined together form a hexomino.
a Investigate how many different hexomino patterns can be made.
(There are more than 30.)
b Show which of the hexominoes you have drawn are nets of cubes.

5 This is a description of a cone.
It has one face that is a circle.
Its only other face is curved.
It has one vertex and only one
edge, which is a circle.

Describe in your own words the following shapes.

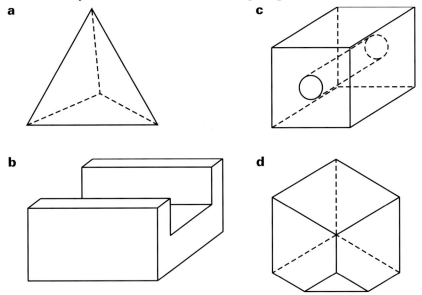

a

c

b

d

6 Which of the solids in Question 5 obey Euler's formula?

7 A room is 5 m long, 4 m wide
and 3 m high. It has two
computer network points on
opposite sides of the room as
shown.
These network points have to be
connected together using the
shortest possible length of cable.

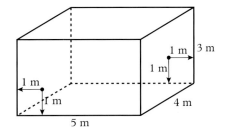

a Using a scale of 1 cm to 1 m, draw a suitable net of the room.
b Mark the positions of the network points on the net and measure
the straight line distance between them.
Hence find the shortest possible length of cable.

8   The diagram shows a
representation of a solid cube. Its
vertices have been lettered *A* to *H*.
Note *G* is below *F*, level with *H*.

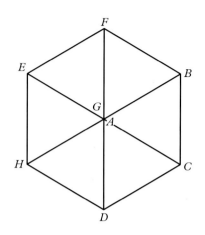

The questions below refer to the
actual 3-D cube, not to the 2-D
diagram.

a   What can you say about the
lengths of the edges *AB*, *BF*,
GH, *EH*, *AE*?

b   Is the length *A* to *C* equal to,
smaller than, or greater than
the length *A* to *B*?

c   Is the length *A* to *C* equal to, smaller than, or greater than the
length *B* to *D*?

d   What can you say about the lengths *AF* and *BE*?

e   Given the following angles, answer (without measuring):

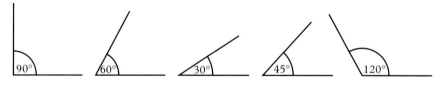

(1) What size is the angle *ADC*?
(2) What size is the angle *EAB*?
(3) What size is the angle *BFA*?
(4) What size is the angle *BDC*?

- In mathematics 3-D shapes are drawn in special ways.
  Hidden edges are shown by dashed lines.

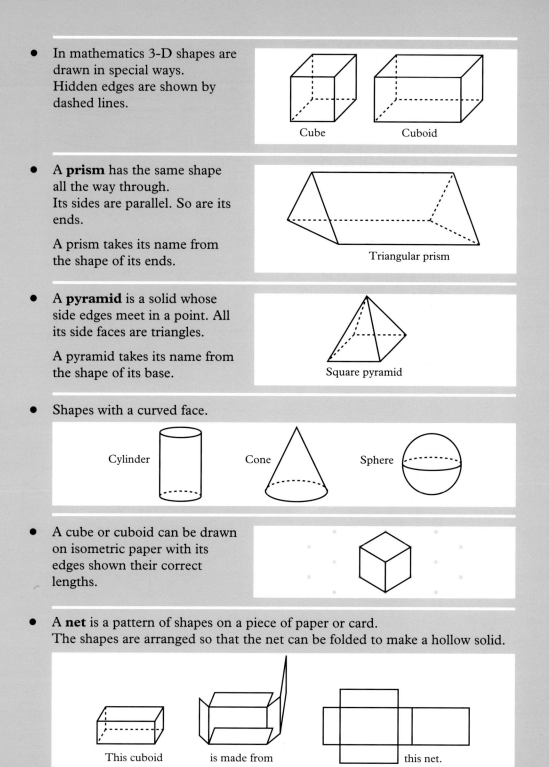

Cube   Cuboid

- A **prism** has the same shape all the way through.
  Its sides are parallel. So are its ends.

  A prism takes its name from the shape of its ends.

Triangular prism

- A **pyramid** is a solid whose side edges meet in a point. All its side faces are triangles.

  A pyramid takes its name from the shape of its base.

Square pyramid

- Shapes with a curved face.

Cylinder   Cone   Sphere

- A cube or cuboid can be drawn on isometric paper with its edges shown their correct lengths.

- A **net** is a pattern of shapes on a piece of paper or card.
  The shapes are arranged so that the net can be folded to make a hollow solid.

This cuboid   is made from   this net.

1 The diagram shows a child's toy 'posting box'. Each of the solids can be 'posted' through one of the holes.

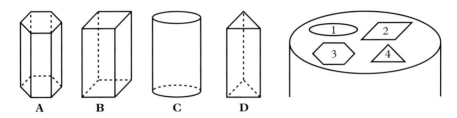

A   B   C   D

a What are the names of the solids?
b Which solid would go through which hole?
c What are the following solids called?

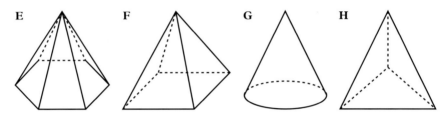

E   F   G   H

d Which of the solids A to H are not polyhedrons?

2 a Write down the length, width and height of this cuboid. It is drawn to scale on 1 cm isometric paper.
b Draw a net of the cuboid.

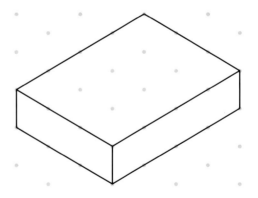

3 a What solid could be made from this net?
b How many edges would the solid have?
c How many faces would it have?
d How many vertices would it have?
e Sketch a different pattern of four triangles that could also be a net of the same solid.

8 Probability

Jacques Bernoulli

The Bernoulli family produced some of the most famous mathematicians in history.

Two brothers, Jacques (1654–1705) and Jean (1667–1748), were probably the most famous. Jacques did a lot of work on probability.

His main book, called 'The Art of Conjecturing', was the first major book about probability. It was not published until 8 years after his death.

A lot of the work on probability is very recent and has been done since 1945.

1 Probability scales

If you watch Breakfast TV you will have seen the weather forecast showing the probability of rain. The presenter may say 'There is a low chance of rain in southern England and a slightly higher chance everywhere else'.

Probability

In maths, **probability** means how likely something is to happen.

Probabilities are often shown on a scale with 'impossible' at one end and 'certain' at the other.

Example

Here is a probability scale.

```
        b                              a           c
        ├────────────────────────────┼───────────┼
  impossible  very unlikely  unlikely  even chance  likely  very likely  certain
```

We have shown on the scale
a A newly born baby will be a girl
b You will live to be 200
c The next person to come into the room will be right-handed.

Exercise 8:1

For each question below, draw a probability scale.
Mark on it points **a**, **b** and **c** to show how likely you think each one is.

1 **a** You will go home from school today
　　b A newly born baby will be a boy
　　c You will walk from London to Glasgow in one day

2   **a**   You will watch TV sometime tonight
     b   You will be late for school at least once this term
     c   It will snow on Christmas Day where you live

3   **a**   A £1 ticket will win the jackpot in the National Lottery
     b   A £1 ticket will win £10 in the National Lottery
     c   You will know the person who wins the jackpot this week

4   **a**   A coin thrown in the air will land heads up
     b   A coin thrown in the air will land tails up
     c   A coin thrown in the air will land on its edge

Random   If a person is chosen at **random** it means that every person has an equal chance of being chosen.

---

5   **a**   A person chosen at random from your school will be left-handed
     b   A person chosen at random in your school will own at least one pet
     c   A teacher chosen at random from your school will be female

To measure probability more accurately we use numbers. We use 0 for 'impossible' and 1 for 'certain'. If something is not certain to happen it must have a probability less than 1.

Probabilities are written as fractions or decimals. Sometimes they are written as percentages. You saw this at the beginning of the chapter.

Our probability scale now looks like this:

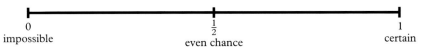

0	$\frac{1}{2}$	1
impossible	even chance	certain

6   Redraw your answers from Questions **1** to **5** on scales like the one above.
For each letter you have marked, give an estimate of the probability.
Write your answer as a decimal or a fraction.

2 How the theory works

Michelle has bought a ticket for a raffle.
100 tickets have been sold altogether.

Michelle says, 'I have a 1 in 100 chance of winning.'
In maths we write the probability of Michelle winning as $\frac{1}{100}$.

Joshua bought five tickets.
The probability of Joshua winning is $\frac{5}{100}$.

Exercise 8:2

1 James has bought one ticket for a raffle.
200 tickets were sold altogether.
What is the probability that James wins first prize?

2 What is the probability of rolling a six on an ordinary dice?

3 A letter is chosen at random from the words KEY MATHS.
What is the probability that the K is chosen?

4 Assume that a coin cannot land on its edge.
What is the probability of a coin landing so that it shows
a heads
b tails

5 Find the probability of getting each of the following when you roll an ordinary dice:
a a two
b an even number
c an odd number
d a prime number
e a score of less than 3

6   Pardeep has one 50p coin and two 10p coins in her pocket.
She takes a coin from her pocket at random.
What is the probability that she takes out a 10p coin?

7   This spinner is spun once.
What is the probability of the
spinner landing on
a   pink
b   green

8   A pupil in 7M is chosen to deliver a message.
7M has 30 pupils. There are 17 boys.
a   What is the probability that the pupil chosen at random will be
a boy?
b   What is the probability that the pupil chosen will be less than
16 years old?

9   One letter is chosen at random from the word ISOSCELES. What is
the probability of choosing
a   the C
b   an E
c   a vowel
d   a consonant

10   A pencil case contains biros of the following colours: 6 black, 6 blue,
2 red and 1 green. One biro is removed from the case without looking.
Find the probability that the biro removed is
a   black
b   green
c   yellow

11   Kieron is changing the fuse in a plug.
He has five identical new fuses in a tray. When he removes the broken
fuse he accidentally drops it into the tray. He cannot tell which is the
broken fuse.
What is the probability that the fuse he chooses to put in the plug will
work?
What do you have to assume to make your answer correct?

12 A packet of 15 fruit drops contains 6 strawberry, 4 lime, 3 orange and
2 lemon sweets.
You choose a sweet without being able to see into the packet.
Find the probability that the sweet chosen is
a strawberry
b orange
c lemon or lime

A pack of playing cards has four suits.
There are two red suits, diamonds ♦ and hearts ♥.
There are two black suits, clubs ♣ and spades ♠.
Each suit has 13 cards.

Here are the hearts:

The jack, queen, king and ace are called picture cards.
A full pack has 16 picture cards and 36 numbered cards, that makes 52 cards
altogether.

---

13 In an ordinary pack of cards,
a how many cards are red?
b how many cards are black?
One card is chosen at random from a pack. Find the probability that it
will be
c red
d black

14 One card is chosen from a pack. Find the probability that it will be
a an ace
b a two
c a heart
d a club
e a black five
f a red queen
g a picture card
h the ace of spades
i an even number
j an odd number

● **15** In her drawer, Charlotte has five pairs of socks. Three pairs are red and two pairs are green.
   a The socks are scattered in the drawer and Charlotte picks one out without looking.
   Find the probability that she chooses a red sock.
   b Assume that Charlotte did choose a red sock.
   Find the probability that the second sock she chooses is also red.

Exercise 8:3 *Higher or lower?*

This card game is for 2 players.
You will need one suit of cards.

Rules
1 Shuffle the cards.
2 Deal the 13 cards face down in a line.
3 Turn over the first card on the left.
4 Player 1 predicts whether the next card will be higher or lower than the first one.
5 Player 1 turns over the next card and scores 1 point if their guess is right.
6 Player 2 does the same with the next card.
7 Continue until all the cards are face up.
   The player with the most points is the winner.

Play the game three times.

Exercise 8:4

William and Stephen are playing 'Higher or lower'.
Each player has a list of the cards.
They cross off the cards that have gone.
The first card turned over is the 5.

William is first.
He sees from his list that 3 of the remaining 12 cards are lower than 5, and 9 are higher.
He calculates that there is a $\frac{9}{12}$ chance of getting a higher card, but only a $\frac{3}{12}$ chance of a lower card.

He says 'higher' and then turns over the next card.

The card he turns over is the 10 so he scores one point and crosses the card off his list.

2 3 4 ~~5~~ 6 7 8 9 ~~10~~ jack queen king ace

Now it is Stephen's turn.

1 What is the probability that the next card will be lower than the 10? (Remember that the 5 has gone.)

2 What is the probability that the next card will be higher than the 10?

3 What should Stephen say, higher or lower?

4 The card Stephen turned over was the 8.
Was his guess correct?

5 Now it is William's turn again.
   a What is the probability that the next card will be lower than 8?
   b What is the probability that it will be higher than 8?
   c Should William say higher or lower?

6 Stephen's turn again.
The next card William turned over was the ace so they now look like this:

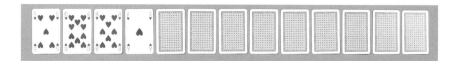

   a What is the probability that the next card will be higher than the ace?
   b What is the probability that the next card will be lower than the ace?
   c What should Stephen say?

7 Stephen turned over the 4.
Work out the probability of the next card being higher or lower than 4.
Decide what William should say.

8 The following pictures were taken in the middle of games of higher or lower.

For each one, calculate the probability of the next card being higher or lower.

Write down which is the best choice, higher or lower.

9 To make the game more interesting, Stephen and William decide to add an extra suit of cards so that there are now 26 cards altogether. They decide that if they turn over a card which is the same as the previous one, they will just ignore it and turn over another one. The first card turned over is a 10.

a What is the probability that the next card will be higher than 10?

b What is the probability that the next card will be lower than 10?

c What is the probability that the next card will also be a 10?

d The next card turned over was in fact an 8. Work out the probabilities to decide what the player should say next.

3   Experiments and games

Probability can help you when you are playing games.

In this section you are going to play some games to see how probability is involved.

Game 1   Odds and Evens 1

This game is for two players.
You need an ordinary dice.

One player is Evens and the other player is Odds.
Take it in turns to throw the dice.

Evens throws first. If the dice shows an even number then score one point. If it is odd, score no points.
Odds goes next and only scores a point if the dice shows an odd number.

Tally your score in a table like this:

Game	Evens	Odds	Winner
1	卌	|||	Evens
2	||||	卌	Odds

The first player to score 5 points wins the game.

Play the game 6 times.

1   How many games did Evens win?

2   How many games did Odds win?

3 Was this what you expected?
Why?

4 What is the probability of scoring an even number on any throw?

5 What is the probability of scoring an odd number on any throw?

Game 2 Two coin chance

This is another game for two players.
You need two coins that are the same.

When you throw two coins, one of three things can happen.
You can get:
    2 heads (HH)
or 2 tails (TT)
or 1 head and 1 tail (HT)
Each player should choose one of these three.

Take it in turns to throw the coins.
You only score a point if your choice appears on your throw.

Tally your score in a table like this:

Game	Player 1	Player 2	Winner	Winning choice HH or TT or HT
1				
2				
3				

The first player to score 5 points wins.

Play the game 6 times.
You may change your choice for each game.

1 How many times was HH the winning choice?

2 How many times was TT the winning choice?

3 How many times was HT the winning choice?

4 Was this what you expected?
Why?

5 What is the probability of getting HH on any given throw?

6 What is the probability of getting TT on any given throw?

7 What is the probability of getting HT on any given throw?

Game 3 Odds and Evens 2

This game is a new version of Odds and Evens.

This time if Odds throws an odd number, they score the number shown on the dice.

If Evens throws an even number, they too score the number shown. The first player to score 30 points wins.

1 Do you think that this is a fair game?
Why?

Play the game 6 times.
Record your results in a table.

2 How many times did Evens win?

3 How many times did Odds win?

4 Have you changed your mind about the fairness of the game?

5 Can you suggest a different way of choosing the numbers for each player to make the game fairer?

6 Does this make the game completely fair?

7 If there are three players, can the game be made fair?

Aisha is planning a probability experiment.
She has 4 red counters and 2 green counters in a bag.
She is going to pick out one counter at random.
She will record its colour. Then she will replace the counter in the bag.

Aisha is going to do this 6 times.
She expects to get 4 red counters and 2 green counters.

She plans to do the experiment 5
times so that she will pick out 30
counters altogether.
She expects:

$$5 \times 4 = 20 \text{ red counters}$$
and $5 \times 2 = 10$ green counters

When she does the experiment, this is what she gets:

Colour	Tally	Frequency
red	ⅢⅢ ⅢⅢ ⅢⅢ ‖	17
green	ⅢⅢ ⅢⅢ ‖‖	13
		Total 30

As you can see, the results are not exactly as she expected, but they are
close.

Exercise 8:5

1 Do Aisha's experiment for yourself.
Record your results in the same way.

2 Are your results the same as Aisha's?

3 If you repeated this experiment lots of times, what do you think would
happen?

4 Change your counters so that you now have 5 red and 1 green.
a If you picked a counter 30 times, how many would you now expect
to be red?
b How many would you expect to be green?

5 Do the experiment described in Question 4.
Record your results.

6 Write a sentence comparing your results with what you expected.

7 Change your counters so that you now have 7 green and 3 red.
a If you picked a counter 50 times how many greens would you
expect?
b How many reds would you expect?

8 Do the experiment described in Question 7.
Record your results.
Are they what you expected?

● **9** Change your counters again so that you now have 7 red, 6 green and 2 blue.

If you picked a counter 60 times, how many of each colour would you expect to get?

● **10** Now do the experiment described in Question **9**.
Comment on your results.

Spot the bias!

Draw the net of a cube with sides of length 3 cm on thin card.
Don't forget to add flaps!

Mark the spots on the net to make it into a dice.
Here is one way of doing this:

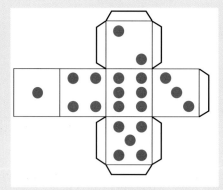

Before you make up the dice, tape a small piece of Blu-tack to the inside of one of the faces.
Write down which face you chose.

Stick the dice together.
You now have a biased dice. This means that it is not fair.

Do an experiment to test the bias of your dice.
Before you start, write down what you expect to happen.

Record your results in a suitable way. Display them using one of the methods you saw in Chapter 1.

Write up your experiment. Include what you expected to happen and whether or not you were right.
Try to explain your results.

When you have finished, swap dice with a partner. Try to find out which face their Blu-tack is on.

4 When the theory doesn't help

Dean is using a biased dice.
He cannot work out the exact probability of each score.

Dean rolls the dice 100 times.
He scores a six 35 times.

| Relative frequency | Dean estimates the probability of throwing a six with his dice. |

Dean estimates the probability of throwing a six with his dice.

He says that it is $\frac{35}{100}$.

This type of estimate is called a **relative frequency**.

Kirsty has a biased dice.
She throws it 1000 times.

Here are her results:

Score on dice	1	2	3	4	5	6
Frequency	200	300	100	150	75	175

As you can see, this is a very strange dice!

We can use this data to estimate the probability of each score.

Score on dice	1	2	3	4	5	6
Estimate of probability (Relative frequency)	$\frac{200}{1000}$	$\frac{300}{1000}$	$\frac{100}{1000}$	$\frac{150}{1000}$	$\frac{75}{1000}$	$\frac{175}{1000}$

Exercise 8:6

1 Tom throws a dice 500 times.
These are his results.

Score on dice	1	2	3	4	5	6
Frequency	25	180	80	70	100	45

Write down estimates for the probabilities of scoring each number on this dice.

2 A biased spinner has 4 coloured sections as shown in the diagram.

Harpinder wants to know the probability of getting each colour.
She spins it 600 times and she records her results.
Here is part of her table:

Colour	B	G	R	Y
Frequency	120	200	110	

a How many times did she spin a yellow?
b Calculate the relative frequency of each colour.
c The spinner is spun 1800 times. How many times do you expect to get each colour?

Research   Sometimes you may not need to do an experiment or collect data yourself.
You can use data collected by someone else.
The data may have been collected over a number of years, e.g. how often it snows in London on Christmas Day.
Finding data in this way is called **research**.

---

3 For each of the following questions, say which method you would choose to work out the probability:

Method 1 Collect your own data or do an experiment
Method 2 Research to find data
Method 3 Use probability theory to calculate it

If you decide to use method 1, then say what you would do.
Also say how much data you would collect or how many times you would repeat the experiment.

a The probability that the next car passing your school will be red.
b The probability that I win a raffle if I buy 5 tickets and 350 are sold.
c The probability that there will be an earthquake somewhere in the world next month.
d The probability that a car will be broken into in Manchester next Saturday night.
e The probability that if someone is chosen at random from your class, their favourite TV programme will be Coronation Street.
f The probability that a shoe pushed off a table will land the right way up.
g The probability of finding Grumpy in a packet of cornflakes if every packet contains one of the Seven Dwarfs.
h The probability that the volcano Mount Etna will erupt in the next year.
i The probability of winning the jackpot on a fruit machine.
j The probability that a drawing pin will land point up if dropped on to a flat surface.

1 On a probability line like the one below, mark on letters to show the probability of the following:

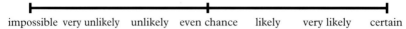

impossible   very unlikely   unlikely   even chance   likely   very likely   certain

   a December following November next year
   b A person chosen at random from your school having brown eyes
   c A piece of toast being dropped butter side down
   d Throwing a five on a dice
   e Snow falling in Sheffield in August

2 Write down the probability of each of the following as a fraction:
   a Throwing a 5 on a normal dice
   b Dealing a red card from a full pack of cards
   c Winning a raffle where you buy 1 of the 300 tickets sold
   d Picking out the one bad egg in a box of six eggs
   e A person chosen at random from your school having been born on a Sunday

3 Write down the probability of each of the following as a fraction:
   a Picking a king from a full pack of cards
   b Picking a heart from a full pack of cards
   c Throwing an odd number on an ordinary dice
   d Throwing an even number on a 10-sided dice numbered 1 to 10
   e Winning a raffle with one of your 5 tickets when 300 have been sold
   f A letter chosen at random from the alphabet being a vowel
   g A number thrown on a 12-sided dice numbered 1 to 12 being a multiple of 3

4 The following pictures were taken in the middle of a game of 'higher or lower', played with one suit of 13 cards.
For each one work out:
(1) The probability of the next card turned over being higher
(2) The probability of the next card turned over being lower
(3) The best answer for the player, higher or lower

5 Gavin is doing a probability experiment.
He puts five blue counters and seven orange counters in a bag.
He picks out a counter at random and writes down its colour.
He then puts the counter back into the bag.
  a What is the probability of pulling out an orange counter?
  b What is the probability of pulling out a blue counter?
  c If Gavin did his experiment 12 times, how many blue counters
    would you expect him to get?
  d If Gavin did his experiment 12 times, how many orange counters
    would you expect him to get?
  e If Gavin did the experiment 24 times, how many of each colour
    should he expect to get?
  f If Gavin did the experiment 36 times, how many of each colour
    should he expect to get?

6 In an experiment, a bag contains three red counters, four blue
counters and five yellow counters.
  a What is the probability of a counter taken out at random being
    (1) yellow (2) blue (3) red (4) orange?
  b A counter is chosen at random. Its colour is recorded and then it is
    replaced in the bag.
    If this is repeated 120 times, how many of each colour would you
    expect to get?
  c Would the answers you gave to part **b** be guaranteed to happen?

7 A simple game consists of a wheel
split into twelve equal sectors as
shown.
The wheel is spun. When it stops
the result is where the arrow
points.
The wheel is not biased.
  a What is the probability of
    winning the star prize?
  b What is the probability of
    winning a normal prize?
  c What is the probability of
    getting a free go?

  d What is the probability of losing?
  e How many times do you think you should spin the wheel in order
    to win a prize or get a free go?
    Explain your answer.
  f If the wheel is spun 180 times, how many times would you expect
    it to fall in each category?

1   Five red counters, four blue counters and three yellow counters are placed in a bag.
    One counter is taken out, its colour is noted and then it is replaced.
    What is the probability that
    a   The counter will be red?
    b   The counter will not be red?
    c   The counter will be either red or yellow?
    d   The counter will be green?

2   Daniel has a set of cards numbered 1 to 20.
    He picks out one card at random and then replaces it in the pack.
    What is the probability that
    a   The number on the card will be even?
    b   The number of the card will be a multiple of 3?
    c   The number on the card will be a prime number?
    d   The number on the card will be a square number?
    e   The number on the card will be a factor of 18?

3   Repeat Question **2** with a set of cards numbered from 11 to 30.
    Make a list showing which answers have changed and another showing which have remained the same.

4   A full pack of 52 cards is shuffled thoroughly. A card is chosen from the pack at random.
    a   What is the probability that the card will be a heart?
    b   If this first card *is* a heart and it is left out of the pack
       (1)   what is the probability that the next card is a heart?
       (2)   what is the probability that this second card is a diamond?

5   Three friends, Ben, Melanie and Sarah sit on a bench.
    a   Make a list of all the different orders that they could sit in.
    b   What is the probability that Ben will be in the middle?
    c   What is the probability that the two girls will be sitting together?
    d   What is the probability that Melanie will be at one end?

6   Twenty coloured counters are placed in a bag.
    One is pulled out and its colour is recorded. It is then replaced in the bag.
    This is repeated 100 times and the results show that a green counter is pulled out 68 times and a red counter 32 times.
    How many of each colour do you think are in the bag?
    Explain why.

- Probability can be marked on scales using words or numbers.

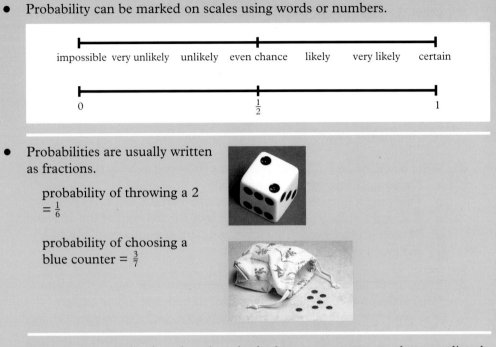

impossible	very unlikely	unlikely	even chance	likely	very likely	certain

0 $\frac{1}{2}$ 1

- Probabilities are usually written as fractions.

    probability of throwing a 2
    $= \frac{1}{6}$

    probability of choosing a
    blue counter $= \frac{3}{7}$

- Experiments can be done but they don't always come out exactly as predicted. Experiments repeated several times often produce different results.

- When probability can't be calculated it can be estimated by doing an experiment. You can do this yourself or you can look at data collected by other people.

1 Make a copy of this probability scale and then mark letters on it to show where the following statements should go.

impossible very unlikely unlikely even chance likely very likely certain

   a A page of a book chosen at random having at least one letter e on it
   b A page of a book chosen at random having at least one letter z on it
   c Throwing an even number on an ordinary dice
   d Snow falling somewhere in Scotland in January
   e Your maths teacher becoming Prime Minister

2 Write down the probability of each of the following as a fraction.
   a Throwing a four on an ordinary dice
   b Throwing a four on a 12-sided dice numbered 1 to 12
   c Winning a raffle when you have bought 5 tickets out of the 325 sold
   d Choosing a red sweet from a box with equal numbers of red, blue and green sweets and no other colours.

3 In a game of 'higher or lower', the game has reached the stage shown below. What is the probability that the next card turned over will be higher?

4 Stefan puts 3 red cubes, 2 green cubes and 5 blue cubes into a bag.
He picks out a cube at random, records its colour and puts it back in the bag.
In all he does this 100 times.
   a How many times would you expect him to get a green cube?
   b How many times would you expect him to get a red cube?
   c How many times would you expect him to get a blue cube?
   d If he picked out a cube 300 times, what would you expect the totals of each colour to be?

5 Gemma throws a dice 600 times.
These are her results.

Score	1	2	3	4	5	6
Frequency	80	110	170	80	70	90

   a Write down estimates for the probabilities of scoring each number on this dice.
   b What frequencies would you have expected from a fair dice?
   c Do you think that this dice is biased?
     Why?

9 Algebra: writing letters

QUESTIONS

EXTENSION

SUMMARY

TEST YOURSELF

The earliest algebra came from Egypt. It is over 5000 years old, dating from around the time the pyramids were built.

The ancient Egyptians used the word 'aha', meaning 'heap', to mean an unknown number. In the same way, we might use the letter x today. Problems have been discovered which were clearly set as exercises for young mathematicians.
One of these was a problem about houses, cats, mice and grain and was a very early version of our rhyme:

As I was going to St Ives,
I met a man with seven wives;
Every wife had seven sacks,
Every sack had seven cats,
Every cat had seven kits.
Kits, cats, sacks and wives,
How many were going to St Ives?

1 Writing simple formulas

Ellen and Jason are doing a sponsored swim. Ellen's sponsors will pay £2 for each length.

Ellen can work out her total sponsor money like this:
The *total* equals
£2 × number of *lengths*
In short form this is
$t = 2 \times l$

Jason's sponsors will pay £3 for each length he swims.
Jason's rule is $t = 3 \times l$

Exercise 9:1

Write down the short form of these rules.
Use the red letters and numbers.

The *total* money raised in a sponsored swim at £5 for each *length*

The *total* money raised on a sponsored walk at £4 for each *mile*

The *total* cost of a weekly magazine at £2 each *week*

The *total* cost of some carpet at £12 per square *metre*

The *recording* time on some video *cassettes* of 3 hours each

The *wages* earned by someone who earns £6 per *hour*

7   The number of *tins* of cat food needed by cats who eat 4 tins a *week*

8   The *total* weight of a number of *cars* weighing 800 kg each

9   The *total* number of children in all the *classes* at a school if there are 27 children in each class

10   The *amount* of money Andy saves if he saves £2.50 a *week*

| Algebra | **Algebra** is a short way of writing mathematical rules. It uses letters and symbols to replace words and numbers. People from many different countries can understand algebra because there are no words to translate. |

Examples

1 Mr Brown's car is 4 m long. He is buying a caravan.
The *total* length will be 4 m plus the length of the *caravan*.
In short form this will be $t = 4 + c$

2 The *money* received by 6 children when a *prize* is shared equally among them.
In short form this would be $m = p \div 6$

Exercise 9:2

Write down in short form these rules.
Use the red letters and numbers.

1 The *total* length of a car 5 m long and a *caravan*.

2 The *total* length of a mini 3 m long and a *caravan*.

3 The *total* length of a large 6 m car and a *caravan*.

4 The *length* remaining on a 10 m roll of carpet when a *piece* has been cut off.

5 The number of *sweets* remaining in a bag of 20 when some have been *eaten*.

6 The *distance* left on a 200 mile journey after travelling a number of *miles*.

7 The *money* received by 4 children when a *prize* is shared equally among them.

8   The *weight* of each cake when some *mixture* is split into 12.

9   The *number* of 3 m pieces that can be cut from a *length* of string.

10   The *sale* price of a CD player with £10 off the normal *price*.

11   The number of *free* seats left in a theatre seating 340 when some seats have been *booked*.

12   The total number of *seats* in a cinema with 16 seats in each *row*.

13   The *total* cost of a meal for *food* and £3 for drink.

● **14**   The *total* cost of a meal for *food* and some *drink*.

● **15**   The *money* received by some *children* when a *prize* is shared equally among them.

● **16**   The *sale* price of a CD player with a *discount* off the normal *price*.

· ·

| **Formula** | A rule written out in algebra is known as a **formula**. |

Examples
$$t = c \times 4$$
$$r = p + k$$
$$c = r - 5$$
$$w = z \div y$$

The formula for the total length of a 3 m car and a caravan is $t = 3 + c$. The value of c can vary but the same formula is used to find the total length.

Example   Use the formula $t = 3 + c$ to find the total length of a 3 m car with
a a 4 m caravan.
b a 3.5 m caravan.

a $t = 3 + 4$ **b** $t = 3 + 3.5$
$\quad = 7\,m$ $\quad = 6.5\,m$

Exercise 9:3

1   **a** Write down a formula for the total length of a 4 m car
        and a caravan.
    b Find the total length if
        (1) The caravan is 5 m long
        (2) The caravan is 7 m long
        (3) The caravan is 4.5 m long.

2   **a** Write down a formula for the distance left to travel on
        a 300 mile journey after travelling a number of miles.
    b Use your formula to find the distance left when you have travelled
        (1) 58 miles
        (2) 120 miles
        (3) 230 miles.

3   **a** Write down a formula for the money received by 5 people
        when a prize is shared equally among them.
    b Find how much each of them receive when the prize is
        (1) £20
        (2) £55
        (3) £125
        (4) £165.

4 A formula for the cost of a meal including food and drink is
   $c = f + d$, where c is the total cost, f is the cost of the food and
   d is the cost of the drink.
   Find c when
   a $f = 30$ and $d = 10$
   b $f = 40$ and $d = 10$
   c $f = 45$ and $d = 15$
   d $f = 24$ and $d = 9$

5 A formula to give the perimeter (distance round the outside) of a
   square is $P = 4 \times L$, where P is the perimeter and L is the length of
   the sides.
   Use this formula to find P when
   a $L = 6$
   b $L = 12$
   c $L = 16.4$
   d $L = 13.2$

2　Two-stage formulas

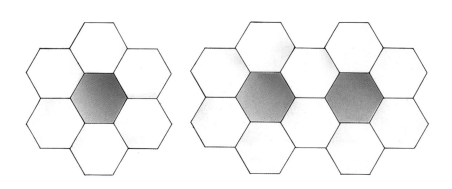

Rod is building a new patio.
He is using red and white slabs. He wants to work out how many
white slabs he needs for each red slab.
He works out a formula to help him.

Algebra and formulas can be used to solve mathematical problems.

Exercise 9:4

1　a　Copy these diagrams.

b　Copy this table and fill it in. Leave 7 more lines to finish it later.

Number of squares S	Number of blue edges B	Number of yellow edges Y	Total number of edges T
1	2	2	
2	4	2	
3	6	2	

c　Look at column **B**.
　　Copy and fill in:
　　　To work out the number of blue edges you .... the number of
　　　squares by ....
d　Look at column **Y**.
　　Copy and fill in:
　　　The number of yellow edges is always ....

e Look at column T.
It is found by adding column B to column Y.
We can put the two parts of the rule together.
Copy and fill in:
    To find the total number of edges you ………. the number of
    squares by ……… and then add ……….
f Write this sentence as a formula. Use the letters S and T.
    $T =$ ………………

You could write $T = B + Y$, but this is not as good. It does not tell
you how to work out the number of edges from the number of squares.
g Use your rule to fill in each column for 4, 5 and 6 squares.
Draw the diagrams to check your answers.
h If you are sure that your formula works, use it to fill in each column
for 7, 8, 9 and 10 squares.

Exercise 9:5

1 a Copy these diagrams.

b Copy this table and fill it in. Leave 7 more lines to finish it later.

Number of hexagons H	Number of blue edges B	Number of yellow edges Y	Total number of edges T
1	4	2	
2	8	2	
3	12	2	

c Copy and fill in:
    To work out the number of blue edges you ………. the number of
    hexagons by ……….
    The number of yellow edges is always ……….
d Look at column T.
    Use your answer to fill in this sentence.
    To find the total number of edges you ………. the number of
    hexagons by ………. and then add ……….

e Write this sentence as a formula using the letters *H* and *T*.

$T =$ ....

f Use your rule to fill in each column for 4, 5 and 6 hexagons.
Draw the diagrams to check your answers.

g If you are sure that your formula works, use it to fill in each column
for 7, 8, 9 and 10 hexagons.

2 Repeat Question **1** but this time use the octagon pattern shown below.
You could use a stencil to draw them.

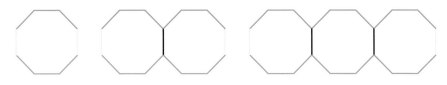

Exercise 9:6

You will need some cubes.

1 a Make these models.

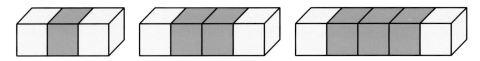

b Copy this table. Leave room for 10 rows altogether.
Fill in the table as far as row 4.

Number of blue cubes *b*	Number of blue faces	Number of yellow faces	Total number of faces *T*
1	4	10	
2	8	10	
3			
4			

c Describe in words how to work out the numbers of blue faces
(column 2) from the number of blue cubes (column 1).

d What can you say about the number of yellow faces (column 3)?

e Write down in words a rule for working out the total number of
faces (column 4) from the number of blue cubes (column 1).

f Write your answer to part **e** as a formula in algebra.

g Fill in the rest of the table up to row 10 by using your rule.

3 How to make everyone understand

〔証明〕 かりに $a+b\sqrt{2}$ が無理数でないとすると，

$$a+b\sqrt{2}=p$$

は有理数である．$b\neq0$ であるから，この式を変形して，

$$\sqrt{2}=\frac{p-a}{b}$$

となるが，a，b，p は有理数であるから，右辺は有理数となる．左辺が無理数であるから，これは不合理である．

　したがって，$a+b\sqrt{2}$ は無理数である．

There are some simple rules that everyone uses.
Algebra is the same in all languages.
You can see the algebra in this Japanese maths book.

Try to learn these rules and use them from now on.

Rules of algebra

We miss out multiplication signs because they look too much like the letter x.

We write the formula $t = 4 \times C + 3$　as　$t = 4C + 3$

$5y$ means multiply 5 by y.
The number is always written first.
We never write $y5$.

Always put the letter you are finding on the left hand side.
Write $t = 4y + z$　not　$4y + z = t$

Miss out any units.
You do not put cm in any formulas involving lengths.

Write divide like a fraction.

Write $5 \div y$　as　$\dfrac{5}{y}$

Exercise 9:7

Rewrite each of these formulas.
Use the rules on the previous page.

1 $F = m \times a$

2 $t = w \times 5$

3 $I \times R = V$

4 $y = 6 \div t$

5 $g \times 3 = t$

6 $8 + t = p$

7 $v \div t = r$

8 $y = 5 \times L + 26$

9 $6 \times C + 32 = t$

10 $u + 10 \times t = v$

Exercise 9:8

Work out a formula for each of these situations.
Write it out using the rules of algebra. The letters you should use are
given at the end of the question.

1   Triangles are drawn corner to corner as shown.
Write down a formula to work out the number of sides if you know the
number of triangles. (T = triangles, S = sides)

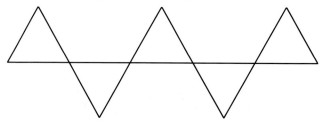

2   Squares are made out of matchsticks as shown.
Write down a formula to work out the number of matches needed
once you know the number of squares. (S = squares, M = matches)

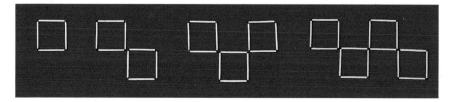

We can find formulas for all kinds of problems.

Example

The Browns hire a car for their holiday.
The cost is £30 for insurance and £50 per day hire charge.
Write down a formula for the total cost. (T = Total, d = days)

Number of days d	Hire charge	Insurance	Total T
1	50	30	80
2	100	30	130
3	150	30	180
4	200	30	230

$T = d \times 50 + 30$
$T = 50d + 30$

3 Hiring lockers at school costs £3 per term and a £5 deposit for the key. Write down a formula to work out the total cost for any number of terms. (C = cost, T = terms)

4 A series of magazines costs £3.50 per week plus £8 for a set of folders. Write down a formula to work out the total cost of the magazines when you know how many weeks it will take to collect them all. (C = cost, W = weeks)

5 For each day's work in a shop, the manager is paid £50 and each of the sales staff is paid £30. Write down a formula to work out the total amount paid to the staff. (T = total, n = number of sales staff)

6

5 m   12 m

A train has an engine 5 m long and some carriages 12 m long. Write down a formula for the total length of the train. (T = total length, c = number of carriages)

7 Year 7 are having a disco. It costs £80 to hire the disco and £2 for each person to have chicken and chips. Write down a formula for the total cost of the evening. (T = total cost, p = number of people)

8 7W are going to the zoo. It costs £60 to hire a coach and £3 entrance for each pupil. Write down a formula for the total amount 7W's form teacher will have to collect. (T = total cost, p = number of pupils)

4 Collecting terms

Cuisenaire rods are coloured rods which are all different lengths. They come in units of 1 to 10.

Different combinations of rods can be fitted together. They then make the same length as other rods.

You are going to write down your findings using algebra.

Exercise 9:9 Cuisenaire investigation

1 Find a green rod.
Make the same length with three white rods.
You can write
    One green rod equals 3 white rods
In algebra
    g = 3w   (notice that you do not write a 1 in front of the **g**)

There is another way that you can make a green rod. Use 1 red rod and 1 white rod.

Copy and fill in:
        One green rod equals 1 .... and 1 ....
Write this sentence as a formula.

g = r + w and **g = w + r** mean the same.
There is no point in writing both of them.

2 Take a pink rod.
Use two other rods to make this length.
Write down your answer as a formula.

Make a four-length using *three* other rods.
Write your answer as a formula, making sure that you write it in the shortest way possible.

Find other ways of making a four-length and write down their formulas.

3 Find as many ways as you can of making a yellow rod.
Write down their formulas.
There are six different formulas.

4 Carry on with some of the longer rods.
Work logically and carefully and find as many rules as you can for each length.
Record how many rules you find for each length.

Katrina and Liam both pay 38 p bus fare each school day.
They work out their totals for the week.

Katrina works like this: Liam does his like this:

                38   38
                38   ×   5
                38   ─────
                38   190
             + 38
             ─────
               190

Obviously they get the same total.

In algebra Katrina would write $t = b + b + b + b + b$
                Liam would write $t = b × 5$ or $t = 5b$

| **Collecting terms** | It is quicker to write $b + b + b + b + b$ as $5b$. This is called **collecting terms**. |

In the same way $c + c + c = 3c$ $3d + 4d = 7d$ and $5e - 3e = 2e$

Exercise 9:10

Collect these terms.

1   $a + a + a + a$

2   $g + g + g + g + g + g$

3   $h + h + h + h + h$

4   $k + k$

5   $d + d + d + d$

6   $3s - 2s$

7   $3c - c$

8   $2p + 2p$

9   $5q - 2q$

10   $6d - 5d$

11   $6m - 6m$

12   $4d - 3d$

13   $4c + 3c$

14   $2p + 6p$

15   $b + b + 2b$

16   $c + 2c + c$

17   $2h + 2h + 2h$

18   $3g + 2g - g$

19   $6k - 4k - k$

20   $7p - p - 2p$

Different letters and numbers are collected separately.

Examples	1 $2a + 3b$ cannot be collected.
	2 $2a + 4a + 3b = 6a + 3b$
	3 $4t + 2 + 3t = 7t + 2$
	4 $3g - 2g + 2h + 4h = g + 6h$

Exercise 9:11

Collect these terms.

1 $2s + 3s + 2t + 4t$

2 $3d + d + e + 2e$

3 $3g + 4g + 2h$

4 $2k + k + 4$

5 $3c + 4d + 2d$

6 $6y + 4z - 2z$

7 $3r + 4s$

8 $6f + g + 2g$

9 $4c + 2b + 2c + 3b$

10 $3y + 2z + 3y + 4z$

11 $5g + 3h + 3h + 2g$

12 $5v + 3w + 2v$

13 $3p + 2q + 3q + p$

14 $2d + 3 + 3d + 2$

15 $3b + 4 + 2b$

16 $5 + 2a + 3 + a + 3a$

17 $5s - 2s + 4t - 2t$

18 $6f - 4f + 6g - 3g$

19 $5k - 3k + 5 - 1$

20 $7y - 5y + 3z - 3z$

● **21** $5b + 4c - 3b - 2c$

● **22** $7r + 6s - 5s - 2r$

● **23** $6 + 4p - 4 - 2p$

● **24** $5a + 5b - 2b + 2a$

5 Substituting in formulas

You can use algebra and formulas to work out codes.
These codes can be used to write messages.

Here is a simple way of numbering the alphabet.

a	*b*	*c*	*d*	*e*	*f*	*g*	*h*	*i*	*j*	*k*	*l*	*m*
1	2	3	4	5	6	7	8	9	10	11	12	13

n	*o*	*p*	*q*	*r*	*s*	*t*	*u*	*v*	*w*	*x*	*y*	*z*
14	15	16	17	18	19	20	21	22	23	24	25	26

Examples

Using $b = 2$, $c = 3$, $d = 4$ and $e = 5$

$$3d = 3 \times d \qquad be = b \times e \qquad c^2 = c \times c$$
$$= 3 \times 4 \qquad\quad = 2 \times 5 \qquad\quad = 3 \times 3$$
$$= 12 \qquad\qquad\; = 10 \qquad\qquad = 9$$

Exercise 9:12

Work these out.

1	$3b$	**6**	cd
2	$4e$	**7**	$3e$
3	$6c$	**8**	b^2
4	ce	**9**	d^2
5	bd	**10**	e^2

Examples The numbers can be used as a code to write messages.

$$c + 5 = 3 + 5 \qquad 2d - f = 8 - 6$$

Use the answers $= 8 \qquad\qquad = 2$
to find new letters: $= h \qquad\qquad = b$

Exercise 9:13

Here are some messages for you to solve.

A **1** $c + 10$ **6** $d + e$

2 $6 - e$ **7** $y - f$

3 $q + 3$ **8** $k - e$

4 $g + 1$ **9** $j + k$

5 $u - 2$ **10** $20 - f$

B **1** d^2 **6** bc

2 c^2 **7** ce

3 $e^2 + a$ **8** $c^2 + c^2$ (this could be written as $2c^2$)

4 $d^2 + j$ **9** $ce + ae$

5 a^2 **10** $e^2 - t$

11 $cg - de$

C **1** $c + g + m$ **7** $3bc + a$

2 $b + f - c$ **8** $3bd - w$

3 $2d + 3e$ **9** $3(b + e)$

4 $3g - 2j$ **10** $be + c^2$

5 $2(c + d)$ **11** $e^2 - ch$

6 $4(g - b)$ **12** $\dfrac{n}{2}$

13 $\dfrac{t}{4}$

14 $be + c^2$

D Use the code to write some messages of your own.

Exercise 9:14

These are some formulas used in science and maths.

1 $P = 4l$ gives the perimeter (distance round) a square.
Find P when $l = 3$.

2 $P = 2l + 2w$ gives the perimeter
of a rectangle.
Find P when $l = 4$ and $w = 3$.

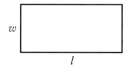

● **3** $P = 2(l + w)$ is another way of writing the perimeter of a rectangle.
Find P when $l = 5$ and $w = 3$.

4 $y = \dfrac{f}{3}$ is a formula for changing feet into yards.
Find y when $f = 6$.

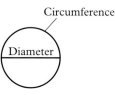

5 $C = 3d$ is a formula for estimating
the circumference of a circle.
Find C when $d = 4$.

6 A formula used in science is $F = ma$ where F is a force.
Find F if $m = 4$ and $a = 10$.

7 $S = \dfrac{D}{T}$ is a formula for finding your speed if you know your distance
and time.
Find S when $D = 100$ and $T = 2$.

8 $p = 8g$ is a formula for changing gallons to pints.
Find p when $g = 3$.

9 $D = \dfrac{M}{V}$ is a formula used in science to find density.
Find D when $M = 12$ and $V = 3$.

10 $D = ST$ is a formula to find distance if you know the speed and time.
Find D when $S = 50$ and $T = 3$.

11 $V = IR$ is a formula used in electricity to calculate voltages.
Calculate V when $I = 3$ and $R = 80$.

● **12** Another formula used in maths and science is $v = u + at$
where v is the velocity (how fast something is travelling).
Find v when $u = 5$, $a = 10$ and $t = 3$.

Exercise 9:15

Here are some problems to solve. The formulas are written in words. You can solve the problems using the words but see if you can write the formula in symbols as well. Use the red letters.

1 The *perimeter* (distance round the outside) of a square is found by multiplying the *length* of one of the sides by 4.
Find the perimeter of a square with sides of length 5 cm.

2 The *perimeter* of a rectangle is found by adding the *length* to the *width* and doubling the answer.
Find the perimeter of a rectangle which is 7 cm long and 2 cm wide.

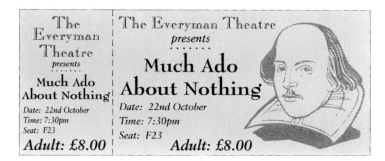

3 The cost of a *child's* ticket at the theatre can be calculated by finding half of the cost of an *adult's* ticket.
How much does a child's ticket cost when an adult's ticket is £8?

4 To estimate the *time* for a journey, divide the *distance* travelled by the average *speed*.
How long will a 200-mile journey take at an average speed of 50 miles per hour?

5 The number of *classrooms* needed in a school can be estimated by dividing the number of *pupils* in the school by the *average* number in a class.
How many classrooms will be needed by a school of 300 pupils with an average of 30 in a class?

6 To calculate a shop assistant's *wages*, multiply the number of *hours* spent serving in the shop by the *rate* of pay per hour.
How much does a shop assistant get after working 8 hours for £3 an hour?

7 The average *s*peed of a runner can be found by dividing the
*d*istance run by the *t*ime taken.
What is the average speed of a runner who covers 100 metres in
10 seconds?

8 To estimate the *c*ircumference of a circle multiply the *d*iameter by 3.
Estimate how far it is around a circular table that is 2 metres across.

9 At a school concert everybody gets a cup of tea in the interval.
To estimate the number of *p*ints of milk needed for the tea, divide the
number of *t*ickets sold by 20.
How many pints of milk will be needed when 400 tickets have been
sold?

10 Count the number of *s*econds between a flash of lightning and the
noise of the thunder. Divide the answer by five.
This gives the distance in *m*iles to the centre of the storm.
How many miles is it to a storm where the lightning and thunder are
separated by 15 seconds?

1 Write down the short form of these rules. Use the red letters and numbers.
  a The *t*otal raised in a sponsored run at £2 a *m*ile.
  b The *t*otal length of a 4 m car with a *b*oat trailer.
  c The *h*eight of a 6 ft post after a *p*iece has been cut off.
  d The *a*mount each receives when 4 friends share a *p*rize.
  e The *t*otal cost of some *b*ags of sweets at *p* pence a bag.
  f The *n*umber in a form when the *p*upils in year 7 are divided into *f* forms.
  g The *l*ength remaining in a *b*all of string when a *p*iece is cut off.
  h The *t*otal length of a building plot for a *h*ouse and a *g*arden.

2 Rewrite each of these formulas. Use the rules of algebra.
  a $P = m \times g \times h$ **e** $S = a \times b + c \times d$
  b $D \div T = S$ **f** $A = s \times s$
  c $m \times v = M$ **g** $s \times 16 = v$
  d $A = b \times h \div 2$

3 **a** The teachers at Stanthorne High are having a Christmas social. It costs £100 to hire a disco and £4 each person to provide a supper. Write down a formula for the total cost.
    (T = total cost, P = number of people)
  b A goods train is made up of an engine pulling some trucks. The engine is 7 metres long and the trucks are each 8 metres. Write down a formula for the total length of the train.
    (L = total length, t = number of trucks)

4 Collect these terms.
  a $b + b + b + b + b$ **f** $7j - 5j + 4k - 2k$
  b $3c + 4c - 2c$ **g** $5a + 4b - b - 3a$
  c $3p + 2p + 7q + 3q$ **h** $8 + 6d + 5 - 5d$
  d $4g + 3h + g + 2h$ **i** $7s - 3s + 5t + t - 2t$
  e $3y + 2y + y + 2z$ **j** $5f + 4g - 5f - 3g$

5 Work these out using $r = 3$, $s = 4$, $t = 6$
  a r^2 **f** $\frac{t}{3}$ **k** $3t - 2r$
  b $s^2 + s^2$ **g** $rs + t$ **l** $\frac{t}{2}$
  c $r + s + t$ **h** $rt - 2s$ **m** rst
  d $r + s - t$ **i** $2r + 2s$ **n** $2rs$
  e $2t - 3s$ **j** $5t - 5r$ **o** $\frac{t}{r}$

6 Solve these problems

a The formula can $R = \dfrac{H \times P}{50}$ can be used to estimate the number of rolls of wallpaper needed to paper a room of height H feet and perimeter (distance round the room) P feet.
Find the number of rolls of wallpaper needed to paper a room of height 7 feet and perimeter 100 feet.

b $O = 16P$ is a formula for changing pounds into ounces.
How many ounces are there in 5 pounds?

c $E = 10mh$ is a formula used in science for calculating energy.
Find the energy when $m = 2$ and $h = 4$.

d A formula sometimes used in maths is $s = \dfrac{a + b + c}{2}$
where s is the distance half way round a triangle.
Find s when $a = 5$ **cm**, $b = 7$ **cm** and $c = 6$ **cm**.

7 In these problems the formula is written in words.
You can solve the problems using the words but see if you can write the formula in symbols as well.
Use the red letters.

a The $p$erimeter (distance round the outside) of a regular octagon can be found by multiplying the length of one $s$ide by eight.
Find the perimeter of a regular octagon of side 5 cm.

b The number of $t$axis needed to get some $g$uests to a wedding is found by dividing the number of guests by five.
Work out how many taxis would be needed for 40 guests.

c The number of carpet $t$iles needed to cover the floor of a room can be found by multiplying the $l$ength of the room by its $w$idth and multiplying the answer by four.
Find the number of tiles needed for a room which is 6 metres long and 4 metres wide.

d To estimate the $d$istance an aeroplane will travel in a given time, multiply the $s$peed of the plane by the $t$ime.
How far would a plane travelling at 600 miles per hour travel in 3 hours?

1 *Cuisenaire investigation extension*

It is possible to write some formulas from a different point of view.
You saw earlier that 1 red rod was the same length as two white rods.
As a formula we wrote this as $r = 2w$
Now think of this the other way around:

> One white rod is the same as half a red one, or one red rod divided by 2.

As a formula this would be $w = \dfrac{r}{2}$

Take a green rod which is the same as three whites or $g = 3w$
Write this formula in a different way starting with $w =$
Write a formula starting with $w =$ for each of the other colours.

Look at the following formulas and see which are true.

a $r = \dfrac{p}{2}$ **d** $t = \dfrac{O}{2}$

b $g = \dfrac{b}{3}$ **e** $w = \dfrac{b}{10}$

c $r = \dfrac{y}{4}$ **f** $y = \dfrac{O}{2}$

Now make up some other formulas about Cuisenaire rods that involve fractions.

2 Simplify these expressions by collecting like terms.

a $3f + 4g + 5h + 2f + 3g + 2h$ **f** $4r + 5 - 4 - 3r - 1 - r$

b $4f + 3 - 2 - 2f + 3g - g$ **g** $3pq + 2rs + 2qp + 4sr$

c $3ab + 2cd + 4ab + 5cd$ **h** $5uv + 4vw + 4wv + 3vu$

d $5ab + 2bc + 3bc + 2bd$ **i** $5a^2 + 7 - a^2 - 3 - 2a^2 + 4$

e $3a + 2ab + 4b - 7$ **j** $2b + 3b^2 + 3b - b^2$

3 Find the value of these. Use $c = 5$, $d = 3$ and $e = 6$.

a $4 + c + d + e$ **f** $cd + ce + de$

b $c^2 + d^2 + e^2$ **g** $3c^2$ ($3 \times c^2$ or $3 \times c \times c$)

c $c(d + e)$ **h** $2d^2$

d $\dfrac{1 + d + e}{c}$ **i** $5e^2$

e $\dfrac{3(c + d)}{e}$

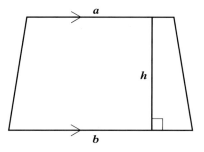

4 a The area of a trapezium is given by the formula $A = \dfrac{h(a + b)}{2}$
where **a** and **b** are the parallel sides and **h** is the height.
Calculate the area of a trapezium of height 6 cm and with parallel
sides of length 8 cm and 10 cm.

b The formula $s = ut + 5t^2$ is used in maths and physics to calculate
the distance **s** moved in time **t**, where **u** is the starting velocity.
Calculate **s** when $u = 0$ and $t = 4$.

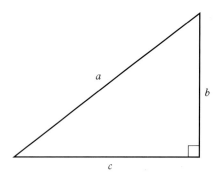

c The formula $a^2 = b^2 + c^2$ connects the three sides of a right-angled
triangle. If $b = 3$ cm and $c = 4$ cm, find a^2. Hence find **a**.

5 Here are some formulas written in words.
Write the formulas in symbols before you solve the problems.

a To get a temperature in degrees Celsius from one given in degrees
Fahrenheit, subtract 32 then divide the result by 9 and multiply by 5.
Change 50 degrees Fahrenheit to degrees Celsius.

b To turn a temperature in degrees Celsius to one in degrees
Fahrenheit, divide by 5 and multiply by 9. Add 32 to the result.
Change 20 degrees Celsius to a temperature in degrees Fahrenheit.

c Gurjeet dropped a stone down a well. He timed the interval to the
splash at the bottom in seconds. The *d*epth of the well in metres is
given by the *t*ime squared multiplied by 5.
How deep is the well if the time to the splash is 4 seconds?

- Algebra is a short way of writing mathematical rules. It uses letters and symbols to replace words and numbers.

- A rule written out in algebra is known as a formula.

- **Rules of algebra**

  We miss out multiplication signs because they look too much like the letter x.

  We write the formula $t = 4 \times C + 3$ as $t = 4C + 3$

  $5y$ means multiply 5 by y.
  The number is always written first.
  We never write $y5$.

  Always put the letter you are finding on the left hand side.
  Write $t = 4y + z$ not $4y + z = t$

  Miss out any units.
  You do not put cm in any formulas involving lengths.

  Write divide like a fraction.
  Write $5 \div y$ as $\dfrac{5}{y}$

- It is quicker to write $b + b + b + b + b$ as $5b$.
  This is called collecting terms.

  Collect different letters and numbers separately.

  1 $2a + 3b$ cannot be collected.

  2 $2a + 4a + 3b = 6a + 3b$

  3 $4t + 2 + 3t = 7t + 2$

  4 $3g - 2g + 2h + 4h = g + 6h$

- You can use algebra and formulas to work out codes.
  Using $b = 2$, $c = 3$, $d = 4$ and $e = 5$

$3d = 3 \times d$	$be = b \times e$	$c^2 = c \times c$	$c + 5 = 3 + 5$
$= 3 \times 4$	$= 2 \times 5$	$= 3 \times 3$	$= 8$
$= 12$	$= 10$	$= 9$	

1. Write down the short form of these rules. Use the red letters and numbers.
   a The *t*otal money raised in a sponsored silence at £2 per *h*our of silence.
   b The *t*otal length of a 7 m van and a *c*aravan.
   c The *l*ength remaining when a *p*iece of dress material is cut off a roll 15 metres long.
   d The *a*mount of money each receives when a *p*rize is shared by 3 sisters.
   e The *t*otal cost of a *c*offee and a *b*iscuit.
   f The *t*otal length of a *c*ar towing a *b*oat.

2. Rewrite each of these formulas using the rules of algebra.
   a $P = m \times f$
   b $M \div V = D$
   c $A = 3 \times a + b$
   d $w \times 10 = b$

3. A mail order company charge £15 each for football shirts plus £5 per order for postage and packing. Write down a formula for the total cost of an order for football shirts.
   (t = total cost, f = number of football shirts ordered)

4. Simplify these by collecting like terms.
   a $k + k + k + k$
   b $7p - 5p + 2p$
   c $5c + 2c + 4b + 3c$
   d $4n + 4 + 3 + 5n$
   e $5r + 4s - 3r - 2s$
   f $5p + 6q - 5q + 2p$

5. Work these out using $f = 2$, $g = 4$
   a f^2
   b fg
   c $\dfrac{g}{f}$
   d $2f + 3g$
   e $3(f + g)$
   f $g^2 - 5f$

6. a $A = \dfrac{bh}{2}$ is a formula often used in mathematics.
      Find the value of A when $b = 6$ and $h = 10$.
   b Use the formula $M = m(v - u)$ to calculate M when $m = 4$, $v = 2$ and $u = 0$.

7. In these problems the formula is written in words.
   You can solve the problems using the words but see if you can write the formula in symbols as well.
   Use the red letters.
   a The *p*erimeter (distance round the outside) of a regular pentagon is five times the length of one *s*ide.
      Find the perimeter of a regular pentagon of side 6 cm.
   b An estimate of the number of *k*ilometres can be obtained from the number of *m*iles by multiplying by eight and dividing the answer by five.
      Estimate the number of kilometres equivalent to 20 miles.

10 Angles

The Earth's orbit

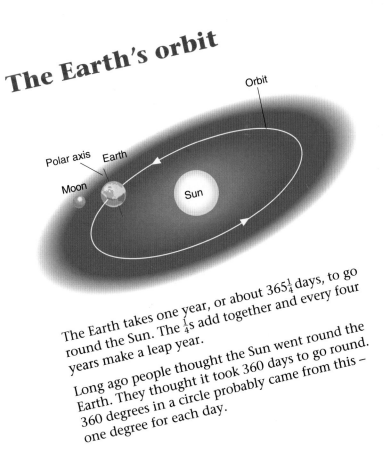

The Earth takes one year, or about $365\frac{1}{4}$ days, to go round the Sun. The $\frac{1}{4}$s add together and every four years make a leap year.

Long ago people thought the Sun went round the Earth. They thought it took 360 days to go round. 360 degrees in a circle probably came from this – one degree for each day.

1 Introducing angles

The pirate ship turns one way.
It then turns back the other way.

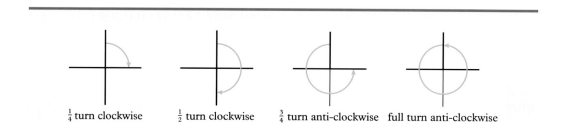

$\frac{1}{4}$ turn clockwise $\frac{1}{2}$ turn clockwise $\frac{3}{4}$ turn anti-clockwise   full turn anti-clockwise

Exercise 10:1

1 For each part write down the fraction of a turn.
Write down if the turning is clockwise or anti-clockwise.

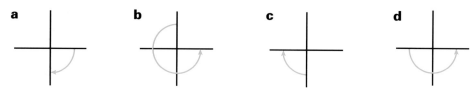

a   **b**   **c**   **d**

2 Copy the map. Write down the
fraction of a turn and say if the
turning is clockwise or anti-clockwise:
  a When Sally goes to school.
  b When Sally goes home from
     school.

3 Describe these journeys in terms of clockwise or anti-clockwise

   a Luke leaves school and goes to the library.

   b Luke walks from the library to his home.

---

right angle

$\frac{1}{4}$ turn is called a **right angle**.

The corners of squares and rectangles are right angles.

A right angle is often shown like this:

$\frac{1}{2}$ turn makes a straight angle or line.

---

4 **a** Draw a square of side 4 cm.

   b Mark the four corners using the sign for a right angle.

5 Take a piece of rough paper.

   a Fold it to make a straight line.

   b Fold it again to make a right angle.

   Keep your right angle to use later.

6 Look for right angles in your classroom.
Write down six things with right angle shaped corners.

degree

We use degrees (written °) to measure angles.

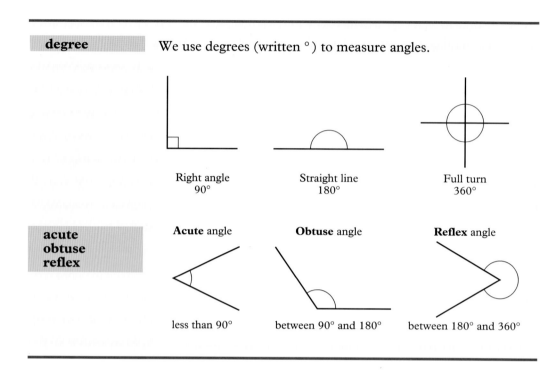

Right angle
90°

Straight line
180°

Full turn
360°

acute
obtuse
reflex

Acute angle

Obtuse angle

Reflex angle

less than 90°

between 90° and 180°

between 180° and 360°

Exercise 10:2

Use your folded right angle to help you with this question.

1 Write down the angles that are:
    a right angles   **c** acute angles   **e** obtuse angles.
    b straight lines   **d** reflex angles

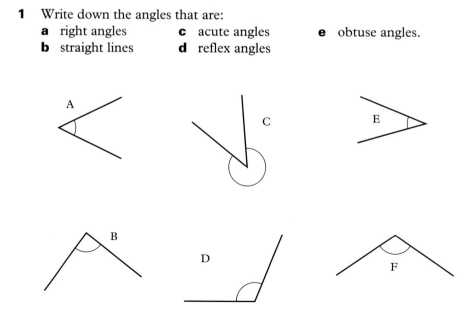

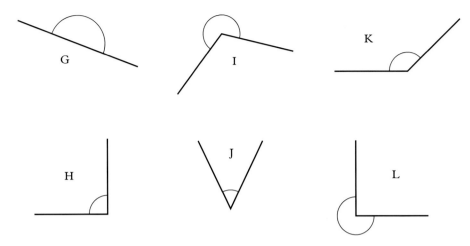

Example   Estimate the sizes of these angles.

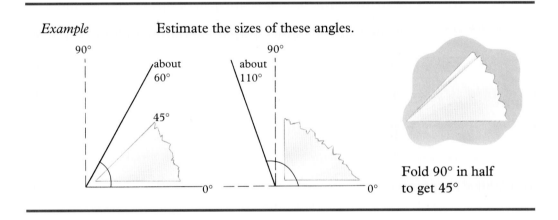

Fold 90° in half
to get 45°

Exercise 10:3

Estimate the size in degrees of each of the angles on the next page.
Use your folded right angle to help you.
Copy this table and fill in your estimates. You will need the 'Actual'
column later.

	Estimate	Actual
1		
2		
3		

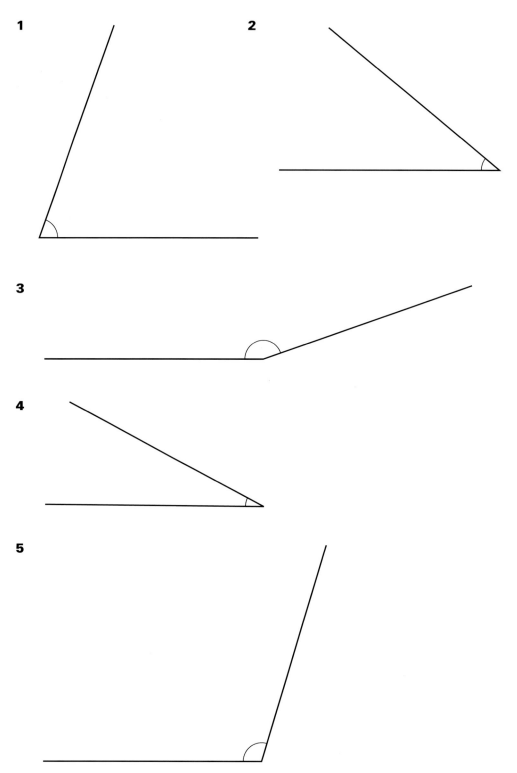

1

2

3

4

5

6

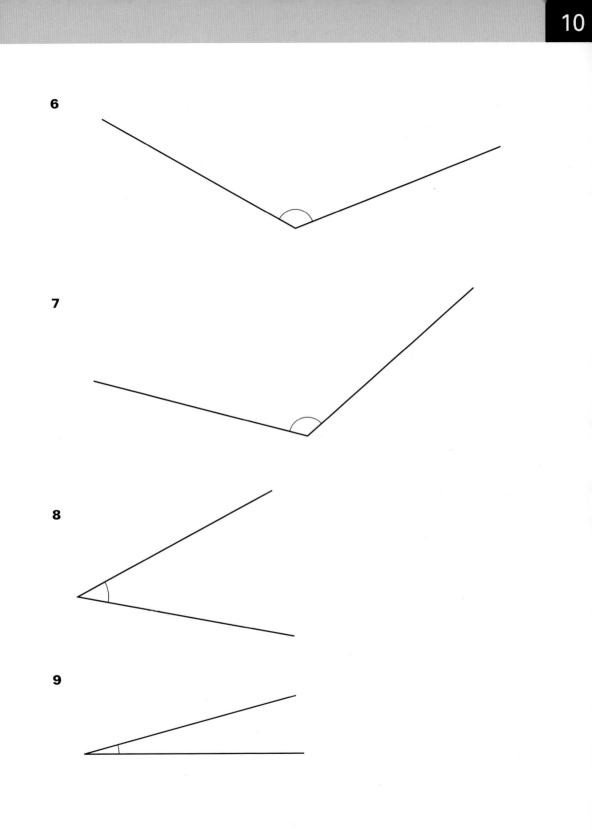

7

8

9

Measuring angles	We use a protractor or angle measurer to measure angles. This can be in the shape of either half or full turns.

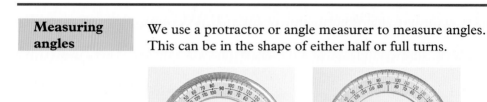

A protractor has a clockwise scale and an anti-clockwise scale.

10 Use your protractor to measure the angles in questions **1–9** accurately.
Write your answers in the 'Actual' column in your table.
Compare your answers with your estimates.

Exercise 10:4

Use your protractor to draw these angles.
Label each angle like this:

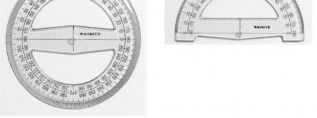

1 60°   **4** 145°   **7** 57°

2 45°   **5** 75°   **8** 168°

3 130°   **6** 105°   **9** 23°

● **10** The sketch shows a pentagon in a house shape.
  a Make an accurate drawing of the pentagon.
  b Measure the angle at the top of the roof.

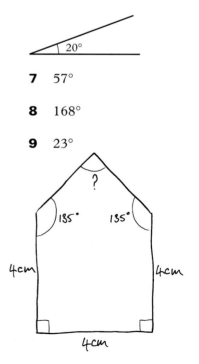

2 Calculating with angles

We do not always find angles by measuring.
We can calculate angles.

The angles on a straight line add up to 180°

Example

Calculate angle *a*

$a = 180° - 80°$
$a = 100°$

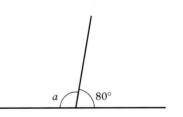

Exercise 10:5

Calculate the angles marked with letters.

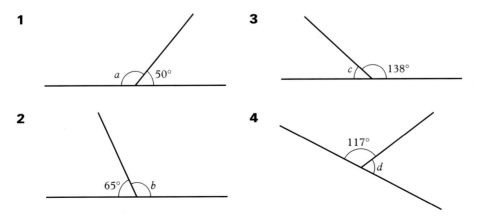

1

a 50°

3

c 138°

2

65° *b*

4

117° *d*

5

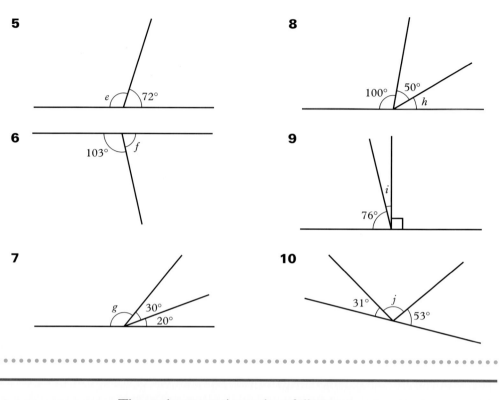

e 72°

8

100° 50° h

6

103° f

9

76° i

7

g 30° 20°

10

31° j 53°

- -

The angles at a point make a full turn.
They add up to 360°

Example   Calculate angle *a*

$a = 360° - 290°$
$a = 70°$

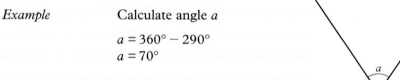

a

290°

Exercise 10:6

Calculate the angles marked with letters.

1

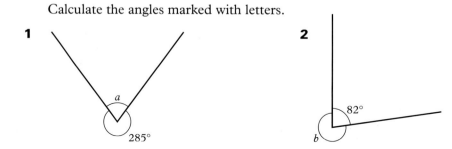

a

285°

2

82°

b

3

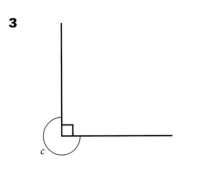

4

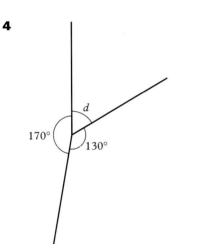

5

6

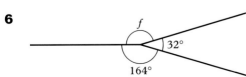

7

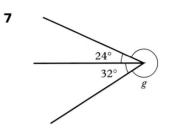

8

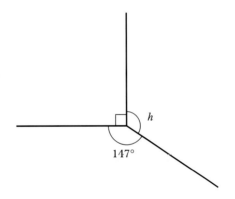

9

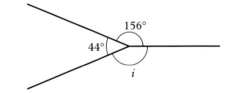

10

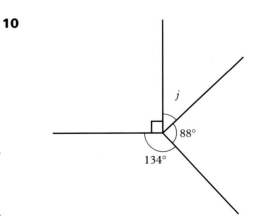

Exercise 10:7

A circular protractor or angle measurer is best for this exercise.

If you have a semi-circular protractor, measure the smaller angle. Subtract the smaller angle from 360°.

Measure these angles.

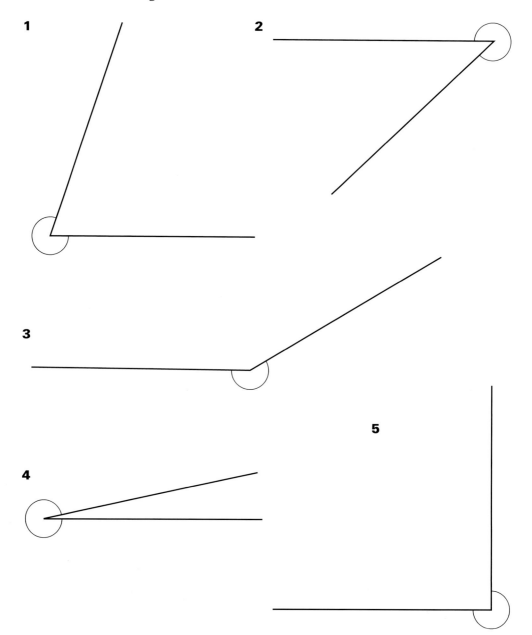

6

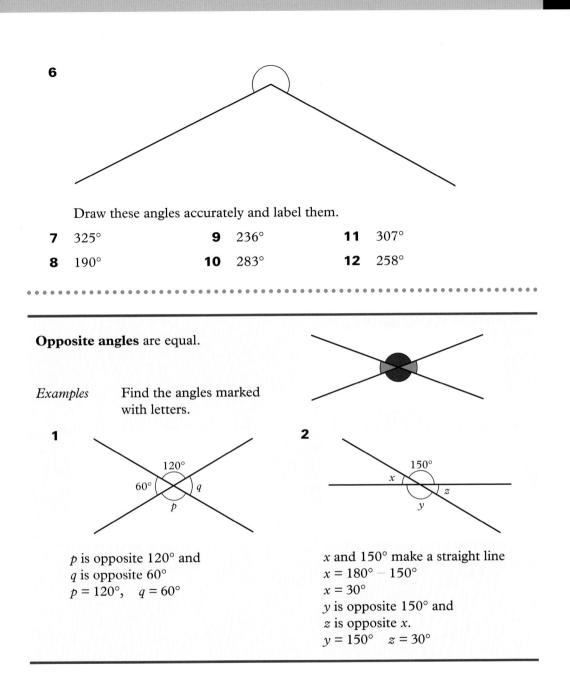

Draw these angles accurately and label them.

7 325°   **9** 236°   **11** 307°

8 190°   **10** 283°   **12** 258°

Opposite angles are equal.

Examples   Find the angles marked
              with letters.

1

120°
60°   *q*
p

2

150°
x
z
y

p is opposite 120° and
q is opposite 60°
p = 120°,   *q* = 60°

x and 150° make a straight line
x = 180° − 150°
x = 30°
y is opposite 150° and
z is opposite *x*.
y = 150°   *z* = 30°

Exercise 10:8

Find the angles marked with letters.

1

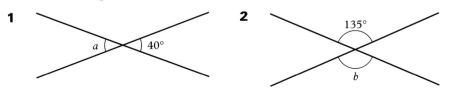

a   40°

2

135°
b

3

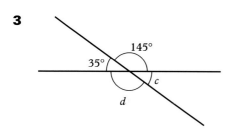

7

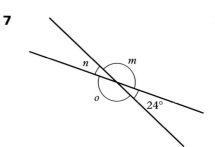

4

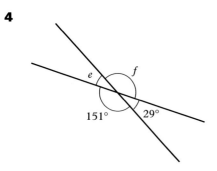

8

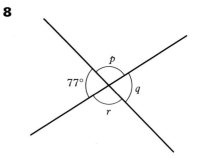

5

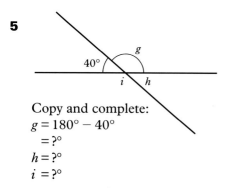

Copy and complete:
$g = 180° - 40°$
$ = ?°$
$h = ?°$
$i = ?°$

9

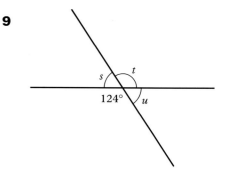

6

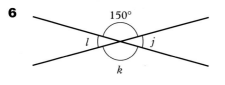

● **10**

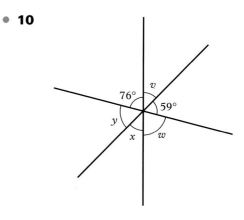

Exercise 10:9

Write down the angles marked with letters.

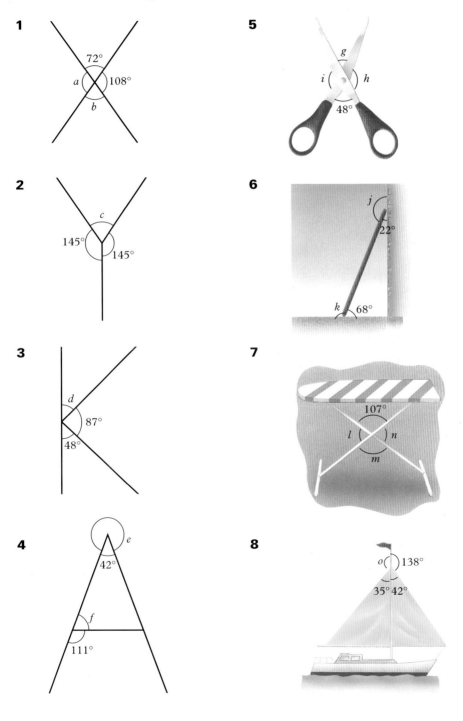

1

72°
a)108°
b

2

c
145° 145°

3

d
87°
48°

4

e
42°
f
111°

5

g
i) h
48°

6

j
22°
k 68°

7

107°
l) n
m

8

o)138°
35° 42°

3 Angles in triangles

Some sets of geometry instruments contain set squares. Set squares are triangles with special angles to help with drawing.

Exercise 10:10

1 Draw a triangle of your own.
Measure the angles of your triangle.
Find the sum of the angles.

2 **a** Measure the angles of a set square.
Find the sum of the angles.
b Repeat for the other shape of set square.

3 **a** Cut out a large triangle from scrap paper.
b Draw round the triangle in your book.
c Tear the three corners from your triangle.
d Stick the torn triangle inside its outline.
(Keep the three corners and stick them in a straight line.)

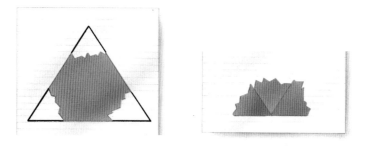

The angles of a triangle make a straight line.

The angles of a triangle add up to 180°.

Example   Calculate angle *a*

$$a = 180° - 85° - 65°$$
$$a = 30°$$

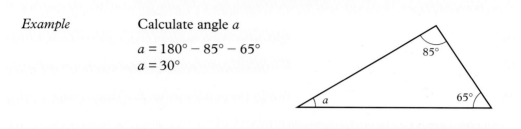

Exercise 10:11

Calculate the angles marked with letters.

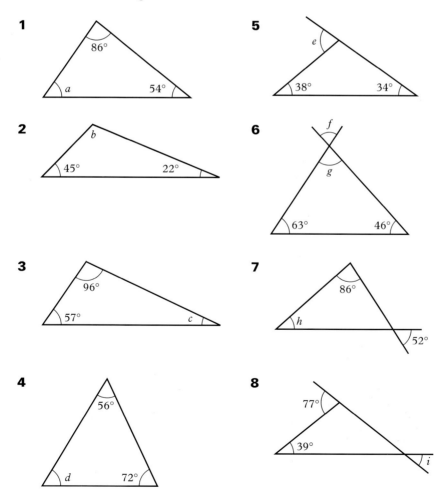

1 86°, *a*, 54°

2 *b*, 45°, 22°

3 96°, 57°, *c*

4 56°, *d*, 72°

5 *e*, 38°, 34°

6 *f*, *g*, 63°, 46°

7 86°, *h*, 52°

8 77°, 39°, *i*

An **isosceles triangle** has two equal angles and
two equal sides.

An **equilateral triangle** has three equal angles
and three equal sides.

Each angle is 60°.

The same mark on sides or angles means that
they are equal.

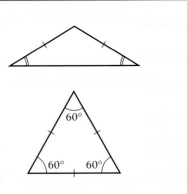

Exercise 10:12

Find the angles marked with letters.

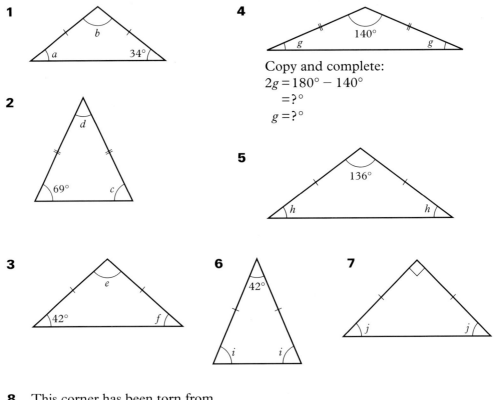

4 Copy and complete:
$2g = 180° - 140°$
$= ?°$
$g = ?°$

● **8** This corner has been torn from
an isosceles triangle. The angle
could belong to two different
shapes of isosceles triangle.
Draw sketches to show them.

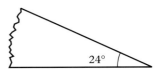

4 Constructions

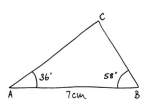

Triangles are very important.
Shapes made from triangles
are very strong.

Example

Construct triangle ABC.

AB = 7 cm   ∠A (angle A) = 36°   ∠B (angle B) = 58°

1 Start with a sketch.

2 Draw a line AB 7 cm long.

A ——————————————————————— B

3 Draw an angle of 36° at A.

A   B

4 Draw an angle of 58° at B.
Label point C.

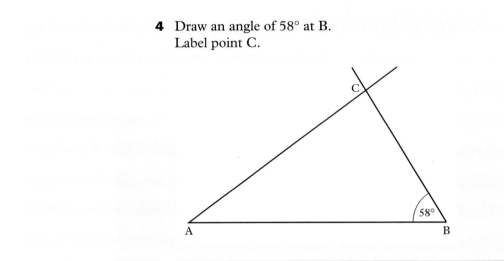

Exercise 10:13

1 Construct triangle ABC as shown in the example.

2 **a** Sketch the triangle LMN.
    b LM = 8 cm, ∠L = 47°, ∠M = 32°
      Label these in your sketch.
    c Construct triangle LMN.
    d Measure side MN.
      Write down its length.

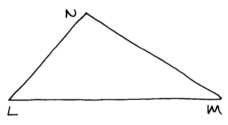

3 **a** Construct triangle PQR.
      PQ = 6 cm, ∠P = 28°, ∠Q = 114°
    b Measure side PR.

4 **a** Construct triangle XYZ.
      XY = 6.5 cm, ∠X = 95°, ∠Y = 43°
    b Measure side XZ.

5 **a** Construct triangle UVW.
      UV = 7.8 cm, ∠U = 38°, ∠V = 38°
    b Measure sides UW and VW.
    c What sort of triangle is UVW?

6 **a** Construct triangle EFG.
      EF = 7.4 cm, ∠E = 53°, EG = 5.6 cm
    b Measure side FG.

7 a Construct triangle ABC.
AB = 6.2 cm, ∠A = 60°, AC = 6.2 cm
  b Measure side BC.
  c What sort of triangle is ABC?

8 a Construct triangle DEF.
DE = 5.6 cm, ∠E = 126°, EF = 5.6 cm
  b Measure ∠D and ∠F.
  c What sort of triangle is DEF?

The kite ABCD has two angles
at B and two angles at D.

The red angle is ∠ABD.
The green angle is ∠DBC

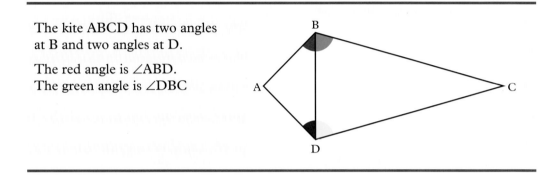

---

9 Sketch kite ABCD.
  a Write down the letter names of:
(1) the blue angle
(2) the yellow angle.
  b Show these on your sketch:
BD = 5.5 cm
∠ABD = 34°
∠ADB = 34°
∠DBC = 66°
∠BDC = 66°
  c Make an accurate drawing of the kite.
  d Measure diagonal AC.

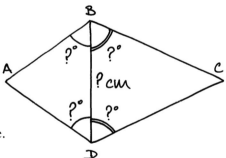

10 a Sketch kite PQRS and label these:
QS = 7.3 cm
∠PQS = 72°
∠PSQ = 72°
∠RQS = 28°
∠RSQ = 28°
  b Make an accurate drawing of the kite.
  c Measure diagonal PR.

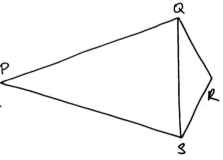

1   **a**   Sketch these quadrilaterals:
rhombus, square, parallelogram, rectangle, trapezium, kite.
    b   Draw in both diagonals in each of your quadrilaterals.
    c   Which quadrilaterals have diagonals that cross at right angles?

2   **a**   Draw a triangle with extended sides.
    b   Colour the equal opposite angles that are outside the triangle.
    c   Measure **one** angle of each colour.
    d   Add your three angles together.
    e   Repeat parts **a** to **d** for a different triangle.
    f   Write down what you notice.

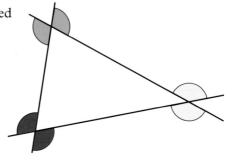

3   Calculate the angles marked with letters.
    a   The side of a bungalow.   **c**   A garden gate.

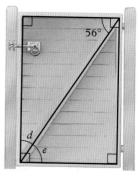

    b   The front of a nesting box.   **d**   The support for a wall.

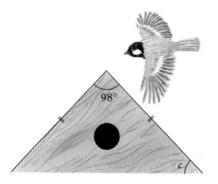

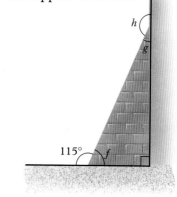

e A picnic hamper.

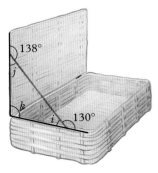

g The support for a hanging basket.

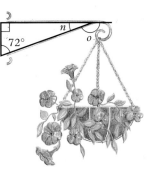

f Part of some stairs.

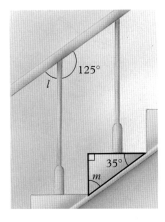

h A pair of tongs.

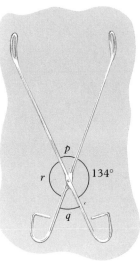

4 Write true or false for each of these.
- **a** A triangle may contain three acute angles.
- **b** A triangle may contain only one acute angle.
- **c** A triangle may contain only one obtuse angle.
- **d** The longest side of a triangle is opposite the largest angle.
- **e** The sides of a triangle could be 7 cm, 4 cm and 3 cm.

5 You need 9-point grids for this question.

These two triangles are congruent. (They would be the same if cut out.)
- **a** How many different triangles can you make using the grid?
- **b** How many triangles contain right angles?
- **c** How many triangles are isosceles?

1 a How much time has passed when the minute hand of a clock has
   turned through:
   (1) 90°   (2) 30°   (3) 120°   (4) 270°?
 b How much time has passed when the hour hand of a clock has
   turned through:
   (1) 90°   (2) 30°   (3) 210°   (4) 300°?
 c The Earth turns once on its axis in 24 hours.
   (1) How many degrees has the Earth turned through after one hour?
   (2) How many hours does it take to turn through 120°?

2 Calculate the angles marked with letters.

a

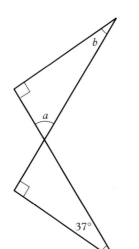

b

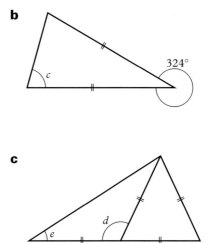

c

3 a One angle of an isosceles triangle is 44°.
   What sizes can the other angles be?
 b One angle of an isosceles triangle is 108°.
   What sizes can the other angles be?
 c Two angles of a triangle are 65° and 50°.
   Could the triangle be isosceles?

4 Construct triangle PQR
   PQ = 6.4 cm, ∠P = 63°, ∠R = 48°

   Measure side RQ.

5 Construct triangle ABC
   AB = 5.6 cm, ∠A = 39°, BC = 3.8 cm

   Measure side AC.

- The **angles at a point** make a full turn. They add up to 360°

The angles on a straight line add up to 180°

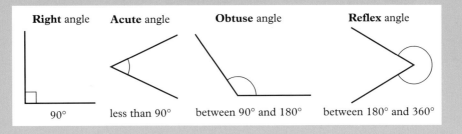

Right angle   **Acute** angle   **Obtuse** angle   **Reflex** angle

90°   less than 90°   between 90° and 180°   between 180° and 360°

- Opposite angles are equal.

  Example

  p is opposite 120°
  q is opposite 60°
  $p = 120°$, $q = 60°$

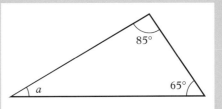

- The angles of a triangle add up to 180°

  Example

  Calculate angle a

  $a = 180° - 85° - 65°$
  $a = 30°$

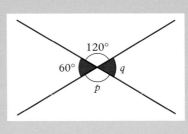

- An isosceles triangle has two equal angles
  and two equal sides.

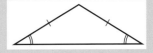

  An equilateral triangle has three equal
  angles and three equal sides.

  Each angle is 60°.

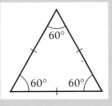

---

1 **a** Draw these angles.
   (1) 212°   (2) 146°   (3) 74°

 b For each part of **a** say whether the angles are acute, obtuse or reflex.

2 Calculate the angles marked with letters.

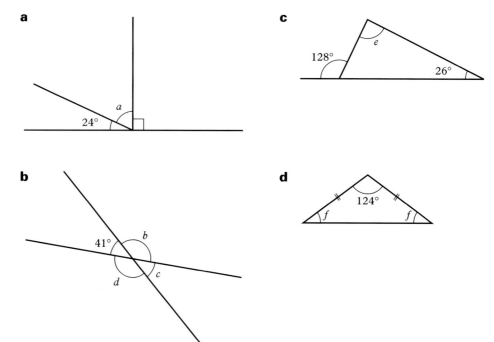

a

24° a

c

128° e 26°

b

41° b c d

d

124° f f

3 Construct these triangles.

 a Triangle PQR where PQ = 6.8 cm, PR = 4.6 cm, ∠P = 74°

   Measure angle Q.

 b Triangle LMN where LM = 5.7 cm, ∠L = 32°, ∠M = 114°

   Measure side LN.

4 Give the letter name of:
 a the red angle
 b the blue angle.

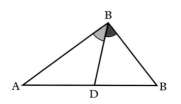

11 Extending the number line

1 Introducing negative numbers

2 Co-ordinates in all four quadrants

3 Graphs of number patterns

QUESTIONS

EXTENSION

SUMMARY

TEST YOURSELF

There are two common systems for measuring temperature.

Gabriel Daniel Fahrenheit (born in Prussia in 1686) put the freezing point of water at 32°F and its boiling point at 212°F.

Anders Celsius (born in Sweden in 1701) put the freezing point of water at 0°C and its boiling point at 100°C. The Celsius scale is sometimes called 'centigrade', meaning '100 degrees'.

Fahrenheit called the coldest temperature he could find 0°F. The coldest temperature possible is approximately −273°C, although Celsius did not know this!

On a very frosty day we might say that it is '−5', using the Celsius scale. On a hot day we often use the Fahrenheit scale: 80°F sounds much hotter than 27°C!

1 Introducing negative numbers

Bill the ice-cream man has to keep his ice cream cold. He uses a Celsius thermometer. The Celsius scale has the freezing point of water at 0 °C. The temperatures below 0 °C have minus signs in front. Bill's ice cream is at −10 °C.

Negative numbers

Positive numbers

Numbers with minus signs in front are called **negative** numbers. Other numbers are **positive**. Positive numbers are sometimes written with a plus sign in front.
Nought is not positive or negative.

Examples   Negative numbers −2, −5, −32.   Positive numbers 7, +3, 25.

Exercise 11:1

1 Write down the temperatures in degrees Celsius (°C) on these thermometers.

   a   **b**   **c**   **d**   **e**   **f**

2 **a** Is 15 °C warmer than −10 °C?
    b Is 10 °C warmer than −20 °C?
    c Is −15 °C warmer than −5 °C?
    d Is −10 °C colder than −2 °C?

3 **a** Which is warmer, 30 °C or −30 °C?
    b Which is colder, −5 °C or −9 °C?
    c Which is colder, −4 °C or 0 °C?
    d Which is warmer, −14 °C or 4 °C?

4 Copy the pairs of temperatures.

	<		>
Replace ? with	less than or colder than	or	more than or warmer than

  a   13 °C ? −26 °C   **d**   24 °C ?   7 °C
  b −50 °C ? −35 °C   **e**   4 °C ? −7 °C
  c −3 °C ?   −6 °C   **f** −24 °C ?   0 °C

5 Write down the temperatures in order, coldest first.
    a 8 °C, −50 °C, 0 °C, −15 °C, −3 °C.
    b −1 °C, 7 °C, −4 °C, 10 °C, −2 °C.

Example

One night the temperature is −4 °C. The next day the temperature is 8 °C.
What is the difference between the day and night temperatures?

The diagram shows part of a thermometer scale.
There are 12 spaces between −4 °C and 8 °C on the scale.
The difference between the temperatures is **12 °C**.

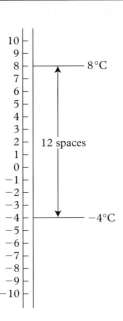

Exercise 11:2

Draw a scale from −10 to 10 up the side of your page, like the one shown in the example on the previous page.

1 Here are some night and day temperatures.
How many degrees difference is there between each pair? Use your scale to help you.

a night −4 °C, day 7 °C   **d** night −8 °C, day 2 °C
b night −10 °C, day −1 °C   **e** night 2 °C, day 10 °C
c night −9 °C, day −3 °C   **f** night −5 °C, day 0 °C

A calculator can be used to help find the answers to temperature questions. A temperature below freezing like −4 °C is put into the calculator using the +/− key.

Example

One night the temperature is −4 °C. The following day the temperature rises to 8 °C.
How many degrees difference is there between the day and night temperatures?

The answer is **12 °C**.

---

2 Check your answers to Question **1** using a calculator.
Use the example above to help you.
Write down the keys you press each time.

3 On a cold night the temperature is −8 °C. The following day the temperature rises to 6 °C.
By how many degrees does the temperature rise?

4 The temperature in a freezer is −18 °C. A frozen chicken is thawed to a room temperature of 20 °C.
By how many degrees does the chicken's temperature rise?

5 Ms Jones has to fly from London to Moscow. It is 5 °C in London and −16 °C in Moscow.
How many degrees colder will Ms Jones find it in Moscow?

6 In deserts it can be very hot in the daytime but very cold at night. The day temperature in a desert is 44 °C and the night temperature is −3 °C.
By how many degrees does the temperature drop at night?

7 We can draw bar charts to show temperatures which are below freezing. This bar chart shows the average temperature for each month. The temperatures are for the city of Montreal in Canada.

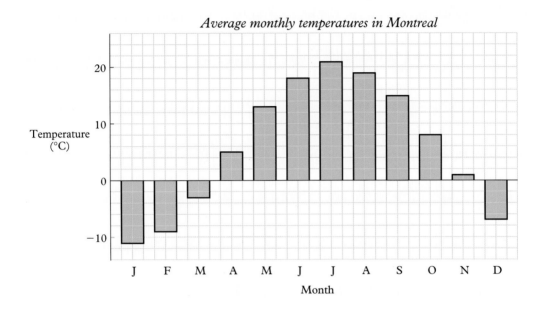

Average monthly temperatures in Montreal

a What is the average temperature for May?
b What is the average temperature for December?
c What is the highest average temperature and in which month does it occur?
d What is the lowest average temperature and in which month does it occur?
e What is the difference between the average temperatures for the hottest month and the coldest month?

8 The table shows the average monthly temperatures for Moscow.
a Draw a bar chart on squared paper or graph paper to show the temperatures.

Month	J	F	M	A	M	J	J	A	S	O	N	D
Temp °C	−10	−9	−4	5	12	17	19	17	11	5	−2	−7

b What is the difference between the average temperatures for the hottest month and the coldest month?

Negative numbers are not just found on thermometers. They have other uses.

Exercise 11:3

1 Here is the control panel of a lift.

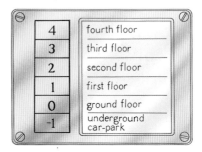

  a What number is used for the ground floor?

  b Where do you go if you press $\boxed{-1}$?

  c You go from the first floor to the fourth floor.
      How many floors do you go up?

  d You go from the third floor to the car-park.
      How many floors do you go down?

2 On a TV quiz show contestants lose 5 points if they interrupt a question but do not know the correct answer.

  a A contestant interrupts the first question and gets the answer wrong.
      How could this be shown on the score-board?

  b The contestant scores 10 points on the next round.
      How many points does he have now?

3 Mr Patel has a points system for his form 7P:
    early 1 point, just in time 0 points, late -2 points.
    Dale is late on Monday, just in time on Tuesday and Wednesday and early on Thursday and Friday.
    How many points does he have at the end of the week?

4 James subtracts one number from another on his calculator and gets the answer 8.
    What would his answer be if he did the subtraction with the second number first?

5 **a** Amy loses her coat and must pay £55 for a new one. She has £26 saved and she earns £15. Amy borrows the rest from her mother.
      How much does she borrow?

  b Amy's aunt gives Amy £20 for her birthday. Amy pays her mother back.
      How much does Amy have left?

6

Sir Isaac Newton (1642–1727)

Einstein (AD 1879): theory of relativity.
Newton (AD 1642): astronomer and mathematician, famous for study of gravity.
Napier (AD 1550): engineer, invented rods or 'bones' for calculating.

AD

2000

1800 **Euler** (AD 1707): wrote books on
1600 maths. Known for his theorem on solids in geometry.
1400 **Pascal** (AD 1623): studied geometry, algebra and physics
1200 of fluids. Known for his number triangle.
Fibonacci (AD 1170):
1000 wrote books on maths and known for
800 his number series.

600

400

200

0 **Erastosthenes**
(276 BC): used angle
200 measure to find the size of Earth and worked out the 'sieve'
400 for prime numbers.

Pythagoras (582 BC):
600 studied geometry. Known for his theorem on right
BC angled triangles.

The time line shows the dates of birth of some famous mathematicians.

a How many years after Newton was Einstein born?

b Pythagoras studied geometry and so did Euler. How many years before Euler was Pythagoras born?

c Erastosthenes was born many years before Napier. How many years exactly?

d If you were to add Archimedes (262 BC) to the diagram, between which two mathematicians would he go?

7 The wreck of the ship *James Egan Layne* lies at 21.6 m. Sea level is zero (0).
A diver is swimming down to look at the wreck. He is 11.2 m below the surface.
a How much deeper does he have to dive?

A helicopter flies overhead at 29.7 m.
b What is the distance between the helicopter and the diver?
c Draw a sketch to illustrate the question.
Show the information and your answers on a number line at the side of your sketch.

30 –
20 –
10 –
Sea level   0 –
10 –
20 –

2 Co-ordinates in all four quadrants

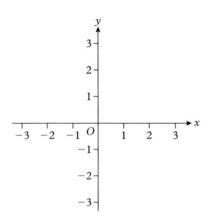

We can draw two number lines at 90° to each other. They can be used as an x axis and a y axis. The two lines cross at the zero value on each axis.

Origin

The point where the x axis and the y axis cross is called the **origin**. The co-ordinates of this point are $(0, 0)$.

Quadrant

The x axis and the y axis divide the space into four **quadrants**. The quadrants are always numbered anti-clockwise.

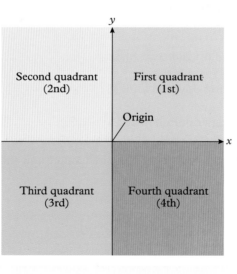

Exercise 11:4

1 Here are the co-ordinates of the points shown.

A (3, 0)
B (3, −2)
C (0, −3)
D (−3, 1)
E (−2, −1)
F (−1, −3)
G (−1, 3)
H (1, 2)

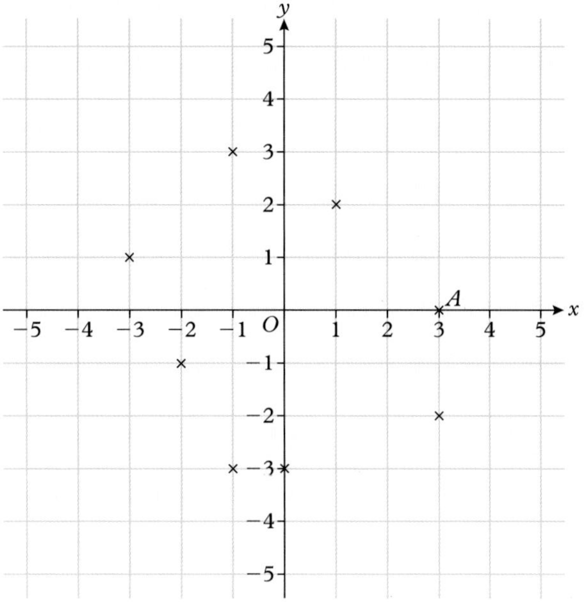

a Copy the diagram on to squared paper.
b Match the letters to the points.
   The first one has been done for you.

2 **a** If the *x* value is positive, in which quadrants could the points be?
   b In which quadrants are the *y* values negative?
   c In which quadrant are both *x* and *y* positive?
   d In which quadrant are both *x* and *y* negative?
   e Add these points to your diagram for Question **1**.
      $I(2, 3), \mathcal{J}(-1, 2), K(-3, -1), L(0, -1), M(2, -1).$

3 **a** Draw axes from −5 to 5 like those in Question **1**.
   b Plot these points and join them up in order: (4, 0), (4, 1), (1, 1),
      (1, 4), (0, 4)
   c Reflect your drawing into the second quadrant.
   d Reflect both sets of lines in the *x* axis.
      You should have a cross.

e Copy this table and fill it in.
Go round the cross anti-clockwise.

Quadrant	Co-ordinates		
First	(4, 1)	(1, 1)	(1, 4)
Second	(−1, 4)	(..., 1)	(−4, 1)
Third	(..., −1)	(−1, ...)	(−1, ...)
Fourth	(..., ...)	(..., ...)	(..., ...)

4 **a** Draw a new pair of axes from −4 to 4.

b Plot these pairs of points.

Join (1, 0) to (0, 4).   Join (3, 0) to (0, 2).
Join (2, 0) to (0, 3).   Join (4, 0) to (0, 1).

c Reflect the pattern into the second quadrant.
Copy these instructions for drawing the lines in the second quadrant.
Fill in the gaps.

Join (−1, 0) to (0, 4).   Join (..., ...) to (..., ...).
Join (−2, ...) to (..., 3).   Join (..., ...) to (..., ...).

d Copy these instructions for the third quadrant.
Use the number patterns to complete them.

Join (−1, 0) to (0, 4).   Join (..., ...) to (..., ...).
Join (−2, ...) to (..., −3).   Join (..., ...) to (..., ...).

Draw the pattern in the third quadrant.

e Complete the pattern in the fourth quadrant.
Write the set of instructions for the fourth quadrant.

5 **a** Copy the diagram.
Reflect shape *P* in
the y axis to get
shape *Q*.

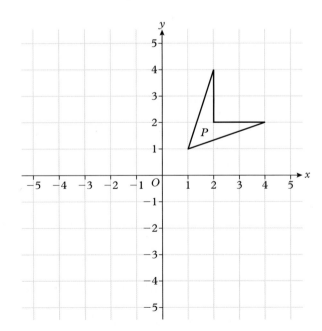

b Copy and complete the table for the reflection.

Co-ordinates of P	(1, 1)	(4, 2)	(2, 2)	(2, 4)
Co-ordinates of Q	(−1, 1)			

c The reflection changes the co-ordinates.
Write down the rule for this change.

d Reflect shape P in the x axis to get the shape S.
Copy and complete the table for the reflection.

Co-ordinates of P	(1, 1)	(4, 2)	(2, 2)	(2, 4)
Co-ordinates of S	(1, −1)			

e Write down the rule for this reflection.

f To complete the pattern shape R could be drawn in the third quadrant. R is a reflection of Q or S.
Use a rule to predict the co-ordinates of R.
Draw R to see if you are right.

Example   A is (1, 2) and B is (5, 8).
M is the mid-point of AB.
Find the co-ordinates of M.

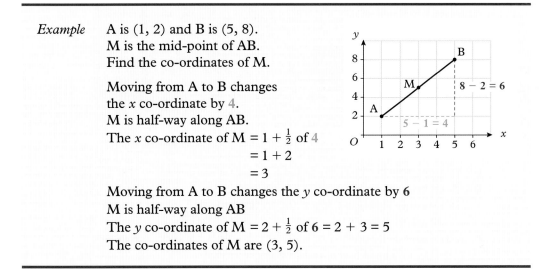

Moving from A to B changes the x co-ordinate by 4.
M is half-way along AB.
The x co-ordinate of M $= 1 + \frac{1}{2}$ of 4
$= 1 + 2$
$= 3$

Moving from A to B changes the y co-ordinate by 6
M is half-way along AB
The y co-ordinate of M $= 2 + \frac{1}{2}$ of $6 = 2 + 3 = 5$
The co-ordinates of M are (3, 5).

---

6 Find the co-ordinates of the mid-point of AB when:
   a A is (1, 2), B is (7, 10)   **c** A is (5, 6), B is (8, 11)
   b A is (5, 6), B is (5, 14)   **d** A is (0, 2), B is (3, 17)

7 Find the co-ordinates of the mid-point of AB when:
   a A is (0, 3), B is (5, 14)   **c** A is (−2, −1), B is (4, 9)
   b A is (−1, 4), B is (3, 6)   **d** A is (−4, 0), B is (5, 11)

3 Graphs of number patterns

Number patterns
can be used to
draw graphs.

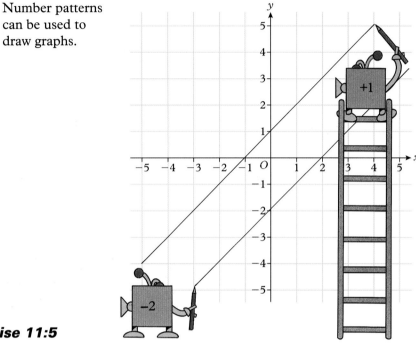

Exercise 11:5

Draw an x axis and a y axis from -5 to 5.

You only need one pair of axes for all the questions in this exercise.

1 a Plot the points (4, 4) (3, 3) (2, 2) (1, 1) and (0, 0).
b Place your ruler against the points.
Draw a line through the points. Extend the line into the third quadrant.
c Write down the co-ordinates of three points on your line in the third quadrant. They should be on your line.
The y value should be the same as the x value in each co-ordinate.
We write $y = x$.
d Label your line $y = x$.
This is the rule for *any* point on that line.
e Copy this co-ordinate table and fill it in.

$y = x$										
x	-4	-3	-2	-1	0	$\frac{1}{2}$	1	2	3	4
y				-1				2		4

2 a Copy and complete the number pattern and co-ordinate table for the rule $y = x + 1$.

$y = x + 1$

x			y
3 →		→	4
2 →		→	3
1 →		→	?
0 →	+1	→	?
−1 →		→	?
−2 →		→	−1
−3 →		→	?

$y = x + 1$							
x	−3	−2	−1	0	1	2	3
y		−1				3	4

b Plot the points.
Join them up with a ruler.
Label the line $y = x + 1$.

3 a Copy and complete the number pattern and co-ordinate table for the rule $y = x + 2$.

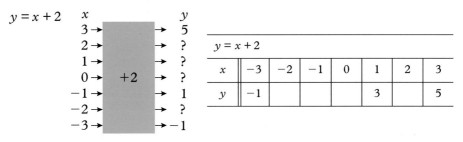

$y = x + 2$

x			y
3 →		→	5
2 →		→	?
1 →		→	?
0 →	+2	→	?
−1 →		→	1
−2 →		→	?
−3 →		→	−1

$y = x + 2$							
x	−3	−2	−1	0	1	2	3
y	−1				3		5

b Plot the points.
Join them up with a ruler.
Label the line $y = x + 2$.

4 Look at your drawings of lines.
 a Write down two facts about the set of lines $y = x$, $y = x + 1$, $y = x + 2$.
 b Use these facts to draw the line $y = x + 3$.

5 The rule for a line is $y = x - 1$.
 a Copy and complete the co-ordinate table.

$y = x - 1$									
x	−3	−2	−1	0	1	2	3	4	5
y								4	

 b Draw and label the line $y = x - 1$.

6 Draw the line $y = x - 2$.

Exercise 11:6 Naming lines of the grid

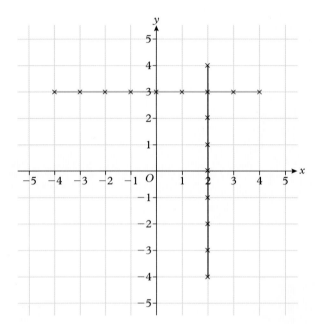

1 **a** Copy the diagram.
Draw the red line and the blue line.
b Copy and complete the co-ordinates.

Red line	Blue line
(..., 4)	(4, ...)
(..., 3)	(3, ...)
(..., 2)	(2, ...)
(..., 1)	(1, ...)
(..., 0)	(0, ...)
(..., −1)	(−1, ...)
(..., −2)	(−2, ...)
(..., −3)	(−3, ...)
(..., −4)	(−4, ...)

c Write what you notice:
(1) about the *x* co-ordinates on the red line.
(2) about the *y* co-ordinates on the blue line.
d The rule for the red line is $x = 2$.
The rule for the blue line is $y = 3$.
Label your lines with these rules.

2 **a** Complete these co-ordinates for other rules.

$x = 1$	$x = -3$	$y = 2$	$y = -4$
(..., 4)	(−3, 4)	(4, ...)	(3, ...)
(..., 2)	(..., 1)	(2, 2)	(1, −4)
(1, 0)	(..., −1)	(−1, ...)	(0, ...)
(..., −2)	(−3, −4)	(−3, ...)	(−2, ...)

b Use the axes you drew for Question **1**.
Plot each set of co-ordinates.
Join each set to make a line.
Label each line with its rule.

3 Use the axes you drew for Question **1**.
Draw and label the lines whose rules are $x = -4$, $x = 3$, $y = 1$, $y = -3$.

4 Write down rules for:
a the x axis.
b the y axis.

5 Write down the co-ordinates of the points where these lines **intersect** (cross).
a $x = 2, y = 3$
b $x = 2, y = -3$
c $x = -4, y = 2$
d $x = 1, y = -3$
e $x = -3, y = -4$

1 Write down these temperatures in order, coldest first.
  a 9 °C, −16 °C, 0 °C, −5 °C, 21 °C, −10 °C.
  b −3 °C, −17 °C, 30 °C, −25 °C, 18 °C, 2 °C.

2 Here are some night and day temperatures.
Use **+/−** on a calculator to find the number of degrees difference
between each pair.
  a night −4 °C, day 9 °C   **d** night 1 °C, day 6 °C
  b night −2 °C, day 8 °C   **e** night −8 °C, day −3 °C
  c night −9 °C, day −2 °C   **f** night 0 °C, day 10 °C

3 **a** Mrs Smith buys some fish at 3 °C. She puts it in her freezer at −18 °C.
    By how many degrees is the fish cooled?
  b Mrs Smith thaws the fish to a room temperature of 17 °C.
    By how many degrees does its temperature rise?

4 Sketch the thermometer. Mark on
it approximately where you think
the temperatures of the following
will be:
  a boiling point of water
  b freezing point of water
  c your body
  d a warm spring day
  e a very cold winter night in Britain
  f the North Pole
  g a can of cola out of the fridge
  h a very hot summer day

5 A crane is lifting gravel from a pit.
Ground level is 0.
The bottom of the pit is −8 m.
Copy and complete the number
line.
Use the line to find:
  a how far the bucket is below
    ground level.
  b how high the crane's top is
    above ground level.

6 **a** Jo owes her father £34 for a broken window. She gives her father her savings of £22 and her father stops £5 from her pocket money. How much does Jo owe her father now?
b Jo gets paid £10 for baby-sitting. She finishes paying for the window. How much does Jo have left?

7 Draw an x axis and a y axis from -6 to 6.
Plot these points in order.
Join them up with a ruler as you go.
a $(-6, 6), (-6, 3), (-3, 3), (-3, 6), (-6, 6)$.
b $(2, 1), (-3, -1), (2, -3), (2, 1)$.
c $(0, 2), (-4, 2), (-6, 0), (-2, 0), (0, 2)$.
d $(5, 1), (3, 1), (3, -5), (5, -5), (5, 1)$.
e $(1, 6), (-1, 4), (1, 2), (5, 4), (1, 6)$.
f $(2, -4), (-2, -3), (-6, -4), (-2, -5), (2, -4)$.
g Label the shapes with their names.
Choose from: rectangle, rhombus, kite, parallelogram, isosceles triangle, square.

8

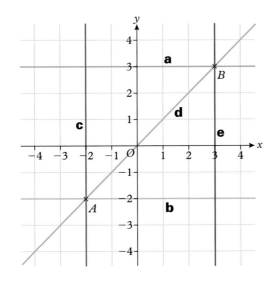

Five lines are drawn. The rules for the lines are
$y = -2, x = 3, y = x, x = -2, y = 3$.
(1) Match the lines **a** to **e** with their rules.
(2) Point A is $(-2, -2)$ and point B is $(3, 3)$. For both the x number equals the y number.
Write down four more points which obey the same rule.

1   **a**   Use [+/−] on a calculator to find the answers to these:

(1) $-4 \times 3 =$ (2) $5 \times -6 =$

  b   Does a negative number multiplied by a positive number always give a negative number?

Use your results from **a** and try some examples of your own to investigate multiplication of negative and positive numbers.

Copy and complete this table:

$\times$	positive	negative
positive		
negative		

Now investigate division of positive and negative numbers. Copy and complete this table:

$\div$	positive	negative
positive		
negative		

2   **a**   Copy and complete this table for the line $y = x$.

$y = x$											
x	-5	-4	-3	-2	-1	0	1	2	3	4	5
y											

  b   Draw a pair of axes from -5 to 5.

Plot the points in your table.

Join them to make the line $y = x$.

Label your line.

  c   Plot the points $(1, 2)$ $(-1, 4)$ $(-4, 4)$ $(-4, 2)$.

Join them to make a trapezium.

  d   Reflect your trapezium in the line $y = x$.

  e   Copy and complete this table.

Original co-ordinates	$(1, 2)$	$(-1, 4)$	$(-4, 4)$	$(-4, 2)$
Reflected co-ordinates	$(2, 1)$			

  f   Use your table to write down the rule for reflections in the line $y = x$.

3 Sometimes temperatures are given in degrees Fahrenheit. The Fahrenheit scale is being replaced by the Celsius scale.

   a On graph paper draw a pair of axes as shown.
      Use a scale of 1 cm to 10 °C on the horizontal axis and 1 cm to 20 °F on the vertical axis.

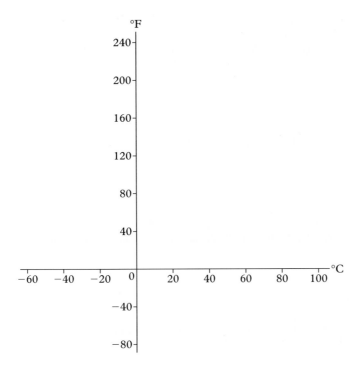

   b Plot the points given in the table.
      Draw a straight line through the points.

°C	−60	0	100
°F	−76	32	212

   c Use your graph to fill in the missing temperatures in this table.

	°C	°F
a cold night	?	20
inside the freezer	−20	?
room temperature	20	?
a hot day	?	90
body temperature	?	98.4

   d Which temperature has the same value on both scales?

4 a Copy and complete these number patterns. Give the rule for each one.

(1) $-3, ?, -1, 0, ?, 2, 3$
(2) $?, -4, -2, 0, ?, 4, 6$
(3) $-9, ?, -3, ?, 3, 6, 9$

b Copy this multiplication table.

$\times$	-3	-2	-1	0	1	2	3
3					3	6	9
2						4	6
1							3
0							
-1							
-2							
-3							

c Complete the table using the number patterns from part **a** to help you. Notice there are vertical patterns as well as horizontal ones.

d Use the completed table to answer these:

(1) $-3 \times 2 =$ (2) $3 \times 3 =$ (3) $2 \times -1 =$ (4) $-2 \times -3 =$

5 Replace ? with < or >.

a $-13 \; ? \;\; -5$
b $\;\; -5 \; ? \;\;\;\; 3$
c $\;\;\;\; 0 \; ? \;\; -4$
d $\;\; -2 \; ? \;\; -8$
e $\;\;\; 17 \; ? \;\; -7$
f $\;\;\;\; 5 \; ? \; -15$

- **Negative numbers** Numbers with minus signs in front are called **negative**
  Positive numbers numbers. Other numbers except nought are **positive**.
  Positive numbers are sometimes written with a plus
  sign in front.
  Nought is not positive or negative.

  Examples Negative numbers -2, -5, -32.
  Positive numbers 7, $+3$, 25.

- *Example* One day the temperature is 9 °C. The next night the temperature
  is -3°C
  What is the difference between day and night temperatures?

  Calculator: | 9 | − | 3 | +/− | = |

  The answer is **12** °C.

- **Origin** The point where an x and y
  Quadrant axis cross is called the **origin**.
  The co-ordinates of this point
  are (0, 0). The two lines
  divide the space into four
  quadrants. The quadrants
  are always numbered anti-
  clockwise.

- A is the point $(-2, 0)$, B is $(-3, 2)$,
  C is -1, -3) and D is $(1, -2)$.
  The lines $x = -3$ and $y = 2$ have been
  labelled with their rules.

  Number patterns can be used to give
  co-ordinates.

  Example $y = x + 1$

$y = x + 1$

x	-2	-1	0	1	2
y	-1	0	1	2	3

1   Write down these temperatures in order, coldest first.
0 °C, 25 °C, −18 °C, −6 °C, 4 °C, −11 °C.

2   **a**   A turkey is stored in a warehouse at −25 °C. Mrs Chandry buys it
and takes it home to be stored at −18 °C.
By how many degrees has the turkey's temperature risen?
    b   Mrs Chandry thaws the turkey to a room temperature of 19 °C.
By how many degrees does the turkey's temperature rise?

3   The diagram shows an octagon
ABCDEFGH.
    a   Write down the co-ordinates
of each point *A* to *H*.
    b   Which point has a negative *x*
co-ordinate and a positive *y*
co-ordinate?
    c   Which points are in the fourth
quadrant?
    d   Which line is a reflection of
GH in the *x* axis?

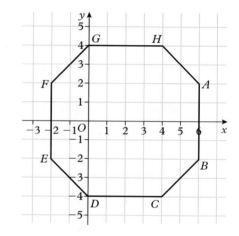

4   **a**   Draw an *x* axis and a *y* axis from −5 to 5.
    b   Copy and complete the co-ordinate table for the rule $y = x + 4$.

$y = x + 4$							
x	−5	−4	−3	−2	−1	0	1
y	−1		1				

    c   Plot the points.
Join them with a ruler.
Label the line $y = x + 4$.
    d   On the same axes draw and label lines for the rules:
      (1) $x = 3$
      (2) $y = −4$
      (3) $y = 2$
    e   Write down the co-ordinates of the point where $y = 2$ crosses
$y = x + 4$.

12 Units of length and scale drawing

The Romans measured in miles. 1 mile was 1000 paces. They counted two steps – left, right – as one pace.

But hands, feet and paces vary. Edward I was the first person in England to set out a system. In 1305, he had standard measures for people to compare, but the units were still complicated. Different measures were in use in different countries. Something better was needed.

In 1795, the French Academy of Science decided to solve the problem. A survey was made of the length of a line from the North Pole, through France to the Equator. This distance was divided into 10 million parts. Each part was called a metre. This was the start of the metric system.

CORINIVM V MILES

1   An introduction to units of length

· ·

In ancient times people used parts of the body to measure length.

thumb	(middle joint to tip)	1 inch
hand	(sideways across wide part)	4 inches
span	(hand stretched wide, thumb tip to little finger tip)	9 inches
cubit	(elbow to middle finger tip)	about 20 inches
foot	(length to tip of big toe)	12 inches
pace	(length of one step)	about 30 inches
yard	(length from nose to finger tip)	36 inches

Exercise 12:1

1   Make a table using the units listed above.

Name of unit	Sketch	Length (inches) (see table above)	My lengths (inches)	(cm)
thumb		1 inch	…	…
hand		4 inches	…	…
span		9 inches	…	…

2   Estimate the answers to these using your table.
  a   How many of your spans are equal to your cubit?
  b   How many of your cubits are equal to your pace?
  c   How many of your thumbs are equal to your foot?
  d   How many of your hands are equal to your foot?
  e   How many of your feet are equal to your yard?

Common Imperial units of length

12 inches (in) = 1 foot (ft)   3 feet = 1 yard (yd)   36 inches = 1 yard

Examples   **1** Convert 2 ft to inches   **3** Convert 4 ft 10 in to inches
                     2 ft = 2 × 12 in   4 ft = 4 × 12 in
                         = 24 in   = 48 in
                                                     48 in + 10 in = 58 in

              2 Convert 4 yd to feet
                   4 yd = 4 × 3 ft
                        = 12 ft

3   Convert these lengths to inches.
  a   3 ft   **c**   10 ft   **e**   3 ft 11 in
  b   5 ft   **d**   4 ft 7 in   **f**   5 ft 3 in

4   Convert these distances to feet.
  a   2 yd   **c**   5 yd   **e**   2 yd 1 ft
  b   6 yd   **d**   1 yd 2 ft   **f**   4 yd 2 ft

5   There are 1760 yd in 1 mile.
  a   How many feet are there in a mile?
  b   How many inches are there in a mile?

6   Dariel's grandmother measures his height as 4 ft 2 in. Last time Dariel
       saw his grandmother his height was 3 ft 9 in.
       How much has he grown?

7   Megan and Shenisse share a piece of ribbon equally between them.
       The piece is 1 yd 18 in long.
       What length of ribbon do they each get?
       Give your answer in inches.

8   Mrs Green wants three new shelves in her kitchen. Each shelf is to be
       2 ft 6 in long.
       What length of wood will she need altogether?
       Give your answer in feet and inches.

Examples

1 Convert 48 in to feet
48 in = 48 ÷ 12 ft
= 4 ft

2 Convert 15 ft to yards
15 ft = 15 ÷ 3 yd
= 5 yd

9 Convert these lengths to feet.

    a 12 in   **b** 36 in   **c** 144 in   **d** 108 in   **e** 84 in

10 Convert these distances to yards.

    a 6 ft   **b** 18 ft   **c** 30 ft   **d** 21 ft   **e** 39 ft

Common metric units of length

10 millimetres (mm) = 1 centimetre (cm)
100 centimetres = 1 metre (m)
1000 metres = 1 kilometre (km)

Example

This line measures 5.7 cm (or 57 mm).

Exercise 12:2

1 Estimate the lengths of these lines in centimetres.

    a ——————————————————

    b ————————————

    c ———————————————————————

    d —————————

    e ———————————————————

2 Check your estimates in Question **1** by measuring the lines accurately.

3 Which units would you use to measure these?
Choose from mm, cm, m, km.

    a The length of the wing of a fly.
    b The length of the classroom.
    c The length of a football pitch.
    d The distance from London to Edinburgh.
    e The height of the classroom.
    f The width of a pencil.
    g The length of a pencil.

4 Copy this table.
Estimate the length of each item.

Write your estimate in the table.

Add five more ideas of your own.

Complete the last column of
the table by measuring.

Distance being measured	Estimate	Actual
Width of exercise book		
Length of classroom		
Height of door		
Length of blackboard		
Length of pen		
...		

Converting units within the metric system

Examples

1 Convert 6.9 cm to mm
6.9 cm = 6.9 × 10 mm
= 69 mm

2 Convert 65 mm to cm
65 mm = 65 ÷ 10 cm
= 6.5 cm

Exercise 12:3

1 Write down the length and width of each rectangle in mm.

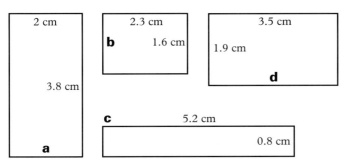

2 cm

3.8 cm

a

2.3 cm

b 1.6 cm

3.5 cm

1.9 cm

d

c 5.2 cm

0.8 cm

2 Work out the length of each line in cm.

a _____ 50 mm _____

b _____ 54 mm _____

c _____ 75 mm _____

d _____ 48 mm _____

e _____ 87 mm _____

3 Kitchen worktops are usually 600 mm wide and 900 mm high.
Convert these lengths to cm.

4 This ordinary first class
stamp is 2 cm by 2.4 cm.
The commemorative stamp
is 4 cm by 3 cm.
Give these sizes in mm.

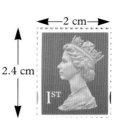

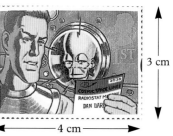

Examples

1 Convert 5.34 m to cm
5.34 m = 5.34 × 100 cm
= 534 cm

2 Convert 148 cm to m
148 cm = 148 ÷ 100 m
= 1.48 m

3 Convert 7.3 km to m
7.3 km = 7.3 × 1000 m
= 7300 m

4 Convert 4500 m to km
4500 m = 4500 ÷ 1000 km
= 4.5 km

---

5 Copy and complete:

5 m = ? cm   700 cm = ? m
1.24 m = ? cm   220 cm = ? m
0.75 m = ? cm   1250 cm = ? m
8.32 m = ? cm   60 cm = ? m
0.08 m = ? cm   95 cm = ? m

6 7M have been measuring items in their classroom. They have measured
in metres.
Convert their measurements to centimetres.

Blackboard 2.5 m by 1.25 m
Pupils' table tops 1.2 m by 0.6 m, height 0.7 m
Door 0.76 m by 2 m
Filing cabinet 0.46 m by 0.62 m by 1.32 m

7 Alex has measured her bedroom furniture for a school project. She has
measured in centimetres. She needs the measurements in metres.
Alex has started a list.
Copy and complete the list.

Bed   190 cm by 90 cm = ... m by ... m
Chest of drawers   85 cm by 45 cm by 120 cm = ...

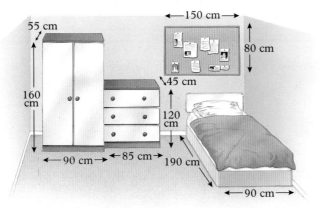

8 Copy and complete:

8000 m = ? km	7 km = ? m
7600 m = ? km	9.8 km = ? m
1700 m = ? km	16.4 km = ? m
605 m = ? km	0.35 km = ? m
405 m = ? km	0.875 km = ? m

9 An athletics club competes in races over these distances:

100 m	400 m	1000 m	2000 m	5000 m
200 m	800 m	1500 m	3000 m	10 000 m

  a Change all these distances to kilometres.
  b The club has one runner in every race.
    What is the total distance they will cover if the distances for each race are added together?
    Give your answer in (1) kilometres and (2) metres.

10 A packet of 500 sheets of paper is 5 cm thick.
    What is the thickness of 1 sheet? Give your answer in mm.

11 Pieces of ribbon each 30 cm long are cut from a 5 m length.
  a How many 30 cm pieces are there?
  b How much ribbon is left over?

● **12** **a** A racing cyclist covers 4 km by making 12 circuits of a cycle track.
      How long is the track? Give your answer in metres.
    b A second cyclist has a puncture 2 circuits from the finish.
      How far has he cycled?

● **13** A4 paper is 210 mm × 297 mm. It is packed in packets 5 cm thick.
    What is the maximum number of packets that could be stacked under a worktop 600 mm wide, 900 mm high and 3 m long?

2 Scale drawings

Actual lengths may not fit on to a sheet of paper. A scale drawing is the same shape as the original but different in size.

 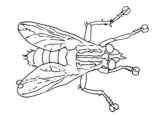

| Scale | The **scale** of a drawing gives the relative size of the actual length to the drawn length. |

Exercise 12:4

1 Rowan makes a scale drawing of a room. The room is 6 m long.
Rowan uses 1 cm on his paper to represent 1 m.
So 6 cm represents 6 m.
He draws this rectangle to represent the floor of the room.
a Measure the width of the room on the drawing.
b What is the actual width of the room?

Rowan decides his drawing is too small.
He draws a new line of length 12 cm to represent the 6 m.
  c How many centimetres represent one metre?
     This is called the **scale** of his drawing.
  d How many centimetres represent 5 m?

2 The scale is 1 cm to 4 m.
Write down the length each line represents.

  a _____   **d** _____
  b _____   **e** _____
  c _____   **f** _____

3 These lines were drawn using a scale of 1 cm to 10 km.
Write down the length each line represents.

  a _____
  b _____
  c _____
  d _____
  e _____
  f _____

4 These lines were drawn using the scale given.
Write down the length each line represents.

  a _____   1 cm to 1 km
  b _____   1 cm to 6 cm
  c _____   1 cm to 20 m
  d _____   1 cm to 8 km
  e _____   1 cm to 4 m
  f _____   1 cm to 6 km
  g _____   1 cm to 12 m
  h _____   1 cm to 5 km

5 Draw lines to represent these lengths.
Use the scale given for each one.

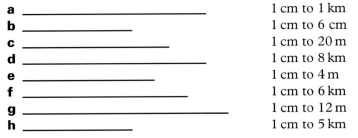

     Length   Scale
  a 4 km   1 cm to 1 km
  b 7 m   1 cm to 1 m
  c $3\frac{1}{2}$ km   1 cm to 1 km
  d 25 miles   1 cm to 5 miles
  e 10 km   1 cm to 2 km
  f 9 km   1 cm to 2 km
  g 500 m   1 cm to 100 m
  h 450 m   1 cm to 100 m

6

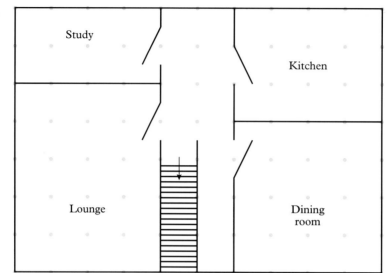

This is a plan of the ground floor of a house.

a Copy and complete this table.

Room	Length (m)	Width (m)
Lounge		
Study		
...		

Scale:
1 cm to 1 m

7 This is the same house as Question **6.** It also shows the garden.

a What is the scale of this plan?

b What are the real length and width of the garden?

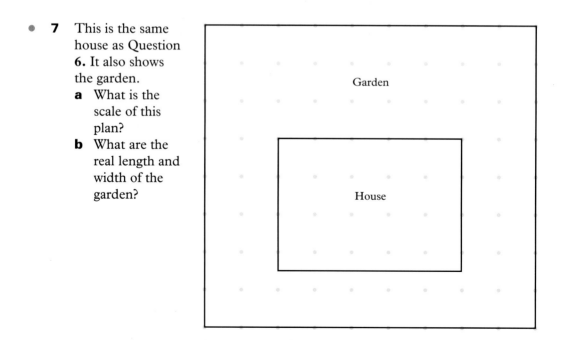

3 Finding lengths

Matthew and Kerry are finding
out how far a plane travels
between London and Paris.

We can use scale drawings to find
lengths.

Exercise 12:5

1 This rectangle is a plan of a swimming pool.
The scale is 1 cm to 1 m.
  a Measure the longer side of the rectangle.
    Write down the length of this side in cm.
    Use the scale to find the actual length of the swimming pool.
  b Use the same method to find the actual width of the pool.
  c What is the actual length of the diagonal of the pool?

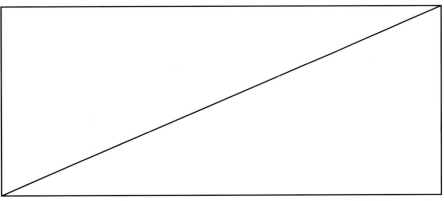

Scale: 1 cm to 1 m

2 A rectangular field has length 80 metres and width 60 metres.
  a Make a scale drawing of the field. Use a scale of 1 cm to 5 m.
  b Use your scale drawing to find the length of the diagonal of the field.

3 Find the shortest distance between the two ships.

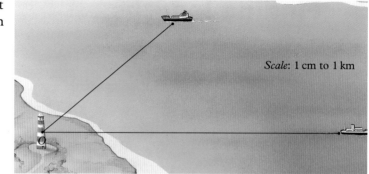

Scale: 1 cm to 1 km

4 A ship starts at A and sails 10 km due West. It then turns to face North. It sails 16 km North until it reaches a point B.

This is a sketch of the journey. It is not drawn to scale.

a Make a scale drawing of the journey. Use the scale 1 cm to 1 km.

b Measure the length of AB on your drawing.

c Use the scale to find the distance between A and B in km.

B|

16 km

10 km — A

N
W — E
S

5 Find the length of the ladder by making a scale drawing.

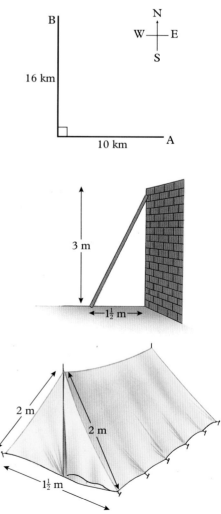

3 m

$1\frac{1}{2}$ m

6 This is a ridge tent.
a Make a scale drawing of the triangular front of the tent.
b Use your drawing to find the height of the tent.

2 m

2 m

$1\frac{1}{2}$ m

7 This diagram shows part of a flight of steps.

Each step is 22 cm deep.
How many steps are there?

←22 cm→

Scale: 1 cm to 1 m

ground

Curved lines

We can find the length of a curved line. We use a piece of string.

This map shows the footpath from Acton to Wesley.

Place the string on top of the curved path.

Mark the string when you get to Wesley.

Measure the marked length of the string.

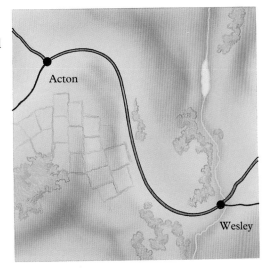

Acton

Wesley

The string is 8 cm long. It represents 8 km.

Exercise 12:6

1 These lines are drawn to the scale 1 cm to 1 km.
Estimate the lengths they represent.

a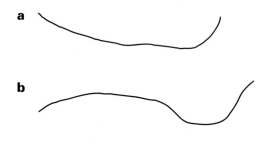

c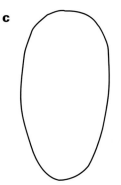

b

2 This is a scale drawing of a lake.

Estimate the length of the path around the lake.

Scale: 1 cm to 2 miles

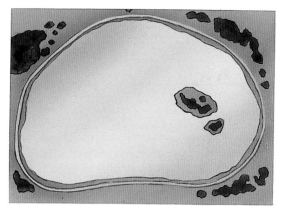

3

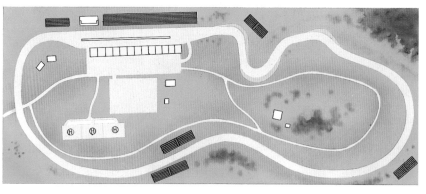

Scale: 2 cm to 1 km

This is a car race track.
Estimate the length of a complete circuit. Give your answer in kilometres.

4 Imperial to metric conversion

. . . .

Katie is 4 ft 11 in tall.
The minimum height for people
allowed to use the ride is 120 cm.
Can Katie go on the ride?

Sometimes we need to
convert lengths given in
Imperial units to metric
units. We can use estimates.

1 inch is about $2\frac{1}{2}$ cm
1 yard is a bit less than 1 metre
1 mile is a bit more than $1\frac{1}{2}$ km

Exercise 12:7

1 Estimate these in metric units:

a	2 inches	**e**	2 yards	**i**	2 miles
b	1 foot (12 inches)	**f**	10 yards	**j**	10 miles
c	6 inches	**g**	50 yards	**k**	50 miles
d	10 inches	**h**	100 yards	**l**	100 miles

---

1 in = 2.5 cm   1 yd = 0.9 m   1 mile = 1.6 km

Examples

1 Convert 9 in to cm
9 in = 9 × 2.5 cm
   = 22.5 cm

3 Convert 3.5 miles to km
3.5 miles = 3.5 × 1.6 km
      = 5.6 km

2 Convert 4 yd to m
4 yd = 4 × 0.9 m
   = 3.6 m

---

2 Copy and complete:

a	1 in = 2.5 cm	**b**	1 yd = ? m	**c**	1 mile = ? km
	2 in = ? cm		3 yd = ? m		3 miles = ? km
	5 in = ? cm		5 yd = ? m		5 miles = ? km
	10 in = ? cm		10 yd = ? m		8 miles = ? km
	12 in = ? cm		15 yd = ? m		10 miles = ? km

3 A wren is 4 inches long.
Convert the lengths of all these birds to cm.

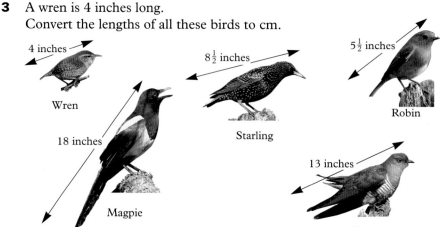

4 inches — Wren

18 inches — Magpie

$8\frac{1}{2}$ inches — Starling

$5\frac{1}{2}$ inches — Robin

13 inches — Cuckoo

4 This chart has the distances in miles.
Copy the chart and fill in the distances in kilometres. Give your answers correct to the nearest whole number.

Cardiff	393	392	152
	Edinburgh	45	403
		Glasgow	400
			London

a How far is it in kilometres from Edinburgh to London?
b How far is it in kilometres from Glasgow to Cardiff?

5 The marathon distance is 26.219 miles (26 miles 385 yd).
a Use 1 mile = 1.609 km to convert the marathon distance to km.
Give your answer correct to three decimal places.
b The marathon distance in metres is actually 42 195 m.
By how many metres does your answer differ from this?

Exercise 12:8

Scales with ten divisions.

1 Write down these lengths.

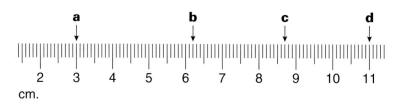

cm.

Write down the numbers the arrows are pointing to:

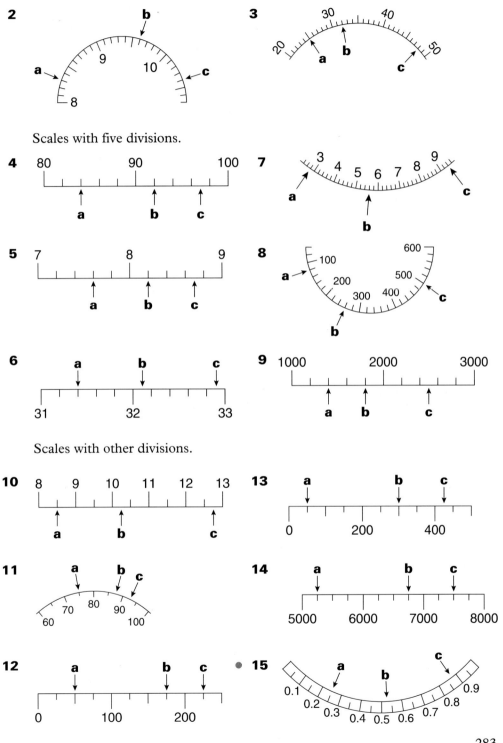

2

3

Scales with five divisions.

4 80 90 100

7

5 7 8 9

8

6

9 1000 2000 3000

Scales with other divisions.

10 8 9 10 11 12 13

13 0 200 400

11 60 70 80 90 100

14 5000 6000 7000 8000

12 0 100 200

15 0.1 0.2 0.3 0.4 0.5 0.6 0.7 0.8 0.9

Exercise 12:9

Use these scales to convert these units.

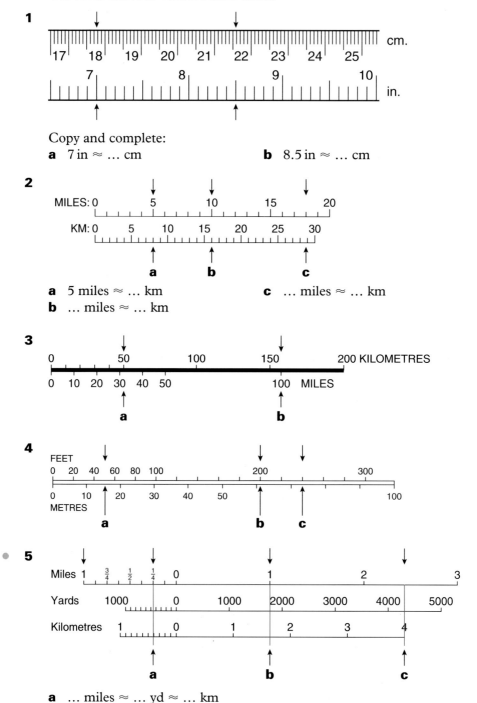

1

Copy and complete:
a 7 in ≈ ... cm   **b** 8.5 in ≈ ... cm

2

a 5 miles ≈ ... km   **c** ... miles ≈ ... km
b ... miles ≈ ... km

3

4

5

a ... miles ≈ ... yd ≈ ... km

1 Change all the imperial units to metric units.

Mr Smith bought an 8" pizza and a 12" pizza. He got into his 15 ft long car and drove the 3 miles to his home. He drove 20 yd along his drive to his house.

2 Furlong, chain and fathom are also imperial units. Find out what you can about them.

3 **a** The length of a pencil case is about:
    (1) 2.5 cm   (2) 2.5 m   (3) 25 mm   (4) 25 cm
  b The length of a bus is about:
    (1) 100 mm   (2) 10 m   (3) 100 cm   (4) 100 m
  c The length of the bristles on a toothbrush is about:
    (1) 90 cm   (2) 9 mm   (3) 9 cm   (4) 0.9 mm
  d When a bus travels three stops it goes about:
    (1) 100 m   (2) 20 km   (3) 1 km   (4) 200 m

4 Copy and complete:
  a 54 mm = ? cm   **e** 650 m = ? km   **i** 340 cm = ? m
  b 1750 m = ? km   **f** 0.7 km = ? m   **j** 0.95 cm = ? mm
  c 27 cm = ? mm   **g** 5400 m = ? km   **k** 85 cm = ? m
  d 2.5 m = ? cm   **h** 8.5 km = ? m   **l** 132 mm = ? cm

5 This map has been drawn to a scale of 1 cm to 10 km.

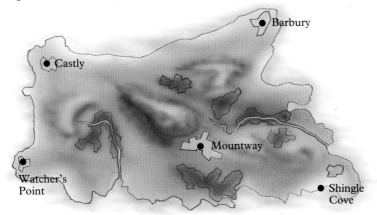

  a Measure the distance between Castly and Barbury on the map in cm.
  b Using the scale calculate the actual distance between Castly and Barbury.
  c Using the same method, find the actual distance between:
    (1) Watcher's Point and Mountway
    (2) Watcher's Point and Shingle Cove
    (3) Barbury and Mountway

6 A model of a Jaguar car is 13.2 cm long. The scale is 1 cm to 36 cm.
What is the length of a real Jaguar car.
a In centimetres?
b In metres?

7 **a** What is the length of the space shuttle?
b What is the width of the space shuttle across the widest part including the wings?

Scale: 1 cm to 6 m

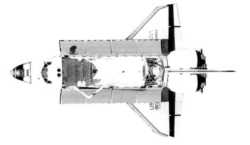

8 Write down the numbers shown by the arrows.

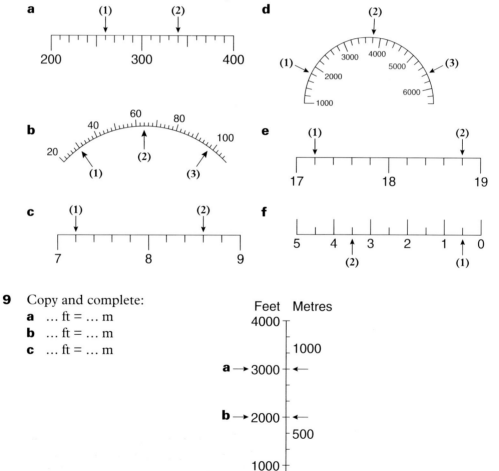

9 Copy and complete:
a ... ft = ... m
b ... ft = ... m
c ... ft = ... m

1 **a** Joseph measures his height with a tape that shows only inches.
Joseph is 63 inches tall. He wants to convert his height to feet and
inches.
Joseph tries using a calculator: $63 \div 12 = 5.25$
Joseph writes down 5 ft 25 in. He knows that this answer must be
wrong.
Explain how Joseph knows.

   b This is how Joseph's teacher tells him to work out the answer.
'Find out how many inches are in five feet. Take that number away
from 63 in. This gives the number of inches left over.
What is Joseph's height in feet and inches?

   c Joseph's friend Kalvinder uses the same method. He is 56 inches tall.
What is this in feet and inches?

   d The teacher is 75 in tall.
What is this in feet and inches?

2 **a** A model of the HMS *Ark Royal* is 16 inches long. The actual ship
is 800 feet long.
(1) What is the scale used to make the model?
(2) How long is the model in cm?

   b An aeroplane has a 50 feet wing span.
(1) What is the wing span of a model aeroplane made to the same
scale as the ship in **a**?
(2) What is the wing span of the actual aeroplane in metres?

3 Model soldiers are made to a scale of 1 cm to 32 cm.
What is the approximate height of a model soldier?

4 The box and these pencils are drawn to different scales.
Which of the pencils will fit into the box?

Scale: 1 cm to 5 cm

Scale: 1 cm to 2 cm

Scale: 1 cm to 4 cm   *Scale*: 1 cm to 2 cm

5 This is a plan of Stonehenge:

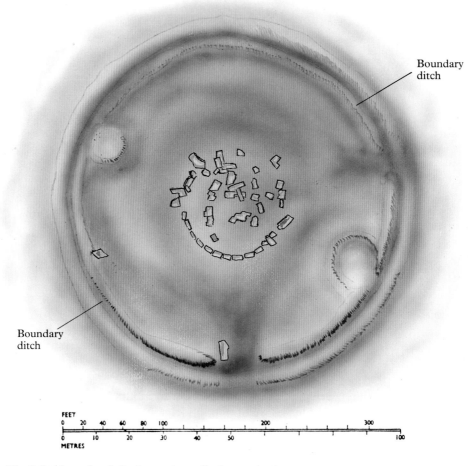

Find the length of the boundary ditch: **a** in feet
b in metres.

6 Noah's Ark was 300 cubits long, 50 cubits wide and 30 cubits high.
Estimate the dimensions of the Ark in metres. (1 cubit ≈ 20 inches)

7 Use this scale to convert these distances.

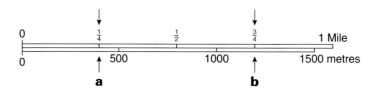

- **Common Imperial units of length**
  12 inches = 1 foot   12 in = 1 ft   3 feet = 1 yard   3ft = 1 yd

- **Metric units of length**
  10 mm = 1 cm   100 cm = 1 m   1000 m = 1 km
  The thickness of a pencil lead is about 1 mm.
  The width of the nail on your middle finger is about 1 cm.
  A door is about two metres high.

- **Converting units within the metric system**
  1 Convert 6.9 cm to mm   **2** Convert 148 cm to m   **3** Convert 7.3 km to m
  6.9 cm = 6.9 × 10 mm   148 cm = 148 ÷ 100 m   7.3 km = 7.3 × 1000 m
  = 69 mm   = 1.48 m   = 7300 m

- A **scale drawing** is the same shape as the original but different in size.
  The scale of a drawing gives the relative size of the actual length to the drawn length.
  Examples of scales are: 1 cm to 1 km; 1 cm to 10 km.
  We can find lengths from scale drawings.
  We use string to measure the length of curved lines.

- **Imperial to metric conversion**
  1 inch is about $2\frac{1}{2}$ cm   1 in = 2.5 cm
  1 yard is a bit less than 1 metre   1 yd = 0.9 m
  1 mile is a bit more than $1\frac{1}{2}$ kilometres   1 mile = 1.6 km

  1 Convert 9 in to cm   **2** Convert 4 yd to m   **3** Convert 3.5 miles to km
  9 in = 9 × 2.5 cm   4 yd = 4 × 0.9 m   3.5 miles = 3.5 × 1.6 km
  = 22.5 cm   = 3.6 m   = 5.6 km

- **Scales** have different numbers of divisions.
  Start by working out what one division represents.

  Here each division is 2   Here each division is 0.2

  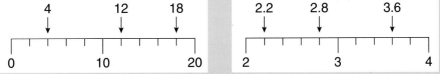

  Scales can be used to convert Imperial to metric units.

1 Convert these lengths to the units given.
   a 3 ft to in   **b** 60 in to ft   **c** 5 yd to ft   **d** 24 ft to yd

2 Copy and complete:
   a 48 mm = ? cm   **c** 3700 m = ? km   **e** 4.6 m = ? cm
   b 240 cm = ? m   **d** 3.7 cm = ? mm   **f** 0.4 km = ? m

3 These lines have been drawn using a scale of 1 cm to 10 km.
   Find the length each line represents.
   a _____   **b** _____

4 This line has been drawn using a scale of 1 cm to 2 km.
   Estimate the actual length it represents.

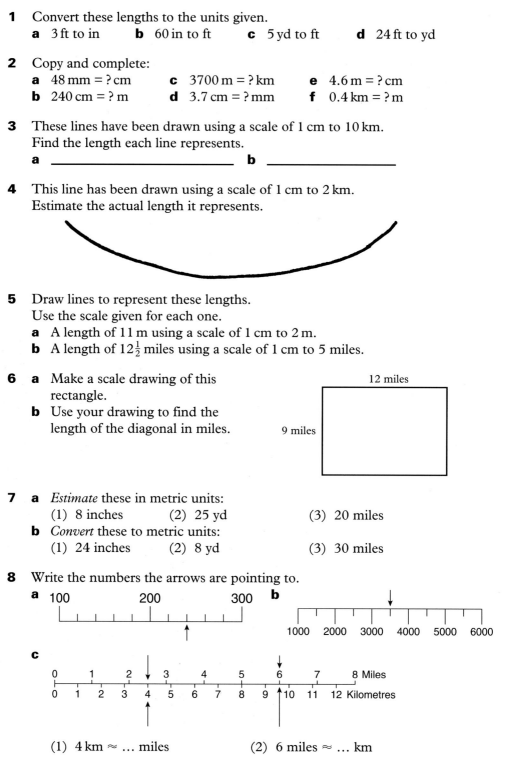

5 Draw lines to represent these lengths.
   Use the scale given for each one.
   a A length of 11 m using a scale of 1 cm to 2 m.
   b A length of $12\frac{1}{2}$ miles using a scale of 1 cm to 5 miles.

6 **a** Make a scale drawing of this rectangle.
   b Use your drawing to find the length of the diagonal in miles.

   12 miles
   9 miles

7 **a** *Estimate* these in metric units:
      (1) 8 inches   (2) 25 yd   (3) 20 miles
   b *Convert* these to metric units:
      (1) 24 inches   (2) 8 yd   (3) 30 miles

8 Write the numbers the arrows are pointing to.
   a 100   200   300   **b**

   1000   2000   3000   4000   5000   6000

   c

   0   1   2   3   4   5   6   7   8 Miles
   0   1   2   3   4   5   6   7   8   9   10   11   12 Kilometres

   (1) 4 km ≈ ... miles   (2) 6 miles ≈ ... km

13 Algebra: into the unknown

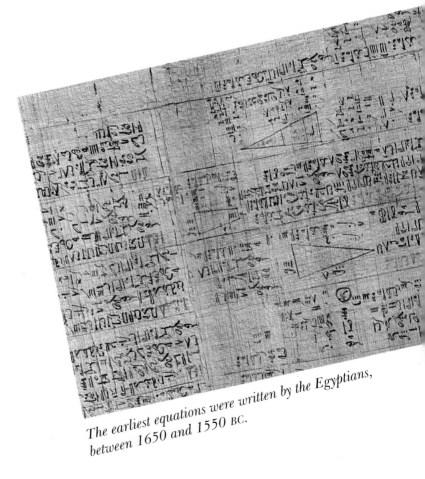

The earliest equations were written by the Egyptians, between 1650 and 1550 BC.

1 Inverse operations

Christopher has knitted a scarf.

His puppy undoes the scarf.

Christopher is back to where he started.
'Undoing the scarf' is called the inverse of 'knitting the scarf'.

Inverse   An **inverse** returns you to where you started.

Exercise 13:1

Write down the inverse of:

1 open the door   **3** turn left   **5** turn the light on

2 walk up the stairs   **4** walk backwards   **6** turn 90° clockwise

7 reflection of the shape
in the red line.

We can find inverses in mathematics.
Start with 3, add 4. The answer is 7.

'Subtract 4' undoes the 'add 4'. It returns 7 to 3.

'Subtract 4' is the inverse of 'add 4'

Exercise 13:2

1 Write down the inverse of these:
    a add 2   **b** subtract 5   **c** multiply by 3   **d** divide by 10

Example   We can use a **function machine** to represent 'add 10'.

Put 8 into this function
machine.
You get the answer 18.

$8 \longrightarrow \boxed{+10} \longrightarrow 18$

We can show the inverse by drawing the function machine
backwards.

Put 18 into this function
machine.
You get the answer 8.

$8 \longleftarrow \boxed{-10} \longleftarrow 18$

We have returned to where we started.

Draw the inverse function machines.
We only draw the screen of the robot.

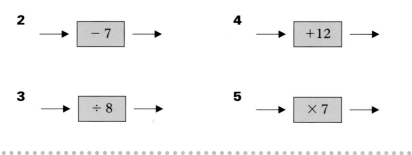

2 $\longrightarrow \boxed{-7} \longrightarrow$

4 $\longrightarrow \boxed{+12} \longrightarrow$

3 $\longrightarrow \boxed{\div 8} \longrightarrow$

5 $\longrightarrow \boxed{\times 7} \longrightarrow$

Example

A function machine can have two steps.

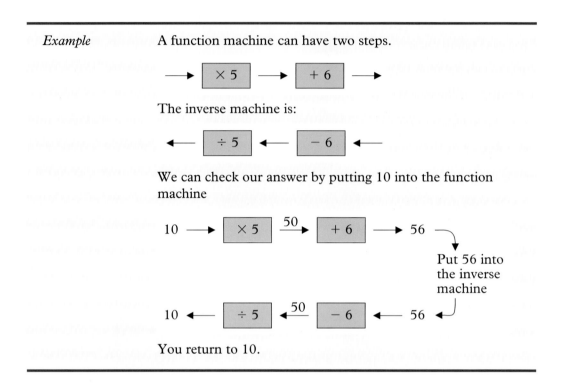

The inverse machine is:

We can check our answer by putting 10 into the function machine

Put 56 into the inverse machine

You return to 10.

Exercise 13:3

Draw the inverse function machines.
Check your answer. Use 10 or choose a number of your own.

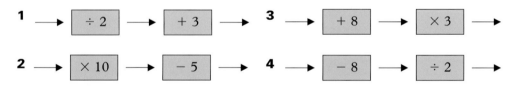

1 → ÷ 2 → + 3 →   **3** → + 8 → × 3 →

2 → × 10 → − 5 →   **4** → − 8 → ÷ 2 →

Can you suggest an inverse for these machines?
Remember you have to get back to where you started.

● **5** → Subtract from 50 →   ● **6** → Subtract from 100 →

What did you notice about the answers to Questions **5** and **6**?

Now try these machines.

● **7** → Divide into 100 →   ● **8** → Divide into 20 →

2 Equations

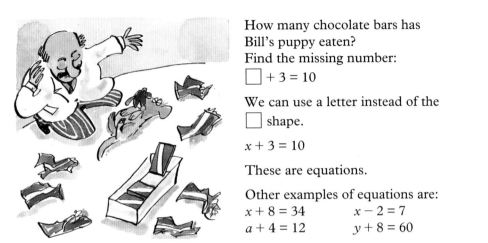

How many chocolate bars has Bill's puppy eaten?
Find the missing number:

$\boxed{} + 3 = 10$

We can use a letter instead of the $\boxed{}$ shape.

$x + 3 = 10$

These are equations.

Other examples of equations are:

$x + 8 = 34$ $x - 2 = 7$

$a + 4 = 12$ $y + 8 = 60$

Example   Solve the equation $x + 3 = 10$ using a function machine.

$$x \longrightarrow \boxed{+ 3} \longrightarrow 10$$

The inverse machine is:

$$7 \longleftarrow \boxed{- 3} \longleftarrow 10$$

Answer: $x = 7$

Exercise 13:4

Solve these equations by drawing function machines.

1 $x + 8 = 34$ **5** $4y = 12$

2 $a - 4 = 10$ **6** $5x = 30$

3 $x + 6 = 24$ **7** $\dfrac{r}{3} = 4$

4 $x - 10 = 36$ **8** $\dfrac{c}{2} = 26$

Example

Solve the equation $3a - 5 = 19$
Remember: $3a$ means $3 \times a$

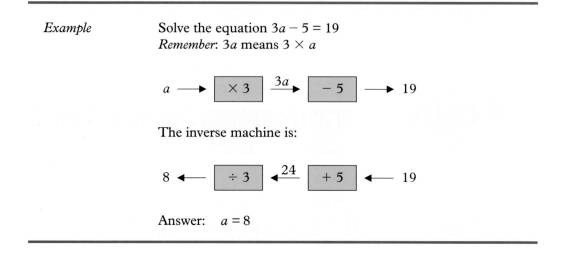

The inverse machine is:

Answer: $a = 8$

Exercise 13:5

Copy these function machines. Fill them in.
Solve the equations.

1 $4x - 10 = 2$

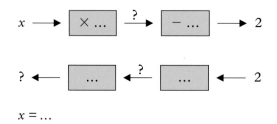

$x = \ldots$

2 $3x - 11 = 10$

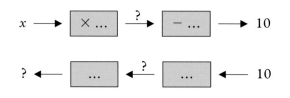

$x = \ldots$

Draw your own function machines and inverse function machines for these.
Solve the equations.

3 $2x + 7 = 19$

4 $6a + 12 = 30$

5 $5x - 8 = 27$

6 $10y + 14 = 44$

7 $5 + 7x = 75$

8 $8 + 3x = 41$

Hint: In Questions **7** and **8** remember to deal with the x term first.

Function machines take a long time to draw.
We can use inverses without drawing the machines.

Examples

1 Solve $x + 10 = 15$
The inverse of $+10$ is -10
We put -10 on both sides of the equation so that both sides remain equal

$$x + 10 - 10 = 15 - 10$$
$$x = 5$$

2 Solve $x - 4 = 6$
The inverse of -4 is $+4$

$$x - 4 + 4 = 6 + 4$$
$$x = 10$$

Exercise 13:6

Solve these equations: Set them out like the examples.

1 $x + 5 = 14$

2 $x + 3 = 10$

3 $a - 10 = 7$

4 $x + 9 = 11$

5 $q - 11 = 20$

6 $x + 14 = 30$

Examples **1** Solve $3x = 12$
The inverse of $\times 3$ is $\div 3$ so we divide both sides by 3.

$$\frac{3x}{3} = \frac{12}{3}$$

$$x = 4$$

$$\left(\text{Note: } \frac{3}{3} \text{ is } 3 \div 3. \text{ It is 1.}\right.$$
$$\left.1x \text{ is just written } x.\right)$$

2 Solve $\frac{a}{5} = 10$

The inverse of $\div 5$ is $\times 5$ so we multiply both sides by 5.

$$\frac{a}{5} \times 5 = 10 \times 5$$

$$a = 50$$

$$\left(\text{Note: } \frac{a}{5} \times 5 \text{ can be written } \frac{5a}{5}.\right.$$
$$\left.\frac{5a}{5} \text{ is } a\right)$$

Exercise 13:7

Solve these equations.

1 $4x = 20$

2 $\frac{a}{3} = 7$

3 $6x = 12$

4 $12y = 60$

5 $\frac{r}{8} = 3$

6 $\frac{x}{2} = 14$

Exercise 13:8

Solve these equations.

1 $3x = 15$

2 $q + 10 = 17$

3 $x - 3 = 7$

4 $\frac{t}{5} = 2$

5 $y + 6 = 14$

6 $2x = 10$

7 $\frac{x}{4} = 8$

8 $a - 5 = 1$

9 $\frac{x}{5} = 12$

10 $7q = 56$

11 $x + 12 = 29$

12 $10x = 350$

Example   We can solve two-stage equations in the same way.

Solve $2x + 5 = 11$

Function machine method:

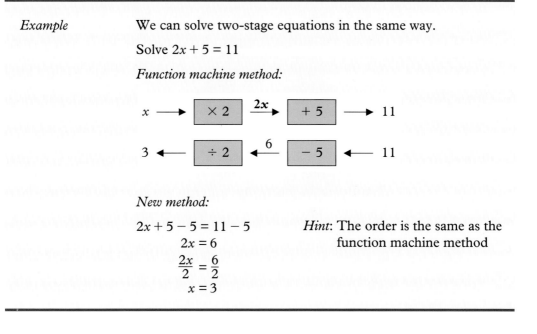

New method:

$$2x + 5 - 5 = 11 - 5$$
$$2x = 6$$
$$\frac{2x}{2} = \frac{6}{2}$$
$$x = 3$$

Hint: The order is the same as the function machine method

Exercise 13:9

Solve these equations using the new method. Show your working.

1 $3x + 4 = 13$

2 $5x + 8 = 28$

3 $2y + 11 = 25$

4 $4x - 3 = 21$

5 $6x - 8 = 46$

6 $3a - 15 = 21$

7 $2x + 5 = 13$

8 $7t + 1 = 36$

9 $3x - 5 = 25$

10 $\frac{r}{2} + 3 = 8$

11 $\frac{x}{5} - 3 = 1$

12 $\frac{k}{6} + 3 = 5$

13 $6 + 2x = 20$

14 $7 + \frac{x}{2} = 11$

15 $20 + 6y = 38$

16 $5x - 6 = 29$

17 $2x - 3 = 19$

18 $16 + 2p = 30$

An equation can be given in words. You have to change the words into algebra.

Example   I think of a number and add 5. The answer is 12. What is the number?

Change the words into algebra.
Call the number x. x
I think of a number and add 5. $x + 5$
The answer is 12. $x + 5 = 12$
Now solve the equation: $x + 5 - 5 = 12 - 5$
                                                                              $x = 7$

Answer: $x = 7$
The number is 7.

Exercise 13:10

Change the words into algebra. Solve the equation to find the number.

1   I think of a number and subtract 3. The answer is 12.

2   I think of a number and multiply it by 3. The answer is 18.

3   I think of a number and multiply it by 3. I then add 5. The answer is 17.

4   I think of a number and multiply it by 10. I then subtract 3.
The answer is 47.

5   I subtract 6 from a number. The answer is 3.

6   I think of a number. The product of this number and 3 is 21.

7   The sum of two numbers is 20. One number is 16. What is the other number?

8   When 6 is added to a number the answer is 9.

9   Paul has x sweets. Jane has 7 sweets. Together they have 19 sweets.
Find the value of x.

10   A class has 28 pupils. There are x boys and 15 girls.
Find the value of x.

Sometimes an equation is given as a diagram.

Example

Remember: angles on a line add up to 180°

We can see that $x + 120 = 180$
We can now solve this equation.

$$x + 120 - 120 = 180 - 120$$
$$x = 60$$

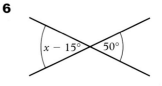

Exercise 13:11

In each question write down an equation and solve it.

1

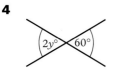

2

3

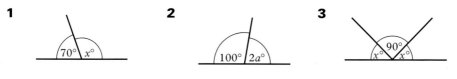

Remember: vertically opposite angles are equal.

4

5

6

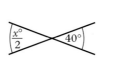

Remember: angles at a point add up to 360°.

7

8

● **9**

Remember: angles of a triangle add up to 180°.

10

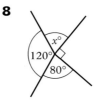

11

● **12**

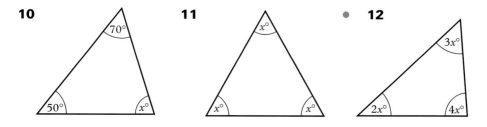

13

In Chapter 9 we wrote down the formula for the total length of
Mr Brown's car and caravan.

$t = c + 4$

't' was the total length and 'c' was the length of the caravan.

We call 't' the **subject** of the formula.
Whatever is written on the
left hand side of the '=' sign is called the subject.

Examples   The subject of the formula $y = 3x + 2$ is y.
                    The subject of the formula $4b = x$ is $4b$.
                    The subject of the formula $3y = a - 2$ is $3y$.

Exercise 13:12

What is the subject of each of these formulas?

1 $a = 3c - 2$ **3** $x = y + z$ **5** $2a = 15 + 3b$

2 $2y = x - 4$ **4** $7d = 12 - x$ **6** $z = a - b$

Look again at $t = c + 4$
This formula gives the total length t of the car and caravan.
We can change it into a formula that gives the length c of the caravan.

Start with $t = c + 4$
Change over sides $c + 4 = t$
Subtract 4 $c + 4 - 4 = t - 4$
                        $c = t - 4$

We now have a new formula for c, the length of the caravan.

Another formula we used was $s = p - 10$
We can make p the subject of this formula in the same way.

Start with $\hspace{6em} s = p - 10$
Change over sides $\hspace{4em} p - 10 = s$
Add 10 $\hspace{6em} p - 10 + 10 = s + 10$
$\hspace{12em} p = s + 10$

The subject is now p.

Exercise 13:13

Change the subject of these formulas to the letter given in brackets.

1 $y = x + 5$ (x) $\hspace{3em}$ **3** $c = z - 3$ (z) $\hspace{3em}$ **5** $p = 4 + q$ (q)

2 $a = b - 2$ (b) $\hspace{3em}$ **4** $m = n + 7$ (n) $\hspace{3em}$ **6** $y = 8 + x$ (x)

Examples $\hspace{2em}$ **1** $\hspace{1em}$ Make q the subject of the formula $p = 7q$

$\hspace{5em}$ Change over sides $\hspace{2em}$ $7q = p$

$\hspace{5em}$ Divide by 7 $\hspace{4em}$ $\frac{7q}{7} = \frac{p}{7}$ $\hspace{1em}$ but $\frac{7}{7} = 1$

$\hspace{5em}$ The subject is now q. $\hspace{1em}$ $q = \frac{p}{7}$

$\hspace{4em}$ **2** $\hspace{1em}$ Make y the subject of formula $x = \frac{y}{3}$

$\hspace{5em}$ Change over sides $\hspace{4em}$ $\frac{y}{3} = x$

$\hspace{5em}$ Multiply by 3 $\hspace{4em}$ $\frac{y}{3} \times 3 = x \times 3$
$\hspace{5em}$ The subject is now y. $\hspace{3em}$ $y = 3x$

Exercise 13:14

Change the subject of these formulas to the letter given in brackets.

1 $y = 4x$ (x) $\hspace{2em}$ **4** $a = \frac{b}{3}$ (b) $\hspace{2em}$ **7** $y = \frac{x}{10}$ (x)

2 $a = 5b$ (b) $\hspace{2em}$ **5** $m = \frac{x}{2}$ (x) $\hspace{2em}$ **● 8** $l = \frac{20}{m}$ (m)

3 $G = 7d$ (d) $\hspace{2em}$ **6** $h = 6f$ (f) $\hspace{2em}$ **● 9** $y = \frac{4}{x}$ (x)

Sometimes we have to do two steps.

Examples **1** Make c the subject of $a = 5c + 3$.

Change over sides $\qquad\qquad 5c + 3 = a$
Subtract 3 $\qquad\qquad\qquad 5c + 3 - 3 = a - 3$
$\qquad\qquad\qquad\qquad\qquad 5c = a - 3$

Divide by 5 $\qquad\qquad\qquad \dfrac{5c}{5} = \dfrac{a-3}{5}$ $\qquad$ *Note:* '$a - 3$' $\div$ 5

The new formula is: $\qquad\qquad c = \dfrac{a-3}{5}$ $\qquad$ is written $\dfrac{a-3}{5}$

2 Make b the subject $a = \dfrac{b}{2} + 7$

Change over sides $\qquad\qquad \dfrac{b}{2} + 7 = a$

Subtract 7 $\qquad\qquad\qquad \dfrac{b}{2} + 7 - 7 = a - 7$

$\qquad\qquad\qquad\qquad\qquad \dfrac{b}{2} = a - 7$

Multiply by 2 $\qquad\qquad\qquad \dfrac{2b}{2} = 2(a - 7)$

The new formula is: $\qquad\qquad b = 2(a - 7)$

We needed to use a bracket to show that all of '$a - 7$' is multiplied by 2.

Exercise 13:15

Change the subject of these formulas to the letter given in brackets.

1 $a = 3b + 1$ (b) $\qquad$ **6** $a = 7b - 6$ (b) $\qquad$ **11** $r = 9w - 8$ (w)

2 $a = 5b - 4$ (b) $\qquad$ **7** $m = 4p - 1$ (p) $\qquad$ **12** $s = 4h + 2$ (h)

3 $p = 2q + 10$ (q) $\qquad$ **8** $q = 9p + 3$ (p) $\qquad$ **13** $a = 12 + 4c$ (c)

4 $m = \dfrac{n}{3} + 10$ (n) $\qquad$ **9** $a = \dfrac{d}{4} + 5$ (d) $\qquad$ **14** $r = 5 + 7f$ (f)

5 $a = \dfrac{c}{5} - 2$ (c) $\qquad$ **10** $f = \dfrac{t}{3} - 7$ (t) $\qquad$ **15** $y = 4 + \dfrac{x}{6}$ (x)

3 Trial and improvement

Aisha is unhappy.

She can't solve equations.

Aisha decides to solve her equations by guessing.
She has to solve $3x + 18 = 57$

Aisha's first guess is 10 .... $3 \times 10 + 18 = 48$..... This is too small.
Aisha tries 20 .... $3 \times 20 + 18 = 78$..... This is too big.
She tries a number between 10 and 20:
She tries 15 .... $3 \times 15 + 18 = 63$..... This is too big.
She tries 13 .... $3 \times 13 + 18 = 57$..... This is correct.
Answer: $x = 13$

Aisha's teacher tells her this method is called **trial and improvement**.
Aisha is happy and wants to solve another equation.

Example   Solve $a^2 = 81$ *Remember*: a^2 means $a \times a$

Aisha tries different numbers.
She writes her results in a table.

Value of a	Value of a^2	
4	$4 \times 4 = 16$	much too small
10	$10 \times 10 = 100$	too big
8	$8 \times 8 = 64$	too small
9	$9 \times 9 = 81$	correct

Answer: $a = 9$

Exercise 13:16

Solve these equations by trial and improvement.
Set your work out in a table.

1 $4x + 21 = 73$

Value of x	Value of $4x + 21$	
10 20		

Continue the table until you find the answer.

2 $27a - 36 = 261$

Value of a	Value of $27a - 36$	

3 $24x + 156 = 948$

Value of x	Value of $24x + 156$	

Now write your own table headings.

4 $4x + 15 = 83$

5 $7a - 21 = 140$

6 $13x + 120 = 588$

7 $57y - 129 = 954$

8 $a^2 = 49$

9 $x^2 = 121$

10 $y^2 = 576$

11 $a^2 = 1849$

12 $x^2 + 574 = 1870$

● **13** $x^3 = 68\,921$

● **14** $x^2 + x = 3192$

● **15** $y^2 + 2y = 399$

Draw the inverse function machine for these:

1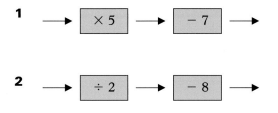

2

Solve these equations:

3 $3x + 8 = 29$

4 $5y - 11 = 19$

5 $\frac{c}{5} + 10 = 16$

6 $8 + 2x = 20$

7 $10 + \frac{x}{3} = 16$

8 $3q + 11 = 11$

In Questions **9–12** change the words into algebra.
Solve the equation to find the number.

9 I think of a number and multiply it by 2. I then add 8.
The answer is 26.

10 I think of a number and divide it by 10. I then subtract 2.
The answer is 6.

11 I add 14 to a number. The answer is 41.

12 I think of a number, multiply it by 11 and then subtract 7.
The answer is 37.

Solve the equations in Questions **13–16** by trial and improvement.

13 $x^2 + 4x = 3965$

14 $x^3 = 512$ *Remember: x^3 means $x \times x \times x$*

15 $x^2 + 5x = 414$

16 $y^3 = 21\,952$

In Quesions **17–19** write down an equation and solve it.

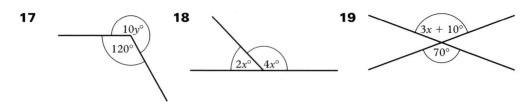

17 $10y°$, $120°$

18 $2x°$ $4x°$

19 $3x + 10°$ $70°$

Crossnumber puzzle

Copy the crossnumber.
Solve each equation and put the answers in your crossnumber.

Across	Down
1 $\frac{x}{2} = 7$	**1** $x - 5 = 10$
2 $4x = 8$	**2** $x + 6 = 30$
3 $x - 5 = 7$	**4** $\frac{x}{5} = 4$
5 $\frac{x}{2} + 11 = 18$	**6** $\frac{x}{5} = 7$
7 $x - 6 = 10$	**7** $2x - 6 = 20$
8 $\frac{x}{5} = 3$	**8** $\frac{x}{3} - 4 = 2$
9 $x - 3 = 20$	**9** $3x + 5 = 80$
11 $4x + 2 = 50$	**10** $\frac{x}{11} + 6 = 8$
12 The value of $5x + 10$ when x is 9	**11** $5x - 60 = 20$
13 The value of $2x + 2$ when $x = 12$	

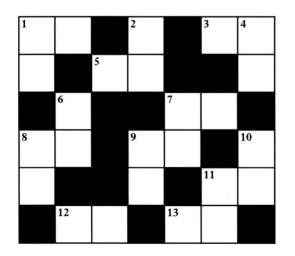

Write down the inverse of:

1   subtract 100

2   subtract from 100

3   divide by 20

4   divide into 20.

In Questions **5–8** write down the equation and solve it.

5

7

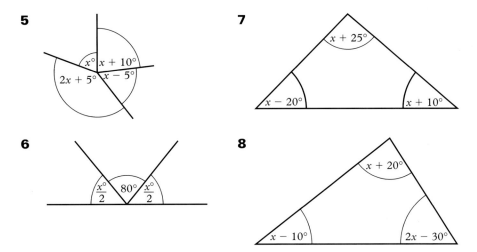

6

8

In Questions **9** and **10** change the words into an equation and solve it.

9   I think of a number and add 7. I then multiply by 8 and the answer is 104.

10   I think of a number and subtract 3. I then divide by 2 and the answer is 5.

In Questions **11–15** change the subject of these formulas to the letter given in brackets.

11 $y = 3x - 7$ (x)

12 $p = 4q + 8$ (q)

13 $y = \dfrac{x}{5} - 3$ (x)

14 $v = 9 + 7t$ (t)

15 $y = \dfrac{3x}{4} - 7$ (x)

In Questions **16–19** solve these equations by trial and improvement.

16 $x^2 + x^3 = 5202$

17 $5x^3 - 3x^2 = 85\,852$

18 $15x^3 - 960 = 0$

19 $x^3 + \sqrt{x} = 117\,656$

20 Some equations have more than one solution.

  a These equations have two whole number solutions between 0 and 10.
Find them both.

    (1) $5x - x^2 = 6$ (2) $9x - x^2 = 8$ (3) $12x - x^2 = 35$

  b This equation has three whole number solutions between 0 and 10.
Find all three.

$$x^3 + 17x - 8x^2 = 10$$

  c This equation has two whole number solutions between 0 and 100.
Find them.

$$100x - x^2 = 1204$$

21 Many equations do not have whole number solutions.

  a The solutions to these equations only work out exactly to one decimal place.
Find one solution between 0 and 10 for each equation.

    (1) $4x^2 = 81$ (3) $5x^2 - x = 130$ (5) $9^x = 243$

    (2) $10x^2 + x = 24$ (4) $\frac{1}{x} + 2x = 3$ (6) $16^x + 4x = 70$

  b These equations have solutions which may never work out exactly.
Find one solution between 0 and 10 for each equation.
Give this solution correct to one decimal place.
(Find the trial solution which is just too big and the one that is just too small. Choose the nearer one.)

    (1) $x^3 = 100$ (3) $2^x = 19$ (5) $x^2 + 5x = 21$

    (2) $3^x = 7$ (4) $x^2 + x = 14$ (6) $x + \frac{1}{x} = 10$

22 This equation has two solutions between 0 and 15.
Find them both.

$$x^2 - 19x + 84 = 0$$

23 This equation has two solutions between 0 and 50.
Find them both.

$$x^2 - 59x + 798 = 0$$

- The inverse returns you to where you started:

Operation	Inverse operation
+3	−3
−5	+5
×4	÷4
÷2	×2

- Equations can be solved using inverse function machines:

Solve $3x + 7 = 31$

$$x \longrightarrow \boxed{\times 3} \xrightarrow{3x} \boxed{+ 7} \longrightarrow 31$$

Answer: $x = 8$

$$8 \longleftarrow \boxed{\div 3} \xleftarrow{24} \boxed{- 7} \longleftarrow 31$$

- Equations can be solved using inverses.

$$3x - 5 = 22$$
$$3x - 5 + 5 = 22 + 5$$
$$3x = 27$$
$$\frac{3x}{3} = \frac{27}{3}$$
$$x = 9$$

- The subject of a formula can be changed using inverses.

Make t the subject $\quad\quad r = t + 8$
Change over sides $\quad\quad t + 8 = r$
Subtract 8 from both sides $\quad t + 8 - 8 = r - 8$
$\quad\quad\quad\quad\quad\quad\quad\quad t = r - 8$

Make t the subject $\quad\quad a = \dfrac{t}{5}$

Change over sides $\quad\quad \dfrac{t}{5} = a$

Multiply both sides by 5 $\quad \dfrac{t}{5} \times 5 = a \times 5$

$\quad\quad\quad\quad\quad\quad\quad\quad t = 5a$

- Equations can be solved by trial and improvement.
Guess what the answer is.
Try a better guess.

Solve $2x + 14 = 50$

Value of x	Value of $2x + 14$	
10	$2 \times 10 + 14 = 34$	too small
20	$2 \times 20 + 14 = 54$	too big
19	$2 \times 19 + 14 = 52$	too big
18	$2 \times 18 + 14 = 50$	correct

Answer: $x = 18$

Draw the inverse function machines for these.

1

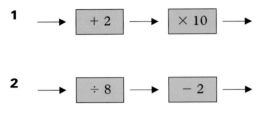

2

Solve these equations:

3 $5y = 30$

4 $\dfrac{c}{4} = 8$

5 $2x - 13 = 17$

6 $\dfrac{x}{2} - 5 = 12$

7   Change these words into algebra and solve the equation.
I think of a number and divide it by 4. I then add 8. The answer is 14.

Write down the equation for each diagram and solve it.

8

9

Change the subject of these formulas to the letter given in brackets.

10 $p = r + 15$ (r)

11 $a = b - 5$ (b)

12 $y = 4x - 5$ (x)

13 $f = 6g + 10$ (g)

14   Solve this equation by trial and improvement.
$$7x + 153 = 384$$

14 Area and perimeter

Four countries make up the United Kingdom. You may be surprised to see the area they cover compared with the number of people who live in each country:

- England has an area of 50 333 square miles and a population of 48.3 million
- Scotland has an area of 30 405 square miles and a population of 4.9 million
- Wales has an area of 8016 square miles and a population of 2.9 million
- Northern Ireland has an area of 5462 square miles and a population of 1.6 million.

But compare all these with Canada, which has an area of 3 851 800 square miles and a population of only 27.7 million.

1 Irregular shapes

Carpet-fitters are covering the floor space of this room. They are using square carpet tiles. Around the edges of the room is the skirting board.

The total distance around the room is the length of skirting board plus the width of the door. This distance is the perimeter of the room.

| **Perimeter** | The total distance around the outside edges of a shape is its **perimeter**.

The perimeter of this shape is 14 cm.

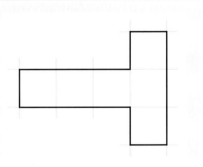

Exercise 14:1

You will need 1 cm squared paper for this exercise.

1 Copy these hexominoes on to squared paper.

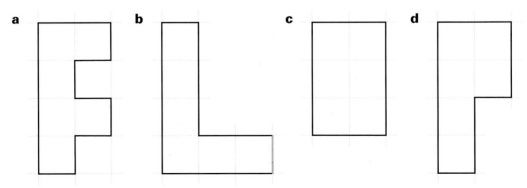

a   b   c   d

Write down the perimeter of each one.

2 **a** Draw a square of side 3 cm on squared paper.
   b What is the perimeter of this square?
   c Which hexomino in Question **1** has the same perimeter as this
      square?

3 **a** Copy this shape on to squared
      paper.
   b Write down the perimeter of
      this shape.
   c Which hexomino in Question **1** has the same perimeter?

4 **a** Copy these on to squared paper.

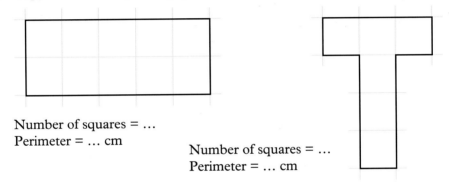

Number of squares = ...
Perimeter = ... cm

Number of squares = ...
Perimeter = ... cm

   b Draw a new shape with a perimeter of 14 cm.
      Write down the number of squares inside your shape.

5 You have drawn shapes with perimeters of 10 cm, 12 cm and 14 cm.
   These are even numbers.
   Draw shapes with perimeters of 11 cm and 13 cm.
   What do you notice?

· ·

Area   The amount of space
         inside a 2-D shape is
         called the **area** of that
         shape.
         Area is measured using
         squares.
         The area of this shape is
         6 cm².

Area is measured in squares. Suppose you have to find the area of a leaf. Here is an easy way of counting bits of squares.

Count whole squares first. There are 30 whole squares.

Now count squares which lie more than half inside the outline. There are 10 of these.

An **estimate** of the area of the leaf is 30 + 10 = 40 squares.

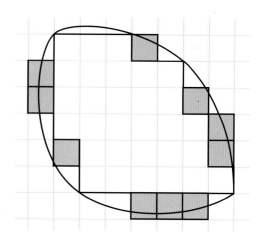

Exercise 14:2

1 Estimate the area of these leaves in cm² by counting squares.

Copy and complete:

a Number of whole squares ....
Number of part squares ....
Estimate of area .... cm²

b Number of whole squares ....
Number of part squares ....
Estimate of area .... cm²

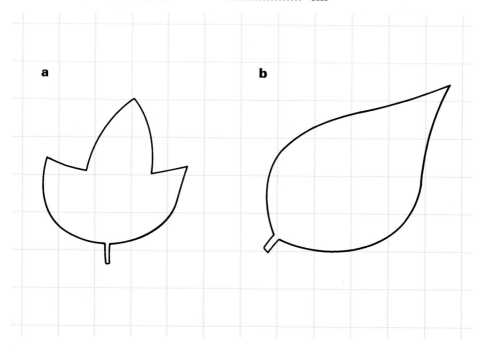

a   b

2   Here is a map of the island of North Ronaldsay, off the north coast of Scotland. Each square of the map represents 1 km² on the ground. Estimate the area of the island in km².

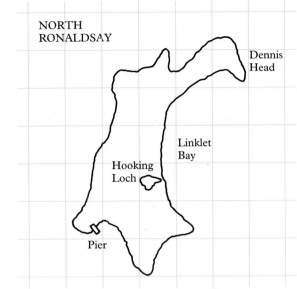

NORTH RONALDSAY

Dennis Head

Linklet Bay

Hooking Loch

Pier

Scale 1 cm represents 1 km

3   The map shows Slaley Forest in Northumberland. The blue lines drawn on the map form squares. Each square represents 1 km².
   a Estimate the area of the forest in km². Use the blue squares.
   b (1) How many 1 cm² squares fit inside one blue square?
      (2) Use a transparent 1 cm square grid or trace on to 1 cm squared paper. Estimate, in cm², the area of the map covered in forest.
      (3) Using (1) and (2) estimate the area of the forest in km².
   c Say which estimate of area, a or b, is more accurate. Explain why.

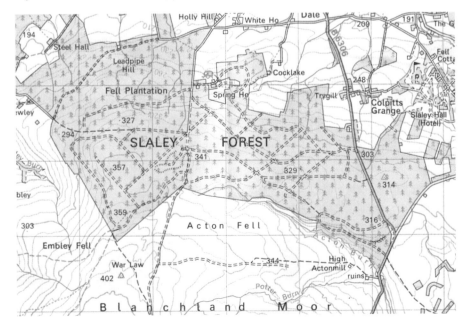

2 Areas of rectangles

Angela is painting a ceiling. The label on her tin of paint gives the area
that the paint should cover.
Angela needs to know the area of the ceiling.

Exercise 14:3

1 **a** Write down the length of this
rectangle.
b Write down the width of this
rectangle.
c Write down the area of this
rectangle.

There is a rule for finding the area of a rectangle.

Area of a rectangle = length × width
$A = l \times w$ or $A = lw$

Example

Calculate the area of the
5 cm by 3 cm rectangle
shown.

$A = lw$
$A = 5 \times 3$
$A = 15\ \text{cm}^2$

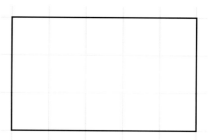

2 These rectangles have sides which are whole numbers of centimetres.
In each case, measure the length. Measure the width.
Use the formula to calculate the area.

a

b

3 Squares are special rectangles.
Use the formula $A = lw$ to calculate the areas of these squares.

a

2 cm

b
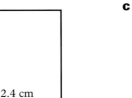
2.4 cm

c

1.5 cm

4 Here are some sketches of rectangles.
Calculate their areas.

a
15 cm
30 cm

b
12 cm
20 cm

c
15 cm
15 cm

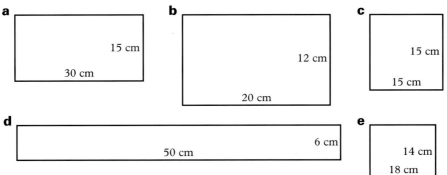

d
50 cm

e
6 cm
14 cm
18 cm

● **5** Draw a square. Make its sides 5 cm long.
  a What is the area of the square?
  b The square you have drawn is called a 5 cm square. Does this mean
    its area is 5 cm²?
    Draw a shape with an area of 5 cm².
  c If a shape has an area of 25 cm² must it be a square?

Exercise 14:4 To find the largest area that will fit inside a loop of string

You need a piece of string and some 1 cm squared paper.

1 Cut a piece of string exactly 24 cm long. Sellotape its ends together like this.

2 Here are two rectangles inside the string. What are their areas?

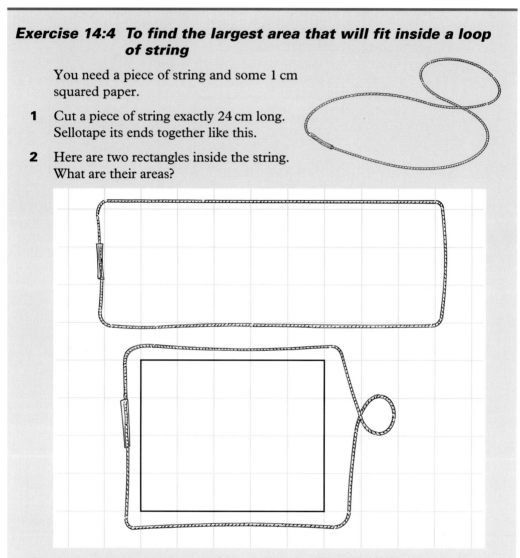

3 Copy this table for your results.

Length l	Width w	Area A
9	3	...
5	4	...

4 Find some more rectangles.

5 What is the largest rectangle that will fit inside the string?

6 Find some other shapes that fit inside.

7 What is the largest area that will fit?

Here are some very small leaves. We need to use very small squares to measure the area of these.

We need to use very large squares to measure the area of the classroom floor.

Units of area   Area is measured in square units. These can be **mm²**, **cm²**, **m²** or **km²**. Imperial units of in², ft², yd² or miles² can also be used. A postage stamp would be in mm² and a garden in m².

Exercise 14:5

1 Suggest units of area to measure these. Choose from mm², cm², m² or km².
  a the page of an exercise book.
  b the floor of your classroom.
  c the city of Liverpool.
  d a fingernail.
  e a television screen.
  f a tennis court.
  g the wing of a fly.
  h the country of Wales.

2 **a** What is the area of this square in cm²?
  b Write down the length of the square in mm.
  c Write down the width of the square in mm.
  d What is the area of this square in mm²?
  e Copy and complete 1 cm² = ... mm².

1 cn

1 cm

3 **a** What is the area of this square in m²?
  b Write down the length of the square in cm.
  c Write down the width of the square in cm.
  d What is the area of this square in cm²?
  e Copy and complete 1 m² = ... cm².

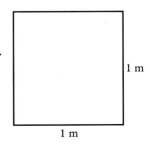

1 m

1 m

321

4 a What is the area of this square in km²?
  b Write down the length of the square in m.
  c Write down the width of the square in m.
  d What is the area of the square in m²?
  e Copy and complete 1 km² = ... m².

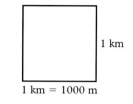

1 km

1 km = 1000 m

5 12 in = 1 ft, 3 ft = 1 yd, 1760 yd = 1 mile.
  a Calculate the number of in² in 1 ft².
  b Calculate the number of ft² in 1 yd².
  c Calculate the number of yd² in 1 mile².

Exercise 14:6

1 A football pitch is 100 m by 72 m.
  Calculate the area of the pitch.

2 A classroom is 8 m by 6 m.
  a What is the area of the classroom floor?
  b To fit carpet costs £10 for 1 m².
    How much would it cost to carpet the classroom?

3 A4 paper is 297 mm long and 210 mm wide
  a Calculate the area of a sheet of A4 paper in mm².
  b How many mm² are there in 1 cm²?
  c Find the area of a sheet of A4 paper in cm².

4 First class stamps are 20 mm by 24 mm.
  a What is the area of one stamp?
  b Stamps are sold in sheets of
    ten stamps in a book.
    What is the area of a sheet of
    ten stamps?

1ST

  c The stamps are arranged upright in two rows of 5.
    Find the length and width of a sheet of stamps.

5 A patio is 4 m by 3 m. The paving stones used are 500 mm square.
  a How many paving stones will fit along the 4 m edge?
  b How many will fit along the 3 m edge?
  c How many paving stones will be needed to make the patio?

6 The headteacher's study is to be fitted with new carpet tiles. The study
  is 3.4 m by 4.5 m. The tiles are 500 mm square.
  What is the minimum number of tiles that it would be reasonable to fit?
  Explain your answer giving your reasons.

Example

Find the width of this rectangle?

28 cm²

7 cm

We know   area = length × width

so   28 = 7   × width

We divide 28 by 7 to find the width.

$$\text{width} = \frac{28}{7}$$

$$= 4\,\text{cm}$$

Exercise 14:7

Find the missing length or width of these rectangles:

1

30 cm²

6 cm

2

80 cm²

8 cm

3

45 m²   5 m

4 The area of a rectangle is 15 cm².
Its length is 5 cm.
What is its width?

5 The area of a roller skating rink is
3000 m². The length is 100 m.
What is the width?

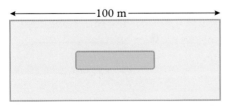
100 m

6 The area of a photograph is 180 cm².
The width of the photograph is 12 cm.
What is the length?

3 Perimeters of shapes

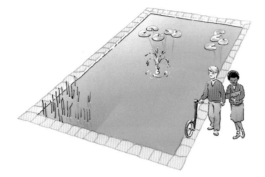

These pupils are measuring the distance around the Stanthorne High School pond.

The perimeter is the distance all the way round the outside of a shape.

Example

Find the perimeter of this rectangle.

Perimeter = 5 + 2 + 5 + 2
        = 14 m

2 m

5 m

Exercise 14:8

1 Find the perimeters of these shapes.
You need to measure the sides.

a

c

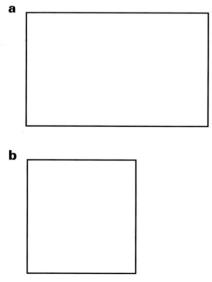

b

d

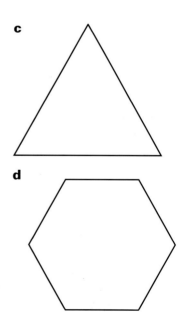

2 Here are some sketches of shapes.
Find the perimeters of the shapes.

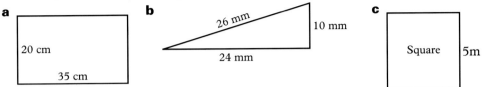

a 20 cm, 35 cm

b 26 mm, 10 mm, 24 mm

c Square 5m

3 A rectangular bookmark has a gold edge. The bookmark is 14 cm by 4 cm.
How long is the gold edge?

4 A cake frill is put round a square cake of side 20 cm. The ends of the
frill overlap by 5 cm.
How long is the frill?

5 A garden is 20 m by 15 m.
A fence is put round the outside of the garden. A 2 m gap is left for a gate.
What is the length of the fence?

6 Skirting board is put round a room 6 m by 5 m. The door is 1 m wide.
What length of skirting board is needed?

● **7** Write down formulas for the perimeters of these shapes: $P = \ldots$
Simplify your formulas by collecting terms.

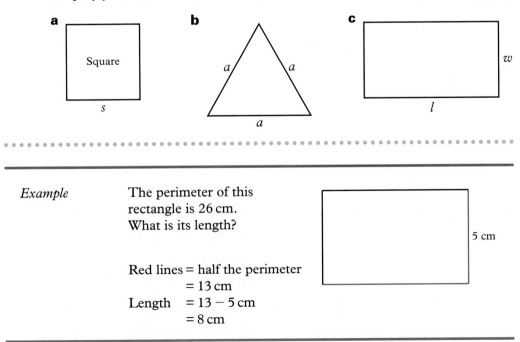

a Square s

b a, a, a

c w, l

Example The perimeter of this
rectangle is 26 cm.
What is its length?

5 cm

Red lines = half the perimeter
= 13 cm
Length = 13 − 5 cm
= 8 cm

Exercise 14:9

1 Find the missing length or width of these shapes.

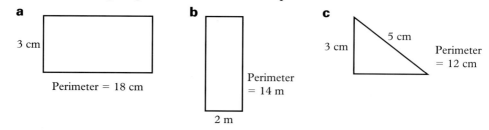

a

3 cm

Perimeter = 18 cm

b

Perimeter = 14 m

2 m

c

3 cm 　 5 cm

Perimeter = 12 cm

2 The perimeter of a square is 32 cm.
What is the length of a side?

3 The perimeter of a regular hexagon is 36 cm.
What is the length of each side?

4 The perimeter of a regular pentagon is 35 cm.
What is the length of each side?

5 The perimeter of an equilateral triangle is 60 cm.
What is the length of each side?

6 The perimeter of a square is 24 m.
What is its area?

7 The area of a square is 81 cm².
What is its perimeter?

● **8** In a rectangle the length is twice the width. The perimeter is 36 cm.
Find the length and width and hence find the area.

● **9** In a rectangle the length is twice the width and the area is 128 cm².
Find the length and width and hence find the perimeter.

● **10** In a rectangle the length is 20 cm more than the width. The perimeter
is 140 cm.
Find the area.

● **11** A rectangular garden has fencing
all round the outside except for
one gate 3 metres wide. The
garden is 24 m long.
Fencing comes in panels of length
1.5 m. Fifty-four panels of fencing
are used.
What is the area of garden?

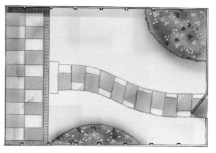

4 Areas of triangles and parallelograms

Richard wants to grow grass on an old flower bed.

The bed is a triangle shape. Richard needs to know the area of the triangle.

He will then know how much grass seed to buy.

Exercise 14:10

1 Copy this table and fill it in.

	Area of rectangle	Area of triangle
a		
b		

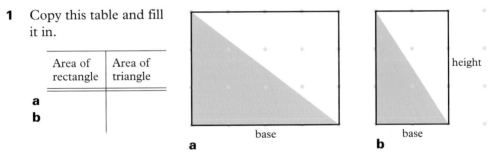

a   **b**

2 Draw some more rectangles and triangles of your own. Put these into your table.
Can you find a rule for finding the area of the triangle? Your rule should use the **base** and the **height** of the triangle.

3 Will your rule work for these triangles?
Explain why.

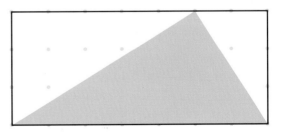

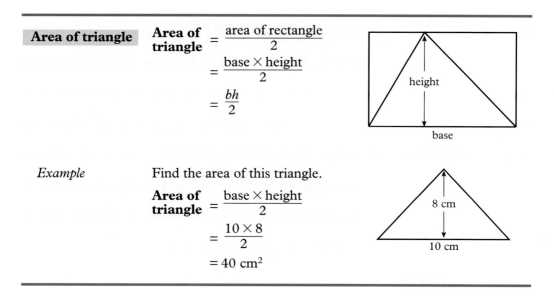

Area of triangle

$$\text{Area of triangle} = \frac{\text{area of rectangle}}{2}$$

$$= \frac{\text{base} \times \text{height}}{2}$$

$$= \frac{bh}{2}$$

Example

Find the area of this triangle.

$$\text{Area of triangle} = \frac{\text{base} \times \text{height}}{2}$$

$$= \frac{10 \times 8}{2}$$

$$= 40 \text{ cm}^2$$

Exercise 14:11

1 Find the areas of these triangles.

a 7 cm 8 cm

b 8 cm 20 cm

c 4 m 8 m

2 Sometimes the triangle can be on its side or even upside down. Copy these triangles and find their areas.

a $\text{Area} = \dfrac{bh}{2}$

$$= \frac{\dots \times \dots}{2}$$

$$= \dots \text{ cm}^2$$

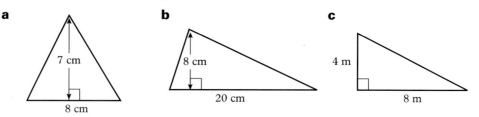

b $\text{Area} = \dfrac{bh}{2}$

$$= \frac{\dots \times 12}{2}$$

$$= \dots \text{ cm}^2$$

20 cm, 9 cm, 12 cm, 10 cm

3 Find the areas of these triangles.

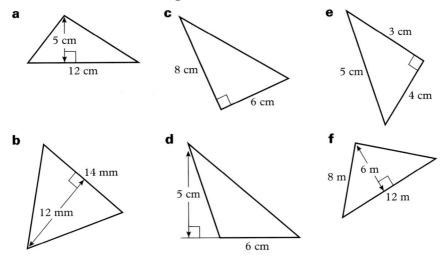

a

5 cm

12 cm

c

8 cm

6 cm

e

3 cm

5 cm

4 cm

b

14 mm

12 mm

d

5 cm

6 cm

f

8 m

6 m

12 m

4 These triangles are drawn accurately.
Find the area of each triangle. Measure any length you need from the diagram.

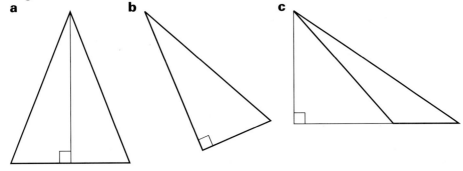

a

b

c

· ·

We can change the parallelogram to a rectangle by moving the triangle

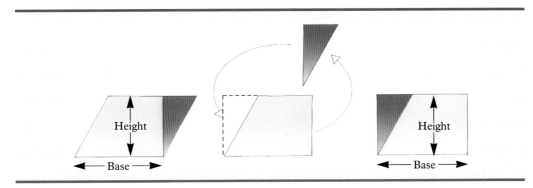

Height

Base

Height

Base

Area of parallelogram

Area of the parallelogram = Area of the rectangle

Area = base × height

$A = bh$

Example

Find the area of this parallelogram.

Area = bh

$= 8 \times 5$

$= 40 \text{ cm}^2$

5 cm

8 cm

Exercise 14:12

Find the areas of these parallelograms.

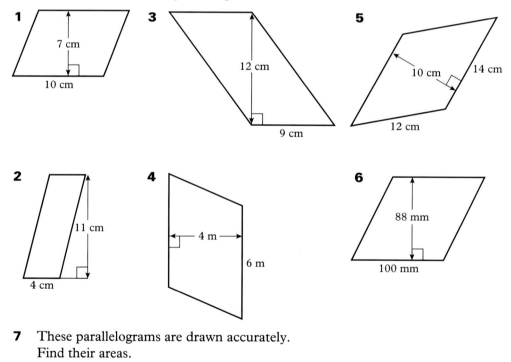

1

7 cm

10 cm

3

12 cm

9 cm

5

10 cm

14 cm

12 cm

2

11 cm

4 cm

4

4 m

6 m

6

88 mm

100 mm

7 These parallelograms are drawn accurately.
Find their areas.

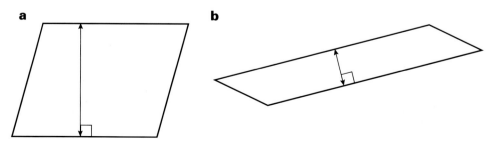

a

b

5 Compound shapes

Andrew is going to carpet a room. He needs to work out the area of the floor.
Andrew has a problem because the room is not a rectangle.

Example

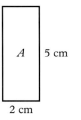

A 5 cm

2 cm

B 2 cm

3 cm

Area of rectangle A is 10 cm².

Area of rectangle B is 6 cm².

The two rectangles are joined.
The dashed line shows the join.

Area of new shape = area of A + area of B
$$= 10 + 6$$
$$= 16 \text{ cm}^2$$

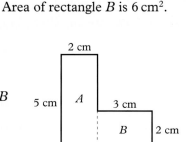

2 cm

5 cm A

3 cm

B 2 cm

Exercise 14:13

1 You can see the two rectangles that have been joined to make this shape.

Copy and complete:

Area of C = ... cm²
Area of D = ... cm²
Area of shape = ... + ...
                = ... cm²

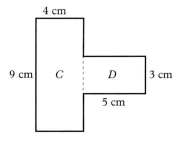

4 cm

9 cm C D 3 cm

5 cm

Find the areas of these shapes.

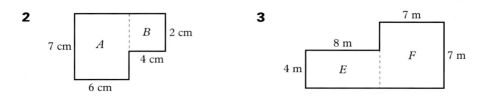

2

7 cm | *A* | *B* | 2 cm
4 cm
6 cm

3

7 m
8 m
E | *F* | 7 m
4 m

Example

Find the area of this shape.

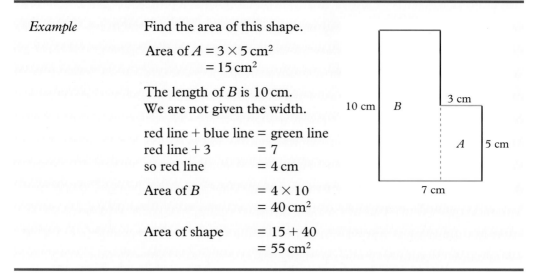

Area of *A* = 3 × 5 cm²

          = 15 cm²

The length of *B* is 10 cm.
We are not given the width.

red line + blue line = green line
red line + 3   = 7
so red line   = 4 cm

Area of *B*   = 4 × 10
                = 40 cm²

Area of shape   = 15 + 40
                = 55 cm²

10 cm   *B*   3 cm
A   5 cm
7 cm

---

4   Find the length of the blue lines in these shapes.

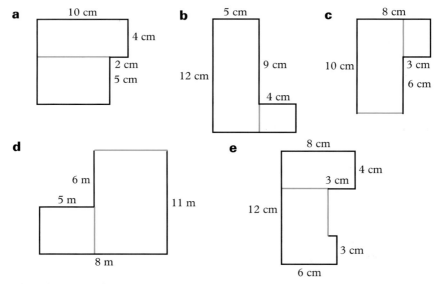

a
10 cm
4 cm
2 cm
5 cm

b
5 cm
9 cm
12 cm
4 cm

c
8 cm
10 cm
3 cm
6 cm

d
6 m
5 m
11 m
8 m

e
8 cm
4 cm
3 cm
12 cm
3 cm
6 cm

5   Find the area of each shape in Question 4.

6 The diagram shows the floor plan of a house.
Find the area of each room.

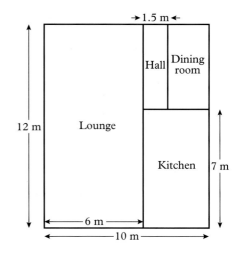

• •

Exercise 14:14

Use 1 cm squared paper for this exercise.

1 a Draw a rectangle 10 cm by 5 cm on squared paper.
Cut it out.
Work out the area of this rectangle.

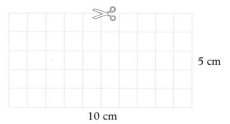

b Draw a rectangle 5 cm by 2 cm inside your rectangle.
Cut this out.
What is the area of the piece cut out?

c The piece you have left looks like this:

What is the area of this piece?

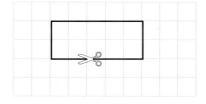

d Copy and complete:
Area of piece left = ... − ...
= ... cm².

e Count the squares on the piece left to check your answer.

2 **a** Draw a new rectangle 6 cm by 9 cm.
Work out its area.

  b Draw a rectangle 4 cm by 3 cm inside your rectangle.
Cut this out. What is the area of the piece cut out?

  c What is the area of the piece you have left?

3 Laura wants to frame a picture.
She has a piece of card 9 cm by
7 cm.

She cuts out a hole 5 cm by 3 cm
to frame the picture.

What is the area of card left?

4 **a** Look at this shape:

  We could find its area by
dividing it into two rectangles.

  Find a different way of finding
the area by subtracting.

  What is the area?

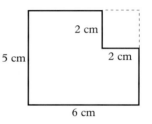

  b Find the area of this shape
using the subtraction method.

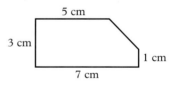

  c Find the areas of these two shapes.

(1)   (2)

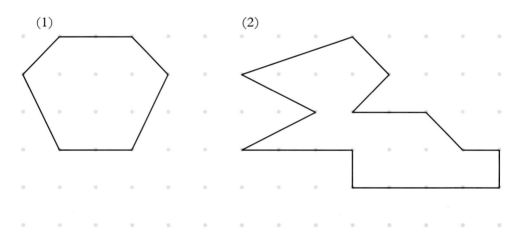

1 Here is a map of Tatton Park. It is just south of Manchester. Each square of the map represents 1 km² on the ground. Estimate the area of Tatton Park in km².

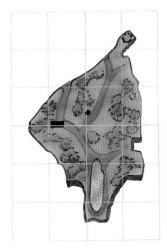

2 A stamp is 40 mm by 30 mm.
   a Calculate the area of the stamp in mm².
   b How many mm² are there in 1 cm²?
   c Find the area of the stamp in cm².

3 **a** A classroom is to have a carpet. The classroom is 7.5 m by 10 m. Calculate the area of carpet needed.
   b The carpet costs £8 for 1 m². How much will it cost to buy the carpet for the classroom?

4 Use 1 cm squared paper to help you with this question.
   A rectangle of paper is 10 cm by 8 cm.
   a What is its perimeter?

8 cm

10 cm

   b A square 2 cm by 2 cm is cut from one corner. What is the perimeter of the shape that is left?

   c Identical squares are cut from the other three corners. What is the perimeter of the shape that is left?
   d What do you notice about the answers to parts **a**, **b** and **c**?
   e How could you cut a square from the edge so that the perimeter changed?

5 Find the area of this stencil with the holes cut out.

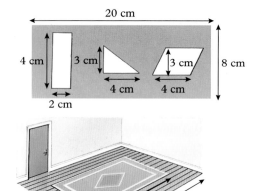

6 The picture shows a rug on a wooden floor.

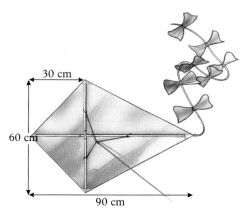

a What area of the floor is covered by the rug?
b What area of the floor is not covered by the rug?

7 What is the area of the shadow cast by the wall?

The wall has a length of 8 m.

8 What is the area of this kite?

9 What is the area of the buckle of this belt?

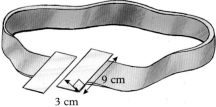

1 **a** What is the perimeter of this rectangle?
   b What is the area of this rectangle?
   c This is a special rectangle.
      The perimeter and area are the same
      number. Only the units are different.
      Find a square which has the same number for its perimeter as for
      its area.

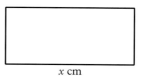

3 cm

6 cm

   d The perimeter of this rectangle
      (not drawn to scale) is 20 cm.
      The length of the rectangle is
      x cm. Write down, in terms of
      x, a formula for the width of
      the rectangle.

x cm

$$w = \ldots$$

   e Copy and complete: $A = lw$
$$A = x(\ldots\ldots)$$

   f Given that the rectangle has the property that its perimeter and area
      are the same number, the equation for the area is $x(10 - x) = 20$
      Use trial and improvement to solve the equation correct to one
      decimal place.
      Hence write down the length of the rectangle.

   g Write down the width of the rectangle.

2 Pooh had wandered into the Hundred
   Acre Wood, and was standing in front
   of what had once been Owl's house. It
   didn't look at all like a house now; it
   looked like a tree which had been
   blown down; and as soon as a house
   looks like that, it is time you tried to
   find another one.

From *The House at Pooh Corner* by
            A.A. Milne

An acre (*pronounced* ay-ker) is an imperial unit of area. It is equal to
4840 yd².
A hectare (*pronounced* heck-tar) is a metric unit of area. It is equal to
10 000 m².
A hectare is just less than $2\frac{1}{2}$ acres.

   a Approximately how many hectares are there in the Hundred Acre
      Wood?

   b Approximately how many m² are there in the Hundred Acre Wood?

   c How many m² are there in 1 km²?

   d Use your answers to **b** and **c** to obtain an estimate of the size of the
      wood in km².

3 Write down formulas for the perimeters of these shapes: $P = \ldots$
Simplify your formulas by collecting terms.

a

b

c

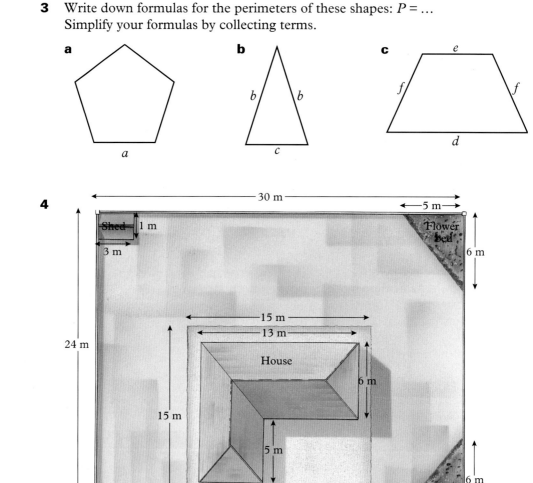

4

This is a plan of Sian's house and her garden.
a What is the area covered by the house?
b The area around the house is paved. What is this area?
c What is the area of one of the two flower beds?
d What is the area of the lawn?
e Lawn fertiliser costs £3 a bag. Each bag covers $10\,\text{m}^2$.
How much will it cost Sian to fertilise the lawn?
f The garden is to be fenced all around except for the gate. The gate
is 3 m wide.
What length of fencing will be needed?
g The fencing is 1.5 m high. It is to be painted on both sides.
What is the total area to be painted?

- Perimeter is the total distance around the outside edges of a shape.

- Area is the amount of space inside a shape.
  It is measured using squares.
  The size of squares you choose depends on the size of the area to be measured.

- Metric units of area are mm^2, cm^2, m^2, km^2
  Imperial units of area are in^2, ft^2, yd^2, $miles^2$

- Formulas: Area of rectangle   = length × width
  = lw

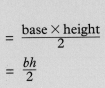

  Area of triangle   = $\dfrac{base \times height}{2}$

  = $\dfrac{bh}{2}$

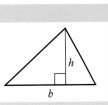

  Area of parallelogram = base × height
  = bh

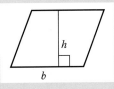

- To find the area of a compound shape we divide it up into simple shapes.

  We can find this area by adding the areas of the two rectangles.

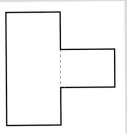

  The green area can be found by subtracting the area of the cut out shape.

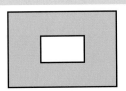

1   **a**   Measure the length and the width of this rectangle.
     b   What is its area?
     c   What is its perimeter?

2   A carpet tile is 50cm square.
     a   What is the area of the tile?
     b   How many of these tiles fit a 1 m square?
     c   How many of these tiles would you need to carpet a room 4 m by 6 m?

3   This rectangle has a perimeter of 36 cm.
What is its length?

3 cm

4   Find the area of each of these shapes.

a

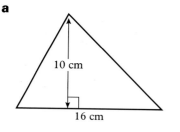

10 cm

16 cm

b

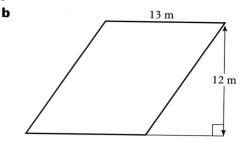

13 m

12 m

5   Find the areas coloured green.

a

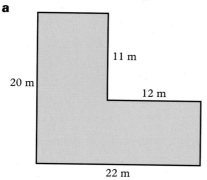

11 m

20 m

12 m

22 m

b

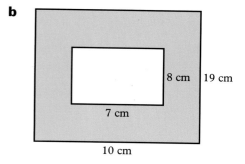

8 cm   19 cm

7 cm

10 cm

15 Small parts

QUESTIONS

EXTENSION

SUMMARY

TEST YOURSELF

In his will a man left his 17 camels to his three sons.
He left $\frac{1}{2}$ of the camels to his oldest son, $\frac{1}{3}$ of them to his
middle son and $\frac{1}{9}$ of them to the youngest son.

When the boys came to divide up the camels they found that
17 was a very awkward number!

The youngest boy who was the cleverest had a good idea.
He borrowed a camel from their neighbour so that they now
had 18.

They now split up the camels:
$\frac{1}{2}$ of $18 = 9$
$\frac{1}{3}$ of $18 = 6$
$\frac{1}{9}$ of $18 = 2$

$9+6+2 = 17$ camels so they could return the last
camel to their neighbour!!

Can you find out how this trick works?

1 Introducing fractions

Tim, Jane and Rachel are sharing a cake.

The cake has been cut into 8 equal parts. They have 1 piece each.

What fraction of the cake is left?

The cake has been cut into 8 pieces.

Each piece is **one eighth**. This is written $\frac{1}{8}$.

Five pieces are left. This is $\frac{5}{8}$.

So five-eighths of the cake is left.

Three pieces have been eaten. This is $\frac{3}{8}$.

So three-eighths of the cake has been eaten.

| Numerator | The top number of a fraction is the **numerator**. This tells you how many pieces you have to talk about. |

| Denominator | The bottom number of a fraction is the **denominator**. This tells you how many pieces the whole was cut into. |

Exercise 15:1

In questions **1–6**, write down:

a the fraction that is left
b the fraction that has been eaten.

Give both of your answers in words and in figures.

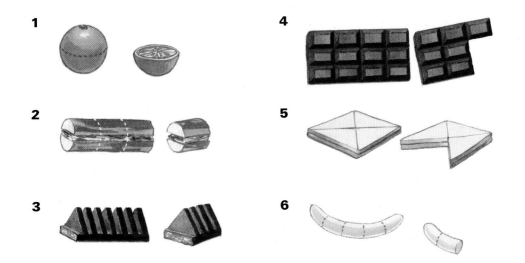

1

4

2

5

3

6

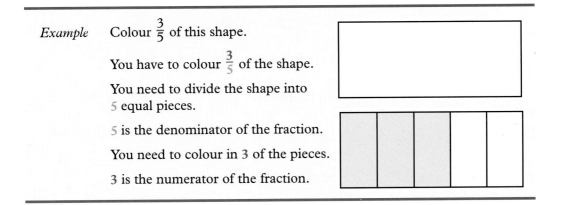

Example   Colour $\frac{3}{5}$ of this shape.

You have to colour $\frac{3}{5}$ of the shape.

You need to divide the shape into 5 equal pieces.

5 is the denominator of the fraction.

You need to colour in 3 of the pieces.

3 is the numerator of the fraction.

In questions **7–10**, colour in the fraction of each shape like this:

a Copy each shape and label it with the fraction that you have to colour.
b Split the shape into the number of equal pieces that the denominator tells you.
c Colour in the number of pieces that the numerator tells you.

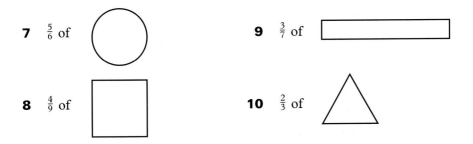

7 $\frac{5}{6}$ of

9 $\frac{3}{7}$ of

8 $\frac{4}{9}$ of

10 $\frac{2}{3}$ of

Exercise 15:2

1 **a** Write down the numerator of the fraction five elevenths.
   b Write down the denominator of seven twelfths.

2 The diagram shows the net of a
tetrahedron.
   a Write down the fraction of the
net that is shaded.
   b Write down the fraction of the
net that is unshaded.

3

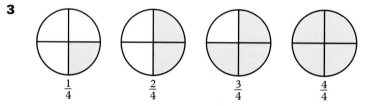

$$\frac{1}{4} \qquad \frac{2}{4} \qquad \frac{3}{4} \qquad \frac{4}{4}$$

   a Why are the denominators all the same?
   b Why are the numerators all different?

Writing one number as a fraction of another number

Make sure that the units are the same before you write down the fraction.

Example   Write 10 minutes as a fraction of an hour.
       1 hour = 60 minutes.

       10 minutes as a fraction of an hour is $\dfrac{10}{60}$

4 Write the first amount as a fraction of the second amount.
   a 5 minutes, 1 hour   **f** 70p, £40
   b 15 minutes, 3 hours   **g** 3 cm, 1 m
   c 4 seconds, 2 minutes   **h** 34 cm, 8 m
   d 23 seconds, 4 minutes   **i** 12 g, 1 kg
   e 10p, £3   **j** 150 g, 3 kg

2 Working with fractions

Paul has 12 sweets. He is sharing them equally with his friends. The three boys get one third ($\frac{1}{3}$) each.

Example   Find $\frac{1}{3}$ of 12 sweets.

$\frac{1}{3}$ of 12 $= 12 \div 3$ (Divide by 3 to get $\frac{1}{3}$)

$\qquad\qquad = 4$ sweets

Exercise 15:3

Find:

1 $\frac{1}{2}$ of eight sweets

2 $\frac{1}{5}$ of ten sweets

3 $\frac{1}{3}$ of nine packets of crisps

4 $\frac{1}{4}$ of 20 p

5 $\frac{1}{5}$ of 15 marbles

6 $\frac{1}{6}$ of 24 biscuits

7 $\frac{1}{4}$ of £1 in pence

8 $\frac{1}{10}$ of £2 in pence

9 $\frac{1}{2}$ of an hour in minutes

10 $\frac{1}{4}$ of an hour in minutes

11 $\frac{1}{2}$ of a minute in seconds

12 $\frac{1}{10}$ of a centimetre in millimetres

Example   Find $\frac{2}{3}$ of 12 sweets.

$\frac{1}{3}$ of 12 sweets $= 12 \div 3$
$= 4$ sweets

$\frac{2}{3}$ of 12 sweets $= 2$ lots of 4 sweets
$= 2 \times 4$
$= 8$ sweets

$\frac{2}{3}$ of 12 sweets

Find:

13 $\frac{2}{3}$ of 15 sweets

14 $\frac{3}{4}$ of eight sweets

15 $\frac{4}{5}$ of ten pence

16 $\frac{7}{10}$ of 20 counters

17 $\frac{3}{8}$ of 16 cans of drink

18 $\frac{5}{6}$ of 18 chocolate biscuits

19 $\frac{2}{5}$ of £1 in pence

20 $\frac{7}{10}$ of £3 in pence

21 $\frac{3}{7}$ of two weeks in days

22 $\frac{3}{4}$ of one metre in centimetres

23 $\frac{5}{8}$ of two metres in centimetres

24 $\frac{3}{10}$ of one minute in seconds

· ·

You do not always get whole numbers as answers to these problems.

Ben, Ned, Kate and Emma have 7 cakes.
They want to share them out equally.
How many cakes will each person get?

They each take a whole cake.
There are only three cakes left. There are not enough cakes to have another whole cake each.

Because there are 4 of them, they cut the rest of the cakes into **quarters**

Each person gets 3 quarters.

Altogether, each person gets $1\frac{3}{4}$ cakes.

Exercise 15:4

1 Share four apples equally between three children.

Answer .... apples each.

2 Share five oranges equally between four children.

Answer .... oranges each.

3 Share these equally. Draw diagrams to help you.

    a   3 cakes between 2 children.   **c**   5 apples between 2 children.

    b   7 bananas between 4 children.   **d**   7 cakes between 3 children.

4 Terry, Louise and Heidi cook 5 small pizzas.
They share the pizzas equally between them.
How many pizzas will each person get?

5 There 10 squares of chocolate in a bar.
Four friends share the bar equally between them.
How many squares will each person get?

6 Nine oranges are shared equally between 4 people.
How many oranges will each person get?

7 30 cakes are shared equally between 8 people.
How many cakes does each person get?

Improper fraction	The fraction $\frac{7}{4}$ has a numerator that is larger than its denominator. It is called an **improper fraction** or top-heavy fraction.

Mixed number	The fraction $1\frac{3}{4}$ is made up of a whole number and a fraction. It is called a **mixed number**.

Examples

1   Change $\frac{13}{5}$ to a mixed number.

    $13 \div 5 = 2$ remainder 3

    So $\frac{13}{5} = 2\frac{3}{5}$

2   Change $2\frac{3}{4}$ to an improper fraction.

    There are four quarters in 1. So 2 is made up of eight quarters.

    This means that $2\frac{3}{4}$ is made up of 11 quarters altogether.

    So $2\frac{3}{4} = \frac{11}{4}$

---

8 Change these to mixed numbers.

   a $\frac{5}{4}$ **c** $\frac{5}{2}$ **e** $\frac{9}{4}$ **g** $\frac{8}{3}$ **i** $\frac{15}{4}$

   b $\frac{4}{3}$ **d** $\frac{8}{5}$ **f** $\frac{7}{2}$ **h** $\frac{17}{5}$ **j** $\frac{19}{6}$

9 Change these to improper fractions

   a $1\frac{1}{2}$ **c** $2\frac{1}{3}$ **e** $3\frac{1}{2}$ **g** $2\frac{5}{6}$ **i** $4\frac{7}{8}$

   b $1\frac{1}{4}$ **d** $2\frac{3}{5}$ **f** $4\frac{2}{3}$ **h** $5\frac{1}{3}$ **j** $3\frac{4}{7}$

Equivalent fractions

Half of each of these shapes is shaded.
Each shape also shows another fraction.
All these fractions must be the same as a half.

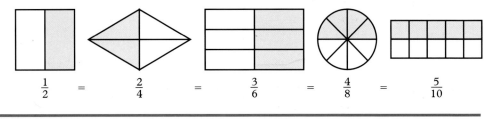

$$\frac{1}{2} \;=\; \frac{2}{4} \;=\; \frac{3}{6} \;=\; \frac{4}{8} \;=\; \frac{5}{10}$$

Equivalent fractions	**Equivalent fractions** are different ways of writing the same fraction.
Example	Write down 4 fractions which are equivalent to $\frac{1}{2}$
	Using the diagrams above, four equivalent fractions are
	$\frac{2}{4}, \; \frac{3}{6}, \; \frac{4}{8}, \; \frac{5}{10}$

Exercise 15:5

Give each of these as two equivalent fractions.

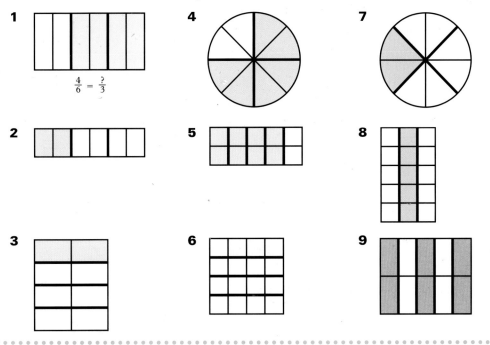

1

$$\frac{4}{6} = \frac{?}{3}$$

2

3

4

5

6

7

8

9

Simplifying fractions

Putting fractions into their simplest form is known as cancelling.

Example   Write each of these fractions in their simplest form:

$$\text{a } \frac{3}{6} \qquad\qquad \text{b } \frac{8}{12}$$

a Look for the biggest number that divides exactly into the numerator and the denominator. 3 divides exactly in to 3 and 6.

$$\frac{3}{6} = \frac{1}{2} \qquad \frac{1}{2} \text{ is the simplest form of this fraction.}$$
(÷3 top and bottom)

b 4 divides exactly in to 8 and 12

$$\frac{8}{12} = \frac{2}{3} \qquad \frac{2}{3} \text{ is the simplest form of this fraction.}$$
(÷4 top and bottom)

Exercise 15:6

Copy and complete these.
You will get each fraction in it's simplest form.

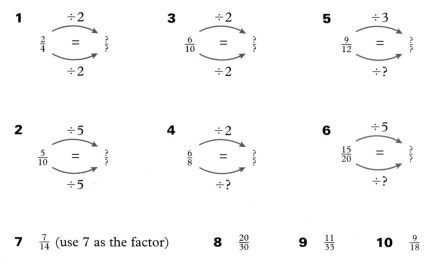

1 $\frac{2}{4} \overset{÷2}{\underset{÷2}{=}} \frac{?}{?}$ **3** $\frac{6}{10} \overset{÷2}{\underset{÷2}{=}} \frac{?}{?}$ **5** $\frac{9}{12} \overset{÷3}{\underset{÷?}{=}} \frac{?}{?}$

2 $\frac{5}{10} \overset{÷5}{\underset{÷5}{=}} \frac{?}{?}$ **4** $\frac{6}{8} \overset{÷2}{\underset{÷?}{=}} \frac{?}{?}$ **6** $\frac{15}{20} \overset{÷5}{\underset{÷?}{=}} \frac{?}{?}$

7 $\frac{7}{14}$ (use 7 as the factor) **8** $\frac{20}{30}$ **9** $\frac{11}{33}$ **10** $\frac{9}{18}$

Adding fractions

To add fractions the bottom numbers **must** be the same.

Example Work out **a** $\frac{1}{3}+\frac{1}{3}$ **b** $\frac{3}{5}+\frac{3}{5}$

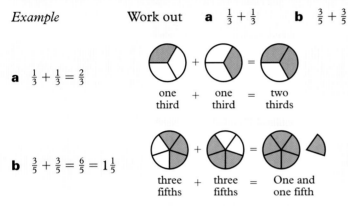

a $\frac{1}{3}+\frac{1}{3}=\frac{2}{3}$

one third + one third = two thirds

b $\frac{3}{5}+\frac{3}{5}=\frac{6}{5}=1\frac{1}{5}$

three fifths + three fifths = One and one fifth

Sometimes the two bottom numbers are different.
Before you can add the fractions you must *make* the bottom numbers the same.
This is called finding a common denominator.

Example Work out $\frac{2}{3}+\frac{1}{6}$

You need to find a number that 3 and 6 both divide into exactly.

Numbers that 3 goes into exactly are:

3 ⑥ 9 12 ...

Numbers that 6 goes into exactly are:

⑥ 12 18 ...

The first number that is in both lists is 6.

Now you need to write both fractions with 6 as the bottom number.

First change the $\frac{2}{3}$

Ask yourself; 'What do I have to multiply the 3 by to get 6?'
The answer is 2. You multiply the top and bottom of the fraction by 2.

$$\frac{2}{3} \xrightarrow{\times 2} \frac{?}{6} \qquad \frac{2}{3} \xrightarrow{\times 2} \frac{4}{6} \qquad \frac{2}{3}=\frac{4}{6}$$

You can see this in a diagram.

The $\frac{1}{6}$ does not need changing.

So $\frac{2}{3}+\frac{1}{6}=\frac{4}{6}+\frac{1}{6}=\frac{5}{6}$

Exercise 15:7

1 $\frac{2}{5} + \frac{1}{5}$ **6** $\frac{1}{4} + \frac{1}{2}$ **11** $\frac{2}{9} + \frac{1}{3}$ **16** $\frac{3}{8} + \frac{5}{7}$

2 $\frac{4}{13} + \frac{6}{13}$ **7** $\frac{1}{6} + \frac{1}{12}$ **12** $\frac{1}{3} + \frac{1}{4}$ **17** $\frac{5}{9} + \frac{3}{7}$

3 $\frac{7}{12} + \frac{5}{12}$ **8** $\frac{2}{5} + \frac{3}{10}$ **13** $\frac{2}{7} + \frac{1}{3}$ ● **18** $\frac{6}{11} + \frac{5}{13}$

4 $\frac{10}{11} + \frac{4}{11}$ **9** $\frac{3}{8} + \frac{1}{4}$ **14** $\frac{2}{5} + \frac{1}{3}$ ● **19** $\frac{1}{2} + \frac{1}{3} + \frac{1}{4}$

5 $\frac{5}{8} + \frac{7}{8}$ **10** $\frac{7}{12} + \frac{1}{6}$ **15** $\frac{2}{7} + \frac{3}{5}$ ● **20** $\frac{2}{7} + \frac{3}{5} + \frac{3}{8}$

Subtracting fractions

Subtracting fractions is very similar to adding.
Again you **must** make sure the bottom numbers of both fractions are the same.
Once you have done this, you take away the top numbers instead of adding them.

Example Work out $\frac{3}{8} - \frac{1}{4}$

You need to write both fractions with 8 as the bottom number.

$$\frac{1}{4} \xrightarrow{\times 2} \frac{?}{8} \qquad \frac{1}{4} \xrightarrow{\times 2} \frac{2}{8} \qquad \frac{1}{4} = \frac{2}{8}$$

The $\frac{3}{8}$ does not need changing.

So $\frac{3}{8} - \frac{1}{4} = \frac{3}{8} - \frac{2}{8} = \frac{1}{8}$

Exercise 15:8

1 $\frac{5}{7} - \frac{2}{7}$ **5** $\frac{3}{8} - \frac{1}{4}$ **9** $\frac{4}{7} - \frac{1}{3}$ **13** $\frac{5}{11} - \frac{2}{9}$

2 $\frac{2}{3} - \frac{1}{3}$ **6** $\frac{5}{12} - \frac{1}{3}$ **10** $\frac{8}{11} - \frac{2}{3}$ **14** $\frac{6}{13} - \frac{3}{11}$

3 $\frac{6}{13} - \frac{2}{3}$ **7** $\frac{1}{3} - \frac{1}{4}$ **11** $\frac{4}{7} - \frac{2}{5}$ ● **15** $\frac{5}{9} - \frac{1}{15}$

4 $\frac{2}{3} - \frac{1}{6}$ **8** $\frac{3}{5} - \frac{1}{6}$ **12** $\frac{8}{9} - \frac{4}{7}$ ● **16** $\frac{1}{20} - \frac{1}{21}$

Multiplying fractions

This box is split into three equal parts.
1 of the 3 parts is red.
$\frac{1}{3}$ of the box is red.

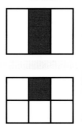

The box is now split in half.
This splits the red part in half.
The box now looks like this.
Only $\frac{1}{6}$ of the whole box is now red.

This means that $\frac{1}{2}$ of $\frac{1}{3}$ is $\frac{1}{6}$

Another way of writing this is $\frac{1}{2} \times \frac{1}{3} = \frac{1}{6}$

To multiply two fractions together: (1) multiply the top numbers together
(2) multiply the bottom numbers together
(3) simplify the answer if you can.

Examples   **1** Work out $\frac{2}{3} \times \frac{3}{8}$

$$\frac{2}{3} \times \frac{3}{8} = \frac{6}{24} \qquad \frac{6}{24} \xrightarrow{\div 6} = \frac{1}{4}$$

2 Work out $\frac{4}{9} \times 1\frac{1}{2}$

You need to change $1\frac{1}{2}$ to an improper fraction.

$$\frac{4}{9} \times \frac{3}{2} = \frac{12}{18} \qquad \frac{12}{18} \xrightarrow[\div 6]{\div 6} = \frac{2}{3}$$

Exercise 15:9

1 $\frac{1}{2} \times \frac{1}{4}$ **5** $\frac{5}{6} \times \frac{2}{3}$ **9** $\frac{3}{11} \times 3$ **13** $2\frac{1}{3} \times 2\frac{1}{3}$

2 $\frac{1}{3} \times \frac{1}{4}$ **6** $\frac{5}{9} \times \frac{2}{7}$ **10** $1\frac{1}{2} \times \frac{1}{3}$ **14** $\frac{7}{9} \times 1\frac{2}{7}$

3 $\frac{2}{3} \times \frac{1}{5}$ **7** $\frac{7}{9} \times \frac{1}{11}$ **11** $2\frac{1}{4} \times \frac{2}{3}$ • **15** $\frac{1}{2} \times \frac{1}{3} \times \frac{1}{4}$

4 $\frac{3}{4} \times \frac{2}{3}$ **8** $\frac{2}{5} \times 3$ (3 is $\frac{3}{1}$)   **12** $1\frac{1}{2} \times 1\frac{1}{2}$ • **16** $\frac{2}{3} \times \frac{3}{4} \times \frac{4}{5}$

Dividing fractions

Adam is making pancakes for himself
and his friends. He is using pancake mix.

It takes $\frac{1}{4}$ of a packet to make each pancake.

Adam has $1\frac{3}{4}$ packets of pancake mix.

He wants to know how many pancakes he
can make.

Adam needs to know how many quarters
there are in $1\frac{3}{4}$.

He counts up in quarters and gets the answer 7

$$0 \quad \frac{1}{4} \quad \frac{2}{4} \quad \frac{3}{4} \quad \frac{4}{4} \quad \frac{5}{4} \quad \frac{6}{4} \quad \frac{7}{4}$$

$$1 \quad 2 \quad 3 \quad 4 \quad 5 \quad 6 \quad 7$$

Asking how many quarters there are in $1\frac{3}{4}$ is the same as doing $1\frac{3}{4} \div \frac{1}{4}$

So $1\frac{3}{4} \div \frac{1}{4} = 7$

A quick way to divide fractions is to turn the second fraction over then multiply.

$$1\frac{3}{4} \div \frac{1}{4} = \frac{7}{4} \div \frac{1}{4} = \frac{7}{4} \times \frac{4}{1} = \frac{28}{4} = \frac{7}{1} = 7$$

Example   Work out $\frac{3}{4} \div \frac{5}{8}$

$$\frac{3}{4} \div \frac{5}{8} = \frac{3}{4} \times \frac{8}{5} = \frac{24}{20} = \frac{6}{5} = 1\frac{1}{5}$$

Exercise 15:10

1 $\quad 1\frac{1}{4} \div \frac{1}{4}$ **5** $\quad \frac{2}{5} \div \frac{2}{3}$ **9** $\quad \frac{3}{7} \div \frac{5}{6}$ **13** $\quad 2\frac{1}{2} \div 3$

2 $\quad 2\frac{1}{2} \div \frac{1}{2}$ **6** $\quad \frac{2}{3} \div \frac{2}{5}$ **10** $\quad \frac{5}{11} \div \frac{2}{3}$ **14** $\quad \frac{5}{9} \div \frac{2}{11}$

3 $\quad \frac{1}{3} \div \frac{1}{2}$ **7** $\quad \frac{1}{7} \div 4$ (4 is $\frac{4}{1}$)   **11** $\quad \frac{2}{3} \div 1\frac{1}{4}$ **15** $\quad \frac{1}{20} \div \frac{1}{21}$

4 $\quad \frac{2}{3} \div \frac{1}{4}$ **8** $\quad \frac{2}{9} \div 3$ **12** $\quad 1\frac{1}{2} \div 1\frac{1}{4}$ **16** $\quad \frac{1}{21} \div \frac{1}{20}$

You can check your answers to this section on your calculator.
Use the calculator help sheet on page 406.

3 Fractions, decimals and percentages

· ·

Parts of a whole can be shown as fractions.
They can also be written as a special fraction, called a percentage.

The large square has 100 small squares.
25 small squares are shaded.

25 out of 100 is the fraction $\frac{25}{100}$

25 out of 100 is 25 per cent.

Percentage

A **percentage** is the same as a fraction out of 100.

There is a special symbol for percentages.
Instead of writing a fraction with a denominator of 100 you use the percentage symbol %.

This is a rearrangement of 100

$$25 \text{ out of } 100 = \frac{25}{100} = 25\%$$

Exercise 15:11

1 Copy this table and fill it in for the grids **a** to **f**.

	Number of squares shaded	Fraction shaded	Percentage shaded
a	?	$\frac{?}{100}$	? %
b	?	$\frac{?}{100}$	? %
c	?		

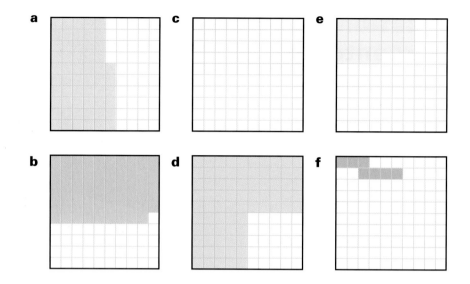

2 Write down the percentage that is coloured if every small square in one of the grids above is coloured.

3 Write these percentages as fractions of 100.
  a 93%   **b** 18%   **c** 5%   **d** 10%   **e** 1%

4 Write these fractions as percentages.
  a $\frac{47}{100}$ **b** $\frac{84}{100}$ **c** $\frac{16}{100}$ **d** $\frac{7}{100}$ **e** $\frac{3}{100}$

5 20% of the pupils in 7M were absent on Monday.
  Write down the percentage that were present.

6 71% of the Earth's surface is water.
  Write down the percentage that is land.

7 Jotinder works in an electrical shop. He pays 15% less than the full price on things that he buys there.
  Write down the percentage of the full price that he pays.

8 The members of a youth club vote for their next trip.
  39% vote to go bowling. The rest vote to go skating.
  Write down the percentage that vote to go skating.

Exercise 15:12

For questions **1–3** copy and complete the lists. Use the diagrams to help you.

1 Copy and complete:

  a $25\% = \frac{25}{100} = \frac{1}{4}$

  b $75\% = \frac{?}{100} = ?$

  c $50\% = \frac{?}{100} = ?$

2 Copy and complete:

  a $10\% = \frac{?}{100} = \frac{1}{10}$

  b $30\% = \frac{?}{100} = \frac{?}{10}$

  c $70\% = ? = ?$

  d $90\% = ? = ?$

3 Copy and complete:

  a $20\% = \frac{?}{100} = \frac{1}{?}$

  b $40\% = \frac{?}{100} = \frac{2}{5}$

  c $60\% = ? = ?$

  d $80\% = ? = ?$

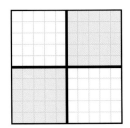 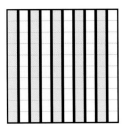 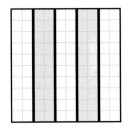

4 Write down:
  a the fraction of the cubes that are blue.
  b the percentage of the cubes that are blue.
  c the percentage of the cubes that are red.

5 **a** What fraction of the squares are red?
  b What percentage of the squares are red?
  c What fraction of the squares are blue?
  d What percentage of the squares are blue?

6 **a** Use squared paper to make a 100 square grid.
  b Colour your grid to show thirds.
  c Copy and complete:
    $\frac{1}{3} = ?\%$ $\frac{2}{3} = ?\%$

7 **a** Draw a grid like the one shown.
  b Colour 20% of the squares red.
  c Colour 10% of the squares green.
  d Colour 30% of the squares blue.
  e Colour the rest yellow.
  f What percentage of the squares are yellow?
  g What fraction of the squares are yellow?

Fractions and percentages are parts of a whole.
You have already seen decimals. They are also part of a whole.

Changing fractions to decimals

A fraction is another way of writing a divide question.

$\frac{3}{5}$ is **three fifths** but it is also 3 divided by 5.

You change this to a decimal by dividing.

$$\begin{array}{r} 0.\,6 \\ 5\overline{)\,3.\,^30} \end{array}$$

3 divided by 5 is 0 with 3 to carry.

Add a decimal point and a nought and carry on.

So $\frac{3}{5} = 0.6$

You can turn any fraction into a decimal like this.

Exercise 15:13

1 Change each of these fractions to decimals.

  a $\frac{1}{2}$ **c** $\frac{2}{5}$ **e** $\frac{1}{10}$ **g** $\frac{7}{10}$

  b $\frac{1}{5}$ **d** $\frac{4}{5}$ **f** $\frac{3}{10}$ **h** $\frac{8}{10}$

Sometimes you need to add more than one nought.

$\frac{3}{4}$ is 3 divided by 4.

3 divided by 4 is 0 with 3 to carry.

$$\begin{array}{r} 0.\,7 \\ 4\overline{)\,3.\,^30} \end{array}$$

Add a decimal point and a nought.

Now do 30 ÷ 4. This is 7 with 2 to carry.

$$\begin{array}{r} 0.\,7\,5 \\ 4\overline{)\,3.\,^30\,^20} \end{array}$$

Add another nought $20 \div 4 = 5$. So $\frac{3}{4} = 0.75$

2 Change each of these fractions to decimals.

  a $\frac{1}{4}$ **c** $\frac{3}{8}$ **e** $\frac{3}{20}$ •**g** $\frac{1}{16}$

  b $\frac{1}{8}$ **d** $\frac{1}{20}$ **f** $\frac{7}{20}$ •**h** $\frac{7}{16}$

Some decimals carry on forever.
They are called **recurring decimals**.
You still work them out in the same way.

Example Change $\frac{1}{3}$ to a decimal.

$\frac{1}{3}$ is 1 divided by 3

1 divided by 3 is 0 with 1 to carry.
Add a decimal point and a nought.
Now do 10 ÷ 3. This is 3 with 1 to carry.
This will carry on forever!

$$\begin{array}{r} 0.33 \\ 3\overline{)1.^10^10^10} \end{array}$$

So $\frac{1}{3} = 0.333\,333\,33...$

You can write this as $0.\dot{3}$ where the dot over the 3 tells you that the 3 *recurs*.

Some decimals recur so that more than one digit repeats.

$0.146\,146\,146\,146\,146...$ is written $0.\dot{1}4\dot{6}$

The two dots tell you where the recurring digits start and stop.

3 Write these recurring decimals using the dot notation.
  a 0.222 22...   **c** 0.141 414 14...   **e** 0.876 587 658 765...
  b 0.666 66...   **d** 0.123 123 123...   • **f** 0.345 656 565 656...

4 Change each of these fractions to recurring decimals.

  a $\frac{2}{3}$ **h** $\frac{7}{9}$ **o** $\frac{6}{7}$

  b $\frac{1}{6}$ **i** $\frac{8}{9}$ **p** $\frac{1}{11}$

  c $\frac{5}{6}$ **j** $\frac{1}{7}$ **q** $\frac{2}{11}$

  d $\frac{1}{9}$ **k** $\frac{2}{7}$ **r** $\frac{1}{13}$

  e $\frac{2}{9}$ **l** $\frac{3}{7}$ • **s** $\frac{1}{17}$

  f $\frac{4}{9}$ **m** $\frac{4}{7}$ • **t** $\frac{1}{19}$

  g $\frac{5}{9}$ **n** $\frac{5}{7}$

Changing decimals to fractions

You need to remember the values of the decimal places to do this.
Look at the column that the last digit is in to see what fraction you need.

units	.	tenths	hundredths	thousandths	
0	.	6			means 6 tenths which is $\frac{6}{10}$ as a fraction.
0	.	2	4		means 24 hundredths which is $\frac{24}{100}$ as a fraction.
0	.	2	7	2	means 272 thousandths which is $\frac{272}{1000}$ as a fraction.

Don't forget that you should cancel the fractions when you can.
Look for a number that divides into the top number and the bottom number.
Don't worry if you need to cancel more than once.
Keep going until you cannot cancel any more.

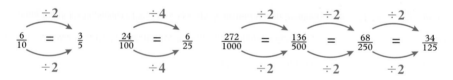

You could do this in one go if you divide by 8.

5 Write each of these as a fraction.
    a 0.3   **c** 0.13   **e** 0.169   **g** 0.2341
    b 0.7   **d** 0.27   **f** 0.499   **h** 0.7911

6 Write each of these as a fraction. Cancel the fraction down as much as you can.
    a 0.4   **e** 0.66   **i** 0.56   **m** 0.875
    b 0.5   **f** 0.24   **j** 0.245   **n** 0.625
    c 0.8   **g** 0.52   **k** 0.125   **o** 0.1875
    d 0.42   **h** 0.32   **l** 0.375   **p** 0.8125

4 Ordering fractions

It can be quite difficult to get fractions into the right order!

It is best to use a number line to help you.

Get in order you 'orrible lot!!!

Exercise 15:14

1 **a** Draw a line 12 cm long.
   Split your line into thirds.
   Leave 4 cm between each mark

   ├──────────────┼──────────────┼──────────────┤

   b Mark the numbers   0 $\frac{1}{3}$ $\frac{2}{3}$ 1   on the number line.

2 **a** Draw another line 12 cm long.
   Line it up exactly under your first line.
   Split your line into quarters.
   Leave 3 cm between each mark
   b Mark the numbers   0 $\frac{1}{4}$ $\frac{1}{2}$ $\frac{3}{4}$ 1   on the number line.

3 **a** Draw another line 12 cm long.
   Line it up exactly under your other lines.
   Split your line into sixths. Leave 2 cm between each mark.
   b Mark the numbers   0, $\frac{1}{6}$, $\frac{2}{6}$, ..., etc. on the number line.

4 **a** Draw another line 12 cm long.
   Line it up exactly under your first line.
   Split your line into eighths. Leave 1.5 cm between each mark.
   b Mark the numbers   0, $\frac{1}{8}$, $\frac{2}{8}$, ..., etc. on the number line.

5 Use your number lines to help you with this question.
Write down each pair of fractions.
Circle the bigger of the two fractions.

a $\frac{1}{2}$ $\frac{1}{3}$ **c** $\frac{2}{3}$ $\frac{1}{2}$ **e** $\frac{7}{8}$ $\frac{4}{6}$ **g** $\frac{7}{8}$ $\frac{5}{6}$

b $\frac{1}{4}$ $\frac{1}{3}$ **d** $\frac{5}{8}$ $\frac{1}{3}$ **f** $\frac{2}{3}$ $\frac{7}{8}$ **h** $\frac{1}{4}$ $\frac{3}{8}$

6 Use your number lines to help you with this question.
Rewrite each set of fractions in order.
Start with the **smallest**.

a $\frac{1}{2}$ $\frac{1}{3}$ $\frac{1}{6}$ $\frac{1}{8}$ $\frac{1}{4}$

b $\frac{2}{3}$ $\frac{1}{6}$ $\frac{5}{8}$ $\frac{5}{6}$ $\frac{2}{4}$

c $\frac{7}{8}$ $\frac{2}{3}$ $\frac{3}{8}$ $\frac{2}{6}$ $\frac{3}{4}$

Sometimes, you can estimate where fractions are on the number line.

Example   Which fraction is bigger, $\frac{4}{7}$ or $\frac{5}{11}$?

$\frac{4}{7}$ is bigger than $\frac{1}{2}$ because 4 is more than half of 7.

$\frac{5}{11}$ is smaller than $\frac{1}{2}$ because 5 is less than half of 11.

On the number line they would look like this.

$\frac{4}{7}$ is the bigger fraction.

Exercise 15.15

1 In each part write down the pairs of fractions.
Circle the bigger fraction.
Use a number line to help you.

a $\frac{3}{5}$ $\frac{3}{7}$ **d** $\frac{1}{3}$ $\frac{4}{7}$ **g** $\frac{2}{5}$ $\frac{4}{7}$

b $\frac{4}{9}$ $\frac{6}{11}$ **e** $\frac{2}{3}$ $\frac{5}{12}$ **h** $\frac{8}{15}$ $\frac{9}{19}$

c $\frac{1}{4}$ $\frac{3}{5}$ **f** $\frac{1}{2}$ $\frac{7}{13}$ •**i** $\frac{11}{20}$ $\frac{9}{16}$

Sometimes it is helpful to think about moving back from the other end of the number line.

You can think of $\frac{8}{9}$ as $\frac{1}{9}$ back from 1

$$0 \quad \frac{1}{9} \quad \frac{2}{9} \quad \frac{3}{9} \quad \frac{4}{9} \quad \frac{5}{9} \quad \frac{6}{9} \quad \frac{7}{9} \quad \frac{8}{9} \quad 1$$

You can think of $\frac{7}{8}$ as $\frac{1}{8}$ back from 1

$$0 \quad \frac{1}{8} \quad \frac{2}{8} \quad \frac{3}{8} \quad \frac{4}{8} \quad \frac{5}{8} \quad \frac{6}{8} \quad \frac{7}{8} \quad 1$$

$\frac{1}{9}$ is smaller than $\frac{1}{8}$ so $\frac{1}{9}$ is a smaller step back from 1.

This means that $\frac{8}{9}$ is the bigger fraction.

2 In each part write down the pairs of fractions. Circle the bigger fraction. Use a number line to help you.

a $\frac{5}{6}$ $\frac{4}{5}$ d $\frac{8}{9}$ $\frac{7}{8}$ g $\frac{3}{5}$ $\frac{4}{6}$

b $\frac{8}{9}$ $\frac{9}{10}$ e $\frac{10}{11}$ $\frac{12}{13}$ h $\frac{11}{13}$ $\frac{12}{14}$

c $\frac{4}{5}$ $\frac{3}{4}$ f $\frac{5}{6}$ $\frac{7}{8}$ i $\frac{17}{20}$ $\frac{16}{19}$

The other way to order fractions is to change them so that they all have the same bottom number. This is called finding a common denominator. It is the method you used in addition and subtraction.

Example   a Write $\frac{3}{5}$ and $\frac{4}{7}$ as fractions with a common denominator.

        b Use your answer to **a** to say which is the bigger fraction.

        a You need to find a number that 5 and 7 both divide into exactly. 5 and 7 both go into 35.
        Now change both fractions,

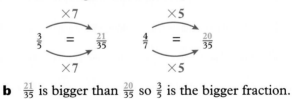

$$\frac{3}{5} = \frac{21}{35} \qquad \frac{4}{7} = \frac{20}{35}$$

        b $\frac{21}{35}$ is bigger than $\frac{20}{35}$ so $\frac{3}{5}$ is the bigger fraction.

3 In each part:
(1) Write the fractions with a common denominator.
(2) Use your answer to (1) to say which is the bigger fraction.

a $\frac{1}{3}$ $\frac{2}{5}$ d $\frac{3}{8}$ $\frac{2}{5}$ g $\frac{5}{11}$ $\frac{4}{9}$

b $\frac{5}{6}$ $\frac{11}{12}$ e $\frac{3}{7}$ $\frac{4}{9}$ h $\frac{3}{11}$ $\frac{4}{13}$

c $\frac{4}{5}$ $\frac{3}{4}$ f $\frac{5}{6}$ $\frac{7}{8}$ • i $\frac{7}{19}$ $\frac{8}{21}$

1　**a**　How many degrees are there in a full turn?

Work out the number of degrees in:

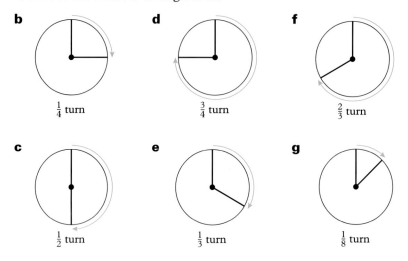

b　$\frac{1}{4}$ turn　　　　**d**　$\frac{3}{4}$ turn　　　　**f**　$\frac{2}{3}$ turn

c　$\frac{1}{2}$ turn　　　　**e**　$\frac{1}{3}$ turn　　　　**g**　$\frac{1}{8}$ turn

2　**a**　Copy the diagram.
　　b　Shade $\frac{1}{4}$ of the diagram.

3　True or false?
　　a　$\frac{9}{16}$ is less than one half.
　　b　If the denominator and the numerator are equal, the fraction is 1.
　　c　If the denominator is twice the numerator, the fraction is equal to a half.
　　d　If you add 1 to the denominator you make the fraction larger.
　　e　If the denominator is more than the numerator, the fraction is less than 1.

4　Give the first quantity as a fraction of the second.
　　Give your answer in its simplest form.
　　a　1 day, 1 week　　　　　　**g**　2 mm, 1 cm
　　b　3 days, 1 week　　　　　　**h**　1 metre, 1 km
　　c　1 week, 1 year　　　　　　**i**　100 m, 1 km
　　d　30 seconds, 1 minute　　　**j**　40 p, £1
　　e　10 seconds, 1 minute　　　**k**　90 p, £1
　　f　50 cm, 1 metre　　　　　　**l**　75 p, £1

5　Work out:
　　a　$\frac{2}{3} + \frac{3}{7}$　　　　　**c**　$\frac{5}{6} - \frac{4}{7}$　　　　　**e**　$\frac{1}{2} + \frac{1}{3} + \frac{1}{4}$
　　b　$\frac{4}{9} + \frac{2}{5}$　　　　　**d**　$\frac{2}{3} - \frac{5}{13}$　　　　**f**　$\frac{2}{3} + \frac{3}{4} + \frac{4}{5}$

6 Rebecca and Julia did a traffic survey.
They recorded the colour of 100 cars.
Here are their results.

Colour of car	Tally
White	llll llll llll llll llll
Black	llll llll
Blue	llll llll llll llll l
Silver/Grey	llll llll ll
Yellow	ll
Red	llll llll llll llll llll ll
Green	lll

    a Which colour is the most popular?
    b What percentage of the cars were yellow?
    c Write the percentage in **b** as a decimal.
    d What percentage of the cars were blue?
    e Write the percentage in **d** as a fraction of a hundred.
    f What percentage of the cars were black?
    g Write the percentage in **f** as a fraction of 100.
       Simplify your fraction.

7 Write each of these decimals as fractions.
Cancel the fraction down as much as you can.
    a 0.1805   **c** 0.3125   **e** 0.488 88
    b 0.9755   **d** 0.130 25   **f** 0.428 46

8 Howard has been trying to change $\frac{1}{3}$ to a decimal.
Here is his working.

$$0.\,3\,3\,3\,3\,3$$
$$3\,\overline{)1\,.\,{}^{1}0\,{}^{1}0\,{}^{1}0\,{}^{1}0\,{}^{1}0}$$

    a What will happen if Howard continues this division?
    b Find out the quick way of writing the answer to this division.
    c Use your answer to **b** to write $\frac{2}{3}$ as a decimal.

9 Rewrite each set of fractions in order.
Start with the **smallest**.
    a $\frac{1}{3}$ $\frac{2}{5}$ $\frac{4}{7}$ $\frac{5}{11}$
    b $\frac{4}{5}$ $\frac{9}{12}$ $\frac{8}{11}$ $\frac{9}{17}$
    c $\frac{5}{9}$ $\frac{6}{11}$ $\frac{7}{15}$ $\frac{9}{17}$

1 Work out:

a $\frac{3}{4} + \frac{2}{3} + \frac{1}{5}$ **c** $\frac{1}{2} \times \frac{1}{4} \times \frac{1}{8}$ **e** $(\frac{5}{8} \times \frac{7}{3}) + \frac{1}{3}$

b $\frac{1}{2} + \frac{1}{4} + \frac{1}{8}$ **d** $(\frac{5}{6} \div \frac{1}{3}) \times \frac{2}{3}$ **f** $\frac{1}{3} \times (\frac{2}{3} \div \frac{5}{7})$

2 **a** Change the following fractions to decimals.

(1) $\frac{2}{21}$ (2) $\frac{5}{21}$ (3) $\frac{8}{21}$ (4) $\frac{11}{21}$

b Write about what you notice.

3 **a** Write down the decimal versions of $\frac{1}{9}, \frac{2}{9}, \frac{3}{9}, ..., \frac{8}{9}$.

b Following the pattern, what is the decimal version of $\frac{9}{9}$?

c $9 \div 9 = 1$. Explain your answer to **b**.

4 Melanie is at the dentist for a checkup. The dentist sees that Mary has all of her 32 adult teeth: 8 incisors, 4 canines, 8 premolars and 12 molars.

What fraction of Melanie's teeth are:
a incisors?   **b** canines?   **c** premolars?   **d** molars?

5 The human skeleton has 206 bones.

     29 are in the skull
     26 in the spine
     32 in each arm
     31 in each leg
     25 in the chest

a Write each set of bones as a fraction of 206 bones.

b What percentage is each set of bones of the whole skeleton? Use the fractions you wrote down in part **a** to help you. Give your answers correct to two decimal places.

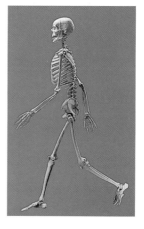

6 Look at the front page of a newspaper.
  a Find the area of the front page.
  b Estimate the total area taken up by pictures.
  c What fraction of the front page is pictures?
  d What percentage of the front page is pictures?

- *Example*   Find $\frac{2}{3}$ of 12 sweets

  $\frac{1}{3}$ of 12 $= 12 \div 3$ (Divide by 3 to find $\frac{1}{3}$)

  $\qquad = 4$

  $\frac{2}{3}$ of 12 $= 4 \times 2$ (Multiply by 2 to find $\frac{2}{3}$)

  $\qquad = 8$

- **Equivalent fractions**

  Equivalent fractions are different ways of writing the same fraction.

  $\frac{2}{4}$ $\frac{3}{6}$ $\frac{4}{8}$ $\frac{5}{10}$ are all equivalent to $\frac{1}{2}$

- **Simplifying fractions**

  Simplifying fractions is also known as cancelling. Look for the biggest number that will divide exactly into the top and bottom numbers.

  $$\frac{8}{12} \xrightarrow[\div 4]{\div 4} \frac{2}{3}$$

- **Adding fractions**

  To add fractions the bottom numbers of both fractions must be the same.

  $$\frac{2}{3} \xrightarrow[\times 2]{} \frac{?}{6} \qquad \frac{2}{3} \xrightarrow[\times 2]{\times 2} \frac{4}{6} \qquad \frac{2}{3} = \frac{4}{6}$$

  The $\frac{1}{6}$ does not need changing.

  So $\frac{2}{3} + \frac{1}{6} = \frac{4}{6} + \frac{1}{6} = \frac{5}{6}$

- **Multiplying fractions**

  To multiply fractions, multiply the top numbers and bottom numbers together, then simplify the answer if possible.

  Example   Work out $\frac{2}{3} \times \frac{3}{8}$

  $$\frac{2}{3} \times \frac{3}{8} = \frac{6}{24} \qquad \frac{6}{24} \xrightarrow[\div 6]{\div 6} \frac{1}{4}$$

- **Dividing fractions**

  To divide two fractions, turn the second fraction over then multiply.

  Example   Work out $\frac{3}{4} \div \frac{5}{8}$

  $$\frac{3}{4} \div \frac{5}{8} = \frac{3}{4} \times \frac{8}{5} = \frac{24}{20} = \frac{6}{5} = 1\frac{1}{5}$$

- **Percentage**

  A **percentage** is a fraction out of 100.

  25 out of 100 $= \frac{25}{100} = 25\%$

- **Fraction to decimal**

  To change a fraction to a decimal, divide the top number by the bottom number.

  $$\frac{3}{5} = 3 \div 5 = 0.6 \qquad 5\overline{)3.0} = 0.6$$

  Remember that some decimals recur. $\frac{1}{3} = 0.333\,333\,3 = 0.\dot{3}$

- **Decimal to fraction** $0.6 = \frac{6}{10}$ $0.24 = \frac{24}{100}$ $0.272 = \frac{272}{1000}$

- **Ordering fractions**

  $\frac{2}{3}$ is the same as $\frac{8}{12}$. $\frac{3}{4}$ is the same as $\frac{9}{12}$

  So $\frac{2}{3}$ is smaller than $\frac{3}{4}$

1 **a** Copy this rectangle.
   b Shade $\frac{2}{5}$ of your rectangle.

2 **a** Find $\frac{1}{3}$ of 15
   b Find $\frac{2}{5}$ of 20

3 Share 5 cakes equally between 3 children.

4 Write $\frac{10}{24}$ as a fraction in its simplest form.

5 **a** Write down the fraction of
      squares that are shaded.
   b Write down the percentage of
      squares that are shaded.

6 **a** Write 10 minutes as a fraction of 1 hour.
   b Write your answer to **a** in its simplest form.

7 Work out
   a $\frac{2}{5} + \frac{2}{5}$ **b** $\frac{2}{5} + \frac{1}{10}$ **c** $\frac{5}{6} - \frac{1}{3}$

8 Work out
   a $\frac{2}{3} \times \frac{4}{5}$ **b** $\frac{5}{7} \div \frac{5}{6}$ **c** $1\frac{1}{4} \times \frac{7}{9}$

9 **a** Change $\frac{4}{5}$ to a decimal.
   b Change $\frac{5}{16}$ to a decimal.
   c Change $\frac{5}{6}$ to a decimal.

10 Write each of these as fractions.
    Cancel the fraction down as much as you can.
    a 0.4   **b** 0.56   **c** 0.175

11 Write down the bigger of these two fractions.
    $\frac{3}{11}$ $\frac{4}{13}$

12 Rewrite these fractions in order of size.
    Start with the smallest.
    $\frac{2}{3}$ $\frac{1}{2}$ $\frac{3}{4}$ $\frac{1}{5}$ $\frac{2}{7}$

16 Statistics: what does it all mean?

An average puzzle to start this chapter:

A stick is broken into two pieces at random. What is the average length of the shorter piece?

1 The mean

Football clubs like to know how many people are likely to come to watch each game. They record the number of tickets sold for each match and then work out the average.

If they play 21 home games in one season, then the average number of tickets sold is the total number of tickets sold divided by 21.

Example

In the 1994/5 season, the total number of tickets sold at Matlock Town was 8100. They played 27 home games.

So the average attendance was $8100 \div 27 = 300$

This type of average is called the **mean**.

Exercise 16.1

1 Copy this table and fill in the mean attendance for each club.

Club	Total attendance (home matches only)	Number of home matches	Mean
Liverpool	808 584	21	
Middlesbrough	239 200	23	
Tottenham Hotspur	570 360	21	
Celtic	514 000	20	
Altrincham	18 312	21	

Example

You may have to work out the total before you can work out the mean.

For example, the heights of five pupils in centimetres are:
    132, 143, 129, 140 and 136.

So the total is:

$132 + 143 + 129 + 140 + 136 = 680$

The mean is $680 \div 5 = 136$ cm

Mean

To find the mean of a set of data:

1 Find the total of all the data values.

2 Divide by the number of data values.

---

2 The heights, in centimetres, of 12 children are:

132	148	141	136	134	129
146	132	137	118	150	141

  a Find the mean height. Show all your working.
  b Find the heights of the people in your class and find the mean height.

3 The cost of a week's shopping for 15 families is:

£45	£56	£53	£32	£56
£48	£34	£64	£71	£49
£61	£41	£29	£61	£65

Find the mean amount they spend.

4 The amounts collected for *Children in Need* by the 8 Year 7 classes were:

£12   £18   £14   £22   £16   £19   £21   £24

Find the mean amount collected.

5 The times taken, in seconds, for the girls in class 7M to run the 100 m race were:

14.1	15.3	15.5	15.6	15.0	14.7	13.9
16.1	15.8	14.5	15.7	14.6	16.3	15.7

  a Find the mean time taken to run the race.
  b How many girls were faster than the mean time?

6 The weekly wages of 21 people chosen at random from a factory are:

£120   £115   £90   £120   £128   £120   £110
£550   £115   £130   £120   £95   £250   £130
£550   £110   £115   £120   £90   £105   £140

a Find the mean wage.
b Write down the number of people who earn less than the mean wage.
c Explain why so many people earn less than the mean.

7 These are the monthly rainfall figures in mm for Sheffield last year:

Jan 93.8   Apr 16.2   Jul 18.9   Oct 128.7
Feb 33.7   May 79.9   Aug 17.3   Nov 32.4
Mar 29.5   Jun 16.6   Sep 134.9   Dec 76.1

a Find the mean rainfall for the year.
b Write down the months that had rainfall lower than the mean.
c Write down the months that had rainfall higher than the mean.

· ·

Sometimes data is given in a table.

Class 7M counted the number of Smarties found in 100 tubes chosen at random.
Many tubes contained the same number of Smarties.
They put their data in a table.

Number of Smarties in a tube	Number of tubes	
34	13 ←	This row shows that 13 of the tubes had 34 Smarties in them.
35	24	This is a total of
36	27	$13 \times 34 = 442$ Smarties
37	22	
38	14	

To work out the total number of Smarties they need to find the total for each row. They add another column to the table so it looks like this:

Number of Smarties in a tube	Number of tubes	Number of Smarties
34	13	13 × 34 = 442
35	24	24 × 35 = 840
36	27	27 × 36 = 972
37	22	22 × 37 = 814
38	14	14 × 38 = 532
		Total = 3600

Mean number of Smarties = $\frac{3600}{100}$ = 36

Exercise 16:2

1 Another 100 tubes of Smarties are chosen at random. The number of Smarties in each tube is shown in the table.

Number of Smarties	Number of tubes
35	14
36	24
37	26
38	20
39	16

Find the mean number of Smarties in a tube.

2 The number of matches in 60 boxes is shown in the table.

Number of matches in a box	Number of boxes
46	6
47	10
48	27
49	12
50	5

The makers claim that the average contents is 48.
Find the mean number of matches in a box.
Do you think the makers are telling the truth?
Write down your reasons.

3 The shoe sizes of the 30 children in 7M are shown in the table.

Shoe size	Number of children
3	4
4	5
5	10
6	9
7	2

Find the mean shoe size of 7M.

4 The number of M&Ms in 40 Family packs is shown in the table.

Number of M&Ms in a Family pack	Number of Family packs
96	2
97	13
98	8
99	17

a Find the mean number of M&Ms in a pack.
b How many packs contained more than the mean number?
c How many packs contained less than the mean number?

Sometimes the mean can give you a strange answer. The mean may not be one of the data values. It may not be a whole number.

The number of people in 10 cars is shown in the table.

Number of people in a car	Number of cars	Total number of people
1	6	1 × 6 = 6
2	2	2 × 2 = 4
3	2	3 × 2 = 6
		Total 16

Mean number of people in a car is $16 \div 10 = 1.6$

You cannot have 1.6 people in a car! But 1.6 **is** the mean. You must **not** round this to the nearest whole number even though you probably think that this is a silly answer.

5 A dice is thrown 100 times. The scores are shown in the table.

Score	Number of times thrown
1	14
2	17
3	16
4	18
5	17
6	18

Find the mean score.

6 The heights of 27 pupils in 7R are shown in the table.

Height in cm	Number of pupils
120	3
125	10
130	6
135	4
140	4

Find the mean height. Give your answer to 1 d.p.

7 One hundred people are asked to give the age of their car. Their answers are shown in the table.

Age of car	Number of people
0	12
1	17
2	13
3	8
4	15
5	18
6	17

  a Why did 12 people say that their car was age 0?
  b Find the mean age of the cars.
  c Thinking about the original data, do you think this answer is accurate?
     Explain your answer.

8 On a golf course, this hole is described as being Par 3. This means that most players would expect to complete the hole in three strokes.

The numbers of strokes taken by 100 players are given in this table.

Number of strokes	Number of people
1	1
2	18
3	30
4	26
5	25

  a Find the mean number of strokes needed to complete the hole.
  b Do you think the hole should be Par 3? Explain your answer.

2 Other types of average

The manager of this shoe shop wants to know the most popular size of shoe sold, so that she doesn't run out of stock.
She decides to work out the average for a month's sales.
The mean shoe sizes are 5.8 for women and 9.2 for men.
She realises that this is not helpful and decides to use a different type of average.

She looks at how many shoes are sold in each size. She writes down the size that sells the most.
For women this is 5 and for men it is 9.
This type of average is called the **mode**.

Mode	The **mode** is the most common or the most popular data value. This is sometimes called the **modal value**.

Exercise 16:3

1 A dice was thrown 100 times. The results were recorded in a tally-chart.

Score	Tally	Total
1	ⵊⵊⵊ ⵊⵊⵊ ⵊⵊⵊ I	
2	ⵊⵊⵊ ⵊⵊⵊ ⵊⵊⵊ	
3	ⵊⵊⵊ ⵊⵊⵊ IIII	
4	ⵊⵊⵊ ⵊⵊⵊ III	
5	ⵊⵊⵊ ⵊⵊⵊ ⵊⵊⵊ ⵊⵊⵊ	
6	ⵊⵊⵊ ⵊⵊⵊ ⵊⵊⵊ ⵊⵊⵊ II	

a Work out the total number of throws for each score.
b Write down the modal score.

2 Boxes of biscuits are labelled 'Average contents 200'. A random sample of 50 boxes was tested.
The results are given in this tally-chart.

Number of biscuits in each box	Number of boxes	
	Tally	Total
198	卌 ‖	
199	卌 卌	
200	卌 卌 ‖‖	
201	卌 卌		
202	卌 ‖‖‖	

a Work out the mean and the mode for these boxes.
b Is the statement 'Average contents 200' true for both types of average?
Explain your answer.

3 These are the number of hours of sunshine on each day in August.
Make a tally-chart and find the modal number of hours of sunshine.

5	8	7	6	8	7	3	10	5
7	6	7	8	9	10	4	6	7
6	3	0	10	7	5	8	7	6
5	7	6	5					

4 A page is chosen at random from a paperback book and the length of each word is recorded. The tally-chart for this data is shown below.

Length of word	Tally	Total
1	‖‖‖	4
2	卌 卌 卌 ‖	17
3	卌 卌 卌 卌 ‖‖	23
4	卌 卌 卌 卌 卌 卌 卌 卌	40
5	卌 卌 卌 卌 卌 ‖‖	28
6	卌 卌 ‖	12
7	卌 ‖‖‖	9
8	‖‖	3
9			1
10	‖	2

a Write down the modal number of letters in the words.
b Work out the mean number of letters.
c Which is the more sensible average?
Explain your answer.

5 This graph shows the favourite colours of class 7B.

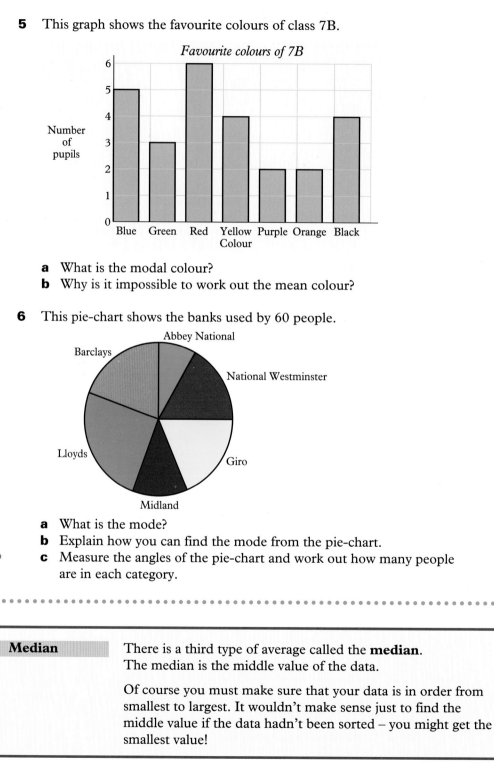

Favourite colours of 7B

a What is the modal colour?

b Why is it impossible to work out the mean colour?

6 This pie-chart shows the banks used by 60 people.

a What is the mode?

b Explain how you can find the mode from the pie-chart.

c Measure the angles of the pie-chart and work out how many people are in each category.

· ·

Median	There is a third type of average called the **median**. The median is the middle value of the data.
	Of course you must make sure that your data is in order from smallest to largest. It wouldn't make sense just to find the middle value if the data hadn't been sorted – you might get the smallest value!

These were the wages in a question that you saw earlier:

£120 £115 £90 £120 £113 £120 £110 £550 £115
£130 £120 £95 £250 £130 £550 £110 £115 £120
£90 £105 £140

You need to re-write this data in order of size to find the median.

£90 £90 £95 £105 £110 £110 £113 £115 £115
£115 £120 £120 £120 £120 £120 £130 £130 £140
£250 £550 £550

There are 21 values so the middle one is the 11th. There are 10 on either side.
The middle value is £120 so this is the **median**.

This is quite different from the mean which is £158.
Next time you hear people arguing about average wages remember that they may have worked out the average in different ways to make their point.

Exercise 16:4

1 Find the median of these numbers.

a 2 3 4 8 12 13 14 18 19
b 3 8 8 9 10 12 14 18 21 23 25

2 Find the median of these numbers.

a 16 12 8 3 4 9 16 1 8
b 2.9 2.4 1.6 2.2 8.6 9.1 12.2 0.7 8.1 7.3 6.2 5.3

3 Find the median height of the 27 pupils in 7R using the data in the table. You might like to write all the heights out separately first.

Height in cm	Number of pupils
120	3
125	10
130	6
135	4
140	4

So far we have found the median when there is an odd number of data values. If there is an even number of values we must look at the middle pair of values.

Example   Find the median of the numbers

$$3 \quad 6 \quad 8 \quad 9 \quad 12 \quad 14 \quad 16 \quad 17$$

The median is halfway between the middle two numbers.

So median $= \dfrac{9 + 12}{2} = 10.5$

Like the mean, the median does not have to be one of the data values.

4 Find the median of each of these sets of numbers.

a 6   8   9   10 11 13 14 15 17 20
b 4   8   12 14 14 15 17 18
c 2   6   7   8   9   9   10 11
d 14 12 2   8   6   14 23 17 6   23 4   5   9   15 18 16

5 The table shows the numbers of strokes taken by 100 players to complete a golf hole.
Find the median number of strokes taken.

Number of strokes	Number of people
1	1
2	18
3	30
4	26
5	25

Exercise 16:5

This exercise is all about choosing the best average to use in different situations.

For each of the following sets of data:
a calculate the mean, median and mode if it is possible to do so.
b say which average you think is the most sensible to use.

1 The totals obtained by throwing two dice and adding the scores together.

6	8	12	5	3	8	10	4	6
7	2	9	11	7	5	9	8	2
11	4	7	9	6	7	7	3	7
6	9	10	7	4	3	7	10	5

2 Test results as percentages in a Year 7 maths test.

61	87	56	90	76	82	74	45	62
56	47	98	79	31	99	75	83	
41	94	69	64	78	73	66	89	

3 Sweatshirt sizes in inches of Year 11 boys.

28	32	34	28	30	30	32	30	34	32	30	36
26	30	34	34	36	32	34	32	34	30	28	30

4 The number of CDs sold in a record shop over a 30-day period.

124	214	126	221	96	320
156	267	201	40	179	411
178	221	231	158	209	347
95	265	189	186	146	324
198	168	237	174	156	379

5 The number of GCSEs gained by a class of 25 students.

8	10	10	8	5	1	10
9	10	6	8	10	7	5
7	8	10	9	10	0	9
10	9	10	7			

3 The range

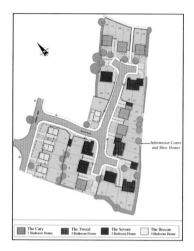

The prices of houses on this new estate start at £56 000 and go up to £90 000.

The difference in price between the cheapest and the most expensive house is
£90 000 − £56 000 = £34 000

This difference is called the **range**.

Range	For any set of data, the **range** is the biggest value take away the smallest value.

Exercise 16:6

1 Find the range of each of these sets of data.

a	4	8	9	10	11	15	16	
b	1	2	4	8	16	17	19	22
c	10 800		15 000		15 500		18 300	21 300
d	2.8	3.1	4.9	8.6	14.3	21.6		
e	7.2	1.3	8.4	2.1	3.6	4.7	9.3	8.4

2 The range of a set of data is 16.
If the biggest data value is 26, find the smallest value.

3 Peter collected data from 10 of his friends about their weekly pocket money. He forgot to write down the last value on his list.

£1 £1.20 £1.15 £1.25 £1 £1.40 £1.90 70 p 90 p

He had worked out that the range was £1.40.
What could the missing value be?

4 Look at the data for hours of sunshine during the year in two different countries.

Month	Jan	Feb	Mar	Apr	May	Jun	Jul	Aug	Sep	Oct	Nov	Dec
Country 1	154	161	165	170	173	185	190	198	187	164	153	140
Country 2	50	80	120	165	190	236	260	301	276	197	101	64

a Work out the mean number of hours of sunshine for each country.
b Draw a bar-chart for each set of data.
c Describe the main differences between the two bar-charts.
d Work out the range for each set of data.
e How does the range help you describe the differences in the two sets of data?

The range tells us how the data is spread out around the mean. If the mean for one set of data is the same or very close to the mean of another set of data, then we can use the range to help us describe the differences between the two sets of data.

5 When you call a taxi you don't usually wait a long time before the taxi arrives. The time it takes for the taxi to arrive is called the response time.
The table shows some response times in minutes for two taxi firms.

Carol's Cars	12	15	9	17	8	13	16	19	10	7	13
Alan's Autos	14	12	11	14	12	10	13	12	13	14	14

a Find the mean and range of the response times for each firm.
b How many times did each company take more than 14 minutes to answer a call?
c How many times did each company take less than 11 minutes to answer a call?
d Mr Jones has an important meeting at another office in 30 minutes. The journey will take 15 minutes.
Which taxi company should he use? Explain why.
e Mr Jones would like a chance for a quick cup of coffee before the meeting starts.
Which taxi company should he use? Explain why.

Exercise 16:7 Simulation

Sometimes it is easier to do experiments than to collect data directly. These experiments are often called **simulations.**

Cereal packets often have cards or models to collect.

You can use dice to do an experiment to simulate how many boxes you would need to buy to collect the whole set.

Six model cars are being given away inside Corn Crunchies packets.

Take an ordinary dice. Each number on the dice represents one of the models.

Draw a table like this to record your results:

Model number	Tally
1	
2	
3	
4	
5	
6	
	Total

Roll the dice and record the number you score in the tally column. Each time that you roll the dice it is like buying a packet of Corn Crunchies.
Keep rolling the dice, but stop as soon as you have rolled all the numbers.

Now add up the total number of rolls. This is the number of packets you would have to buy to get all six models.

Repeat the experiment at least ten times.

Find the mean number of packets you would have to buy.

Find the range of the number of packets you would have to buy.

What would happen if there were 8 or 10 models to collect?
Change the experiment and try it for one of these.
Is the range different?

4   Misleading statistics

The Minister of Health and Social Security is presenting information during an election campaign. His charts show increases in spending on the National Health Service.
Do the charts give a fair picture of the figures?

Changing the scale of a diagram can have a big effect on its appearance. When you read statistical diagrams, you should always look carefully at the scale or the key.

Look at the two diagrams below.
The one on the left was drawn by a record company that specialises in selling singles.
The one on the right was prepared by a company that sells CDs of chart hits.

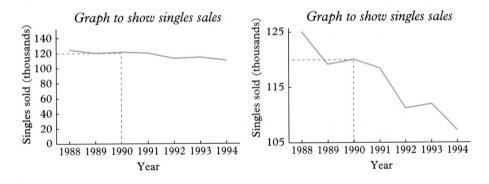

The two graphs show exactly the same information. They look very different because the scales are different.
Read off the figure for 1990 on each graph, shown by the red dotted line.
You will see that they both give the same figure.

Exercise 16:8

1 For each of the following questions there are two graphs. They show
the same information but look different because of the scales.
Read the explanation that goes with each pair.
Say which graph each person would choose and why.

  a A car sales manager is trying to prove to one of the sales staff that
he is not selling enough cars and that he is in danger of losing his
job.

    The salesperson is trying to show that he is doing well.

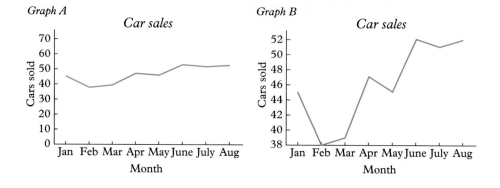

  b The government is trying to prove to the voters that unemployment
is holding steady.

    The opposition wants to show that it is rising steeply.

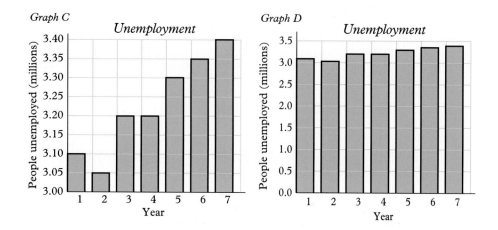

c A new DJ has taken over the breakfast show on a local radio station and wants to show that the audience figures have gone up.
The station manager is not impressed. She thinks that the new DJ is not doing a good job.

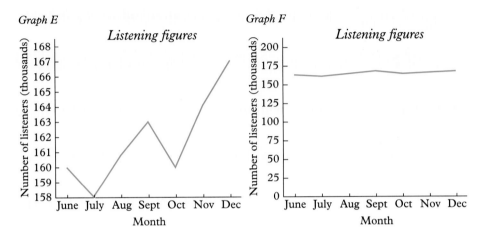

2 The audience figures for a theatre over a period of eight weeks are shown below.
The person in charge of the box office wants to show that the audiences are increasing because she wants some extra staff.
The manager does not want to pay any more staff and so he wants to show that the audiences are staying at about the same level.

Week 1	840	Week 5	870
Week 2	860	Week 6	870
Week 3	855	Week 7	875
Week 4	867	Week 8	878

Draw one graph for each person.
Choose your scale carefully and say who would use each graph.

3 A publishing company launched a new teenage magazine for a six-month trial period. At the end of the trial period, the editor and staff want to keep the magazine going but the publishers are not so sure.

Using the sales figures given below, draw two graphs, one for the editor and one for the publisher.
Say who would use each and why.

January	320 000	April	305 000
February	290 000	May	300 000
March	295 000	June	298 000

Exercise 16:9

You are now going to use all the statistics skills you have learned to produce a new advertising campaign.

You are going to advertise a new breakfast cereal.

You will need to show how good it is compared with another breakfast cereal that you can already buy. You will need the details from the panel at the side of a cereal packet showing the energy, fibre and vitamin contents.

Below are the details of your new cereal:

Nutritional Content (per 100 g)		
Energy	320 Kcal	Vitamins:
Protein	8 g	B6 1.6 mg
Fat	1.6 g	B2 1.7 g
Carbohydrate	68 g	B1 0.8 μg
Fibre	9.8 g	D 2.3 μg
		B12 1.8 μg
		Iron 7.3 μg

Look at these details carefully and compare them with your cereal packet. You need to pick out the things in this new cereal that are better and produce some diagrams to make it look really good by choosing your scale carefully.

If the things in the new cereal are not as good then alter the scale on the graph so that it looks as if there is very little difference.

Produce an advertisement for a magazine and a more detailed information sheet to be sent to shop managers to tell them about the new product.

Remember that you must not lie, but you must use your skill to make the new cereal look as good as possible. You will also need to give it a name and decide on the price.

▼   To see how the Government produces its statistics, ask your teacher for the 'Social Trends' worksheets.

1   The weekly wages of 20 people chosen at random from a factory are:

 £135 £119 £113 £135 £113 £135 £110
 £490 £119 £130 £135 £127 £245 £130
 £490 £110 £119 £135 £105 £160

 a Find the mean wage.
 b Write down the number of people who earn below the mean wage.

2   Bags of sweets are labelled 'Average contents 100'. A random sample
 of 50 bags was tested.
 The results are shown in the table.

Number of sweets in each bag	Number of bags
98	卌 I
99	卌 卌 II
100	卌 卌
101	卌 卌 III
102	卌 IIII

 a Work out the mean and the mode for these bags of sweets.
 b Is the statement 'Average contents 100' true for both types of average?
  Explain your answer.

3   The times taken by 90 snails to finish a race are shown on below.

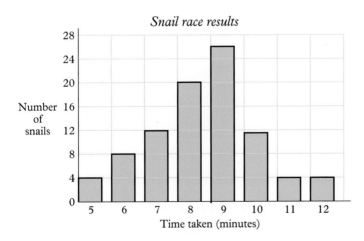

Snail race results

 a What is the modal time taken?
 b Calculate the mean time taken.
 c How many snails took more than the mean time to finish the race?

4 Find the median of each set of data.

   a 23   28   34   27   31   30   42   34   39

   b 24   28   37   40   24   26   29   31   35   38

5 The owner of a small shop is applying for a bank loan. She sends the bank manager this graph to show her profits over the past 6 months.

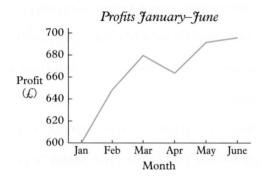

   a What has the shop-owner done to the graph to make her profits look very good?

   b This is the data she used:

Jan	Feb	Mar	Apr	May	Jun
£600	£650	£680	£670	£690	£695

     Plot another version of the graph with the profits starting at 0 on the side scale.

   c Describe how the profits look on your graph compared with the first one.

6 These are the heights in centimetres of 10 pupils in Sally's class:

    124   136   118   127   143

    131   129   122   138   134

Sally works out the mean height and gets 102.3 cm.

Explain why Sally must be wrong. Do not work out the mean.

1 In a mental arithmetic test, a class of 28 pupils obtained the marks shown in the table.

Marks	3	4	5	6	7	8	9	10
Number of Pupils	2	2	6	7	4	3	3	1

  a Calculate the mean mark.
  b Calculate the median mark.
  c Calculate the modal mark.
Two pupils were absent at the time of the test and took it late.
These pupils scored 7 and 8 when they took the test.
  d Without calculating the new mean, say whether it will be higher or lower when these pupils are added in.
  e Calculate the new mean and check your answer to **d**.

2 In an exam, the 17 boys in a class scored a mean mark of 32.
The 13 girls scored a mean of 34.
  a Calculate the total marks scored by the boys and the girls.
  b Use your answer to **a** to calculate the mean mark for the whole class to 2 d.p.

3 The waiting time in days for orders to arrive from a mail-order catalogue are:

    13   18   21   25   17   28   32   28   23   26   19   23
    17   27   25   32   19   26   23   56   12   19   24   27

  a Find the mean (to 2 d.p.) and the median of this data.
  b Find the range of this data.
  c If one more result is included in the data the mean changes to 25. Find the value of the extra result.

4 The total sales of Chunks Dog Food over a six-month period were reported to be falling.
The actual sales figures were:

    Jan   125 000   Apr   116 700
    Feb   123 000   May   109 000
    Mar   119 400   Jun   105 500
  a Plot a graph on a suitable scale to make it look as if the figures are holding steady.
  b If you were the sales manager for this company, would you use the mean or the median of this data to promote your sales? Explain your answer.

- To find the **mean** of a set of data:
  1. Find the total of all the data values.
  2. Divide by the number of values.

  For example, the mean of the numbers 2, 4, 7, 9 and 13 is

  $$\frac{2 + 4 + 7 + 9 + 13}{5} = \frac{35}{5} = 7$$

- When data is in a **table**, add another column to work out the total.

  Example
  Number of Smarties in 100 tubes

Number of Smarties in a tube	Number of tubes	Number of Smarties
34	13	$13 \times 34 =$ 442
35	24	$24 \times 35 =$ 840
36	27	$27 \times 36 =$ 972
37	22	$22 \times 37 =$ 814
38	14	$14 \times 38 =$ 532
		Total = 3600

  Mean number of Smarties $= \dfrac{3600}{100} = \mathbf{36}$

- The **mode** is the most common data value – the one which appears the most.
  The **median** is the middle value of the data when it is in order from smallest to largest.
  For an even number of values find the middle two. Then find the number in the middle of these by adding them and dividing by 2.

  For example, the mode of 2, 4, 6, 7, 8, 7, 5, 9, 6, 4, 8, 5, 8 is 8 because there are more 8s than anything else.

  To find the median, write the data out again in order:
     2, 4, 4, 5, 5, 6, **6**, 7, 7, 8, 8, 8, 9
  The median is 6 as this is the middle number.

- The range is the biggest value take away the smallest value.
  The range tells us how spread out the data is. The bigger the range the more spread out the data.

  The range of 2, 4, 6, 7, 8, 7, 8, 5, 9, 6, 4, 8, 5, 8 is $9 - 2 = 7$

- Statistics can be **misleading** if you draw axes which do not start at 0. Always look very carefully at the scale when you are reading any type of diagram.

1   The cost of a week's shopping for 12 families is:

£45   £54   £29   £32   £39   £42
£78   £47   £23   £46   £76   £29

Find the mean amount they spend.

2   Packets of crisps are marked 30 g **e** which means that 30 g is the average contents.

Here are the weights of 30 packets of crisps, chosen at random from the production line.

Weight	Number of packets
28 g	4
29 g	5
30 g	11
31 g	7
32 g	3

   a   Find the mean weight of these packets.
   b   Is the company's claim true?
   c   What is the mode for these packets?
   d   Does this average make the company's claim true?

3   Howard is testing his reaction times using a computer program. His times in seconds are:

0.23   0.24   0.29   0.24   0.34   0.25   0.34   0.23
0.34   0.23   0.29   0.34   0.32   0.41   0.39   0.21

   a   Find the range of these reaction times.
   b   Find the mean reaction time and say how many results are below the mean.
   c   Find the median reaction time.

393

4 The sales figures for eight weeks in a furniture shop are:

Week	Sales (£)
1	8500
2	8800
3	8650
4	9200
5	9000
6	9400
7	9550
8	9400

The figures are put on to a graph as shown.

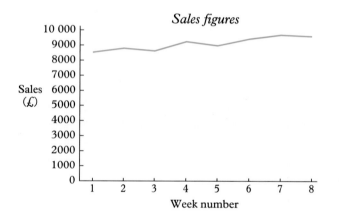

a Describe how this graph makes the sales figures look.

The manager of the shop is not impressed with the graph as she wants the figures to look better. She redraws the graph using a different scale.

b Re-draw the graph yourself as the manager would like to see it.

c Describe how your graph makes the sales figures look.

Help yourself

1 Adding

You should set out additions in columns.

Example

13 + 2   should be set out like this:

```
  1 3
+   2
  1 5
```

Here are some more examples.

27 + 21

```
  2 7
+ 2 1
  4 8
```

431 + 26

```
  4 3 1
+   2 6
  4 5 7
```

542 + 136

```
  5 4 2
+ 1 3 6
  6 7 8
```

Sometimes we need to 'carry'. This happens when a column adds up to 10 or more.

Example

13 + 9

```
  1 3
+   9
  2 2
    1
```

Here are some more examples.

27 + 29

```
  2 7
+ 2 9
  5 6
    1
```

246 + 28

```
  2 4 6
+   2 8
  2 7 4
      1
```

558 + 67

```
  5 5 8
+   6 7
  6 2 5
    1 1
```

Exercise 1

Copy these into your book.
Work out the answers.

1
```
  1 6
+   3
```

2
```
  2 4
+ 3 2
```

3
```
  3 6
+ 1 2
```

4
```
  4 3 1
+ 1 3 4
```

5
```
  6 2 1
+   4 8
```

6
```
    2 7
+ 6 3 2
```

7
```
  5 0 4 2
+   6 2 7
```

8
```
  3 6 0 9
+ 4 2 9 0
```

9 11 + 6

10 32 + 26

11 542 + 37

12 541 + 126

Exercise 2

Copy these into your book.
Work out the answers.

1
```
  1 8
+   6
```

2
```
  3 8
+ 2 7
```

3
```
  1 7 8
+ 2 1 9
```

4
```
  3 2 4
+ 1 6 7
```

5
```
  4 3 5
+ 1 7 5
```

6
```
  4 2 3
  1 2 2
+   4 8
```

7
```
  3 9 7
+ 4 8 3
```

8
```
  1 4 7 6
+   6 4 6
```

9 $36 + 27$ **11** $2488 + 512$

10 $243 + 361$ **12** $7959 + 929$

Other words

All these words can also mean **add**.

   plus   **sum**   **total**

Examples
Work out 24 **plus** 13
Find the **sum** of 24 and 13
Find the **total** of 24 and 13

```
             2 4
all mean  +  1 3
             3 7
```

---

2 Subtracting

Subtractions should also be set out in columns.

Example

$28 - 10$ should be set out like this:

```
     2 8
  -  1 0
     1 8
```

Here are some more examples.

```
 29 - 16     436 - 25     587 - 226
    2 9         4 3 6         5 8 7
 -  1 6      -    2 5      -  2 2 6
    1 3         4 1 1         3 6 1
```

Exercise 3

Copy these into your book.
Work out the answers.

1
```
     5 6
  -  2 3
```

2
```
     3 6 8
  -  1 4 4
```

3
```
     4 6 9
  -  1 3 5
```

4
```
     8 6 4
  -    4 1
```

5
```
     6 4 3
  -  1 0 2
```

6
```
     1 8 2 6
  -    4 0 5
```

7
```
     3 8 6 1
  -    5 1 0
```

8
```
     6 2 1 3
  -    1 0 2
```

9 $648 - 26$

10 $493 - 281$

11 $193 - 181$

12 $4291 - 1111$

Sometimes we need to 'borrow'. This happens when the number on the bottom of a column is bigger than the one on the top.

Example

$42 - 19$

The 4 is worth
4 lots of 10.
We can 'borrow' →   4 2
one of these 10s.   − 1 9 ← The 9 is
We change it into   bigger
ten ones.   than
                      the 2.

Our working now looks like this:

$$\begin{array}{r} {}^{3}\cancel{4}^{1}2 \\ -\ 1\ 9 \\ \hline 2\ 3 \end{array}$$ ← We can now take the 9 away from the 12.

Here is another example:

$64 - 28$

$$\begin{array}{r} 6\ 4 \\ -\ 2\ 8 \\ \hline \end{array} \rightarrow \begin{array}{r} {}^{5}\cancel{6}^{1}4 \\ -\ 2\ 8 \\ \hline \end{array} \rightarrow \begin{array}{r} {}^{5}\cancel{6}^{1}4 \\ -\ 2\ 8 \\ \hline 3\ 6 \end{array}$$

Here are some more difficult examples:

$82 - 67 \qquad 231 - 119 \qquad 623 - 487$

$$\begin{array}{r} {}^{7}\cancel{8}^{1}2 \\ -\ 6\ 7 \\ \hline 1\ 5 \end{array} \qquad \begin{array}{r} 2\,{}^{2}\cancel{3}^{1}1 \\ -\ 1\ 1\ 9 \\ \hline 1\ 1\ 2 \end{array} \qquad \begin{array}{r} {}^{5}\cancel{6}^{11}\cancel{2}^{1}3 \\ -\ 4\ 8\ 7 \\ \hline 1\ 3\ 6 \end{array}$$

Exercise 4

Copy these into your book.
Work out the answers.

1
$$\begin{array}{r} 3\ 2 \\ -\ 1\ 8 \\ \hline \end{array}$$

5
$$\begin{array}{r} 8\ 4\ 2 \\ -\ 7\ 9\ 1 \\ \hline \end{array}$$

2
$$\begin{array}{r} 4\ 2 \\ -\ 2\ 7 \\ \hline \end{array}$$

6
$$\begin{array}{r} 9\ 1\ 1 \\ -\ 6\ 3\ 5 \\ \hline \end{array}$$

3
$$\begin{array}{r} 2\ 1\ 7 \\ -\ 1\ 2\ 3 \\ \hline \end{array}$$

7
$$\begin{array}{r} 6\ 4\ 3 \\ -\ 2\ 5\ 7 \\ \hline \end{array}$$

4
$$\begin{array}{r} 6\ 4\ 2 \\ -\ 3\ 2\ 9 \\ \hline \end{array}$$

8
$$\begin{array}{r} 1\ 4\ 2\ 3 \\ -\ \ \ 9\ 7\ 9 \\ \hline \end{array}$$

9 $83 - 29$ **11** $521 - 156$

10 $432 - 86$ **12** $1240 - 736$

You cannot borrow from the next column if there is a zero in it.
You may need to borrow across more than one column.

Example

$$\begin{array}{r} 3\ 0\ 0 \\ -\ 1\ 9\ 6 \\ \hline \end{array} \rightarrow \begin{array}{r} {}^{2}\cancel{3}^{1}0\ 0 \\ -\ 1\ 9\ 6 \\ \hline \end{array} \rightarrow \begin{array}{r} {}^{2}\cancel{3}\,{}^{9}\cancel{0}^{1}0 \\ -\ 1\ 9\ 6 \\ \hline 1\ 0\ 4 \end{array}$$

Exercise 5

Copy these into your book.
Work out the answers.

1
$$\begin{array}{r} 3\ 0\ 0 \\ -\ 1\ 7\ 4 \\ \hline \end{array}$$

3
$$\begin{array}{r} 5\ 0\ 0\ 0 \\ -\ \ \ 2\ 8\ 7 \\ \hline \end{array}$$

2
$$\begin{array}{r} 4\ 0\ 6 \\ -\ 1\ 3\ 8 \\ \hline \end{array}$$

4
$$\begin{array}{r} 6\ 0\ 0\ 0 \\ -\ 5\ 2\ 4\ 6 \\ \hline \end{array}$$

Other words

All these words can also mean **subtract**.

   take away   **take**
      minus   **difference**

Examples
Find 73 **take away** 24
Work out 73 **take** 24
Find 73 **minus** 24
Find the **difference** between 73 and 24

Checking

You can always check a subtraction by adding.

Example

$256 - 183$

$$\begin{array}{r} \overset{1}{2}\overset{1}{5}6 \\ -\ 183 \\ \hline 73 \end{array} \qquad \text{check} \qquad \begin{array}{r} 183 \\ +\ 73 \\ \hline 256 \end{array}$$

Go back to your answers for Exercise 5. Check each of them by adding.

3 Multiplying

When we are adding lots of the same number it is quicker to multiply.

Example

$$\begin{array}{r} 31 \\ 31 \\ 31 \\ 31 \\ +\ 31 \\ \hline 155 \end{array} \quad \text{is the same as} \quad \begin{array}{r} 31 \\ \times\ \ 5 \\ \hline 155 \end{array}$$

To do $\begin{array}{r} 31 \\ \times\ 5 \\ \hline \end{array}$ first do 5×1 $\begin{array}{r} 31 \\ \times\ 5 \\ \hline 5 \end{array}$

then do 5×3 $\begin{array}{r} 31 \\ \times\ 5 \\ \hline 155 \end{array}$

Remember to keep your numbers in columns.

Here are some more examples:

$$\begin{array}{r} 62 \\ \times\ 4 \\ \hline 248 \end{array} \qquad \begin{array}{r} 51 \\ \times\ 9 \\ \hline 459 \end{array}$$

Exercise 6

1 $\begin{array}{r} 32 \\ \times\ 4 \\ \hline \end{array}$ **3** $\begin{array}{r} 42 \\ \times\ 4 \\ \hline \end{array}$

2 $\begin{array}{r} 43 \\ \times\ 3 \\ \hline \end{array}$ **4** $\begin{array}{r} 423 \\ \times\ 3 \\ \hline \end{array}$

Sometimes we need to carry.

Example

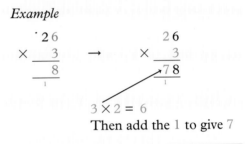

$3 \times 2 = 6$
Then add the 1 to give 7

Exercise 7

1 $\begin{array}{r} 26 \\ \times\ 2 \\ \hline \end{array}$ **6** $\begin{array}{r} 627 \\ \times\ 3 \\ \hline \end{array}$

2 $\begin{array}{r} 35 \\ \times\ 2 \\ \hline \end{array}$ **7** $\begin{array}{r} 56 \\ \times\ 7 \\ \hline \end{array}$

3 $\begin{array}{r} 46 \\ \times\ 3 \\ \hline \end{array}$ **8** $\begin{array}{r} 78 \\ \times\ 6 \\ \hline \end{array}$

4 $\begin{array}{r} 124 \\ \times\ 4 \\ \hline \end{array}$ **9** $\begin{array}{r} 247 \\ \times\ 5 \\ \hline \end{array}$

5 $\begin{array}{r} 253 \\ \times\ 3 \\ \hline \end{array}$ **10** $\begin{array}{r} 605 \\ \times\ 4 \\ \hline \end{array}$

Other words

These words can also mean **multiply**.

times　　　**product**　　　**of**

Examples

Find 24 **times** 16
Find the **product** of 24 and 16
Find one half **of** 24

4　Multiplying by 10

When we multiply by 10, all the digits move across one column to the **left**. This makes the number 10 times bigger.
We can use the headings **Th H T U** to help.
They mean **Th**ousands, **H**undreds, **T**ens and **U**nits. Units is another way of saying 'ones'.

Example

$23 \times 10 = 230$

H　T　U

2　3
2　3　0

Here are some more examples:

Th　H　T　U

4　6　　$46 \times 10 = 460$
4　6　0

2　5　3　　$253 \times 10 = 2530$
2　5　3　0

6　0　1　　$601 \times 10 = 6010$
6　0　1　0

Exercise 8

Multiply each of these numbers by 10.

1　27　　　**4**　823　　　**7**　8000

2　36　　　**5**　635　　　**8**　9001

3　326　　**6**　7426

5　Multiplying by 100, 1000, ...

When we multiply by 100, all the digits move across two columns to the left.
This makes the number 100 times bigger.
This is because $100 = 10 \times 10$. So multiplying by 100 is like multiplying by 10 twice.

Example

$74 \times 100 = 7400$

Th　H　T　U

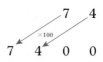

7　4　0　0

When we multiply by 1000 all the numbers move across three columns to the left.

This is because $1000 = 10 \times 10 \times 10$. This means that multiplying by 1000 is like multiplying by 10 three times.

Example

$74 \times 1000 = 74\,000$

TTh　Th　H　T　U

7　4　0　0　0

Exercise 9

Write down the answers to these questions.

1 63 × 100

2 91 × 100

3 42 × 1000

4 873 × 100

5 2770 × 100

6 605 × 1000

7 4321 × 100

8 400 × 1000

9 2001 × 1000

10 634 × 10 000

11 206 × 10 000

12 435 × 100 000

Exercise 10

Work out:

1 23 × 20

2 26 × 20

3 17 × 30

4 32 × 30

5 18 × 30

6 26 × 30

7 12 × 40

8 23 × 50

9 42 × 50

10 123 × 20

11 247 × 30

12 132 × 70

6 Multiplying by 20, 30, ...

When we multiply by 20 it is like multiplying by 2 then by 10. This is because 20 = 2 × 10.

Example

To do 18 × 20:

first do

$$\begin{array}{r} 18 \\ \times 2 \\ \hline 36 \\ \scriptstyle 1 \end{array}$$

Then do   36 × 10 = 360

So   18 × 20 = 360

In the same way multiplying by 30 is the same as multiplying by 3 and then multiplying by 10.

Example

To do 26 × 30:

first do

$$\begin{array}{r} 26 \\ \times 3 \\ \hline 78 \\ \scriptstyle 1 \end{array}$$

Then do   78 × 10 = 780

So   26 × 30 = 780

7 Long multiplication

When we want to multiply two quite large numbers we have to do it in stages.
Here are two methods. You only have to know one of them.

Method 1

Example 146×24

First do 146×4

$$\begin{array}{r} 1\,4\,6 \\ \times \quad 4 \\ \hline 5\,8\,4 \\ \tiny{1\ 2} \end{array}$$

Then do 146×20

$$\begin{array}{r} 1\,4\,6 \\ \times \quad 2 \\ \hline 2\,9\,2 \\ \tiny{1} \end{array}$$

$292 \times 10 = 2920$

Now add the two answers together.

$$\begin{array}{r} 5\,8\,4 \\ +\ 2\,9\,2\,0 \\ \hline 3\,5\,0\,4 \end{array}$$

Usually the working out looks like this:

$$\begin{array}{r} 1\,4\,6 \\ \times \quad 2\,4 \\ \hline 5\,8\,4 \\ 2\,9\,2\,0 \\ \hline 3\,5\,0\,4 \end{array}$$

Here is another example.

$$\begin{array}{r} 2\,2\,3 \\ \times \quad 3\,6 \\ \hline 1\,3\,3\,8 \leftarrow (223 \times 6) \\ 6\,6\,9\,0 \leftarrow (223 \times 30) \\ \hline 8\,0\,2\,8 \\ \tiny{1\ 1} \end{array}$$

Method 2

Example 125×23

First set out the numbers with boxes, like this:

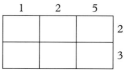

Now draw in the diagonals like this:

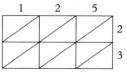

Fill in like a table square then add along the diagonals like this:

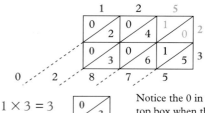

$1 \times 3 = 3$

Notice the 0 in the top box when the answer is a single digit.

So the answer is **2875**

Here is another example.
When the diagonal adds up to more than 10, we carry into the next one.

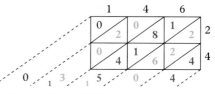

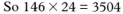

So $146 \times 24 = 3504$

Exercise 11

Use the method you prefer to work these out.

1 43×25

2 56×32

3 123×32

4 241×37

5 361×25

6 248×73

7 481×52

8 572×64

9 634×33

10 721×56

11 863×74

12 999×99

Exercise 12

Work these out.

1 $18 \div 3$

2 $16 \div 4$

3 $24 \div 6$

4 $25 \div 5$

5 $28 \div 4$

6 $28 \div 7$

7 $36 \div 9$

8 $50 \div 10$

9 $18 \div 2$

10 $30 \div 6$

11 $56 \div 8$

12 $63 \div 9$

8 Dividing

Multiplying is like doing lots of additions. In the same way dividing is like doing lots of subtractions.

To find out how many 4s make 12 we can see how many times we can take 4 away from 12.

$12 - 4 = 8$ (once)
$8 - 4 = 4$ (twice)
$4 - 4 = 0$ (three times)

So there are 3 lots of 4 in 12.

We can say   12 divided by 4 is 3

or $12 \div 4 = 3$

Example

$15 \div 3 = ?$
$15 - 3 = 12$ (once)
$12 - 3 = 9$ (twice)
$9 - 3 = 6$ (three times)
$6 - 3 = 3$ (four times)
$3 - 3 = 0$ (five times)

So $15 \div 3 = 5$

When the numbers get bigger, this method takes too long. We need a new way to work it out.

Example

$68 \div 2$

$$2 \overline{)68}$$

First work out $6 \div 2 = 3$. Put the 3 above the 6:

$$2 \overline{)6 \, 8}^{\;3}$$

Now work out $8 \div 2 = 4$. Put the 4 above the 8:

$$2 \overline{)6 \, 8}^{\;34}$$

So $68 \div 2 = 34$

Here is another example: $84 \div 4$

$$4 \overline{)8 \, 4}^{\;21}$$

So $84 \div 4 = 21$

Exercise 13

Work these out.

1 $2\overline{)46}$ **4** $69 \div 3$

2 $3\overline{)96}$ **5** $82 \div 2$

3 $6\overline{)66}$ **6** $448 \div 4$

Sometimes we need to 'carry'. This happens when a number does not divide exactly.

Example

$$72 \div 4$$

$$4\overline{)72}$$

First do $7 \div 4$. This is 1 with 3 left over.
Put the 1 above the 7 and carry the 3 like this.

$$4\overline{)7^3 2}^{\,1}$$

Now do $32 \div 4$. This is 8. Put the 8 above the $^3 2$ like this

$$4\overline{)7^3 2}^{\,18}$$

So $72 \div 4 = 18$

Here is another example: $85 \div 5$

$$5\overline{)8^3 5}^{\,17}$$

So $85 \div 5 = 17$

Exercise 14

Work these out.

1 $2\overline{)36}$ **2** $3\overline{)48}$

3 $96 \div 4$ **8** $96 \div 8$

4 $52 \div 4$ **9** $436 \div 4$

5 $91 \div 7$ **10** $256 \div 2$

6 $68 \div 4$ **11** $387 \div 3$

7 $90 \div 6$ **12** $294 \div 7$

9 Dividing by 10

When we divide by 10, all the digits move across one column to the **right**. This makes the number smaller.

Example

$230 \div 10 = 23$

H	T	U
2	3	0

$\div 10$

	2	3

Here are some more examples.

Th	H	T	U
	5	8	0

$580 \div 10 = 58$

$\div 10$

| | | 5 | 8 |

| 2 | 4 | 6 | 0 |

$2460 \div 10 = 246$

$\div 10$

| | 2 | 4 | 6 |

Exercise 15

Divide each of these numbers by 10.

1 630   **5** 9010

2 70   **6** 2900

3 4960   **7** 3000

4 740   **8** 400 000

10 Dividing by 100, 1000, ...

When we divide by 100, all the digits move across **two** columns to the **right**. This is because $100 = 10 \times 10$. So dividing by 100 is like dividing by 10 twice.

Example

$7400 \div 100 = 74$

Th	H	T	U
7	4	0	0

$\div 100$

7　4

When we divide by 1000, all the numbers move across **three** columns to the **right**.

Example

$74\,000 \div 1000 = 74$

TTh	Th	H	T	U
7	4	0	0	0

$\div 1000$

7　4

11 Dividing by 20, 30, ...

When we divide by 20, it is like dividing by 2 then by 10. This is because $20 = 2 \times 10$.

Example

To do $360 \div 20$

first do

$$\begin{array}{r} 1\,8\,0 \\ 2\,\overline{)3^{1}6\,0} \end{array}$$

Then do　$180 \div 10 = 18$

So　　　$360 \div 20 = 18$

In the same way dividing by 30 is the same as dividing by 3 then by 10.

Example

To do $780 \div 30$

first do

$$\begin{array}{r} 2\,6\,0 \\ 3\,\overline{)7^{1}8\,0} \end{array}$$

Then do　$260 \div 10 = 26$

So　　　$780 \div 30 = 26$

Exercise 16

Work these out.

1 $6300 \div 100$ 　　**5** $87\,000 \div 100$

2 $6700 \div 100$ 　　**6** $87\,000 \div 1000$

3 $8600 \div 100$ 　　**7** $800\,000 \div 1000$

4 $24\,000 \div 1000$ 　**8** $800\,000 \div 10\,000$

Exercise 17

Work these out.

1 $520 \div 20$ 　　**5** $1320 \div 20$

2 $720 \div 30$ 　　**6** $1740 \div 30$

3 $2080 \div 40$ 　　**7** $3240 \div 90$

4 $1450 \div 50$ 　　**8** $16\,160 \div 80$

These words can also mean **divide**.

　　share　　**quotient**

Share 240 by 12　⎫
Find the **quotient**　⎬ both mean
of 240 and 12　　⎭ $240 \div 12$

To enter a fraction on your calculator use the $a^{b/c}$ key.

To enter $\frac{1}{2}$ key in 1 $a^{b/c}$ 2

ssssssss

Your display should show $1 r 2$

To enter $1\frac{3}{4}$ key in 1 $a^{b/c}$ 3 $a^{b/c}$ 4

Your display should show $1 r 3 r 4$

Example   Find $\frac{2}{3}$ of 12 sweets.

You want to find $\frac{2}{3} \times 12$

Key in 2 $a^{b/c}$ 3 × 1 2 =

The answer is 8 sweets.

You can also use the $a^{b/c}$ button to work out sharing problems.

Example   Share 5 oranges equally between 3 children.

Key in 5 $a^{b/c}$ 3 =

Your display should show $1 r 2 r 3$

The answer is $1\frac{2}{3}$ oranges.

Examples

1 $\frac{3}{4} + \frac{1}{2} =$ 3 $a^{b/c}$ 4 + 1 $a^{b/c}$ 2 = $1 r 1 r 4$

Answer is $1\frac{1}{4}$

2 $2\frac{1}{3} - 1\frac{5}{6} =$ 2 $a^{b/c}$ 1 $a^{b/c}$ 3 − 1 $a^{b/c}$ 5 $a^{b/c}$ 6 = $1 r 2$

Answer is $\frac{1}{2}$

3 $\frac{2}{3}$ of $4\frac{1}{2} = \frac{2}{3} \times 4\frac{1}{2} =$ 2 $a^{b/c}$ 3 × 4 $a^{b/c}$ 1 $a^{b/c}$ 2 = 3

Answer is 3

4 $6\frac{3}{4} \div 9 =$ 6 $a^{b/c}$ 3 $a^{b/c}$ 4 ÷ 9 = $3 r 4$

Answer is $\frac{3}{4}$

CHAPTER 1

1 **a** 20 pupils (UK is twice USA)   **c** UK has largest angle

b 5 pupils (France is half USA)   **d** 40 pupils altogether

e

Country	UK	USA	Spain	France
Number of pupils	20	10	5	5

2

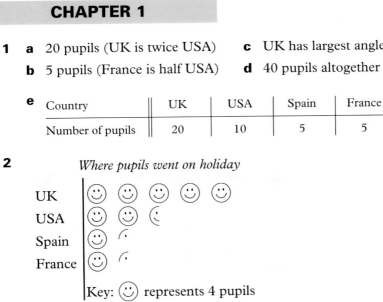

Where pupils went on holiday

Key: ☺ represents 4 pupils

3 **a**

Results	Tally	Total
1–20	卌 |	6
21–40	|||	3
41–60	卌 卌	10
61–80	卌 |||	8
81–100	卌	5
	Total	32

b

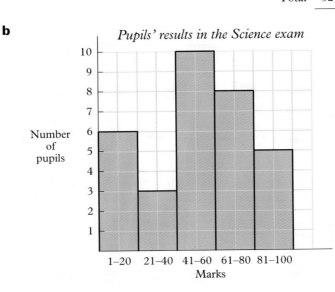

Pupils' results in the Science exam

4 a

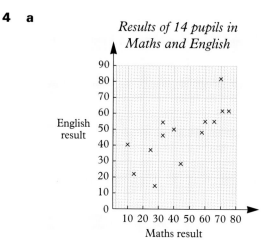

Results of 14 pupils in Maths and English

b There is weak correlation. In general, as the results in Maths go up so do the English results.

CHAPTER 2

1 a   **b**

2 a   **b**

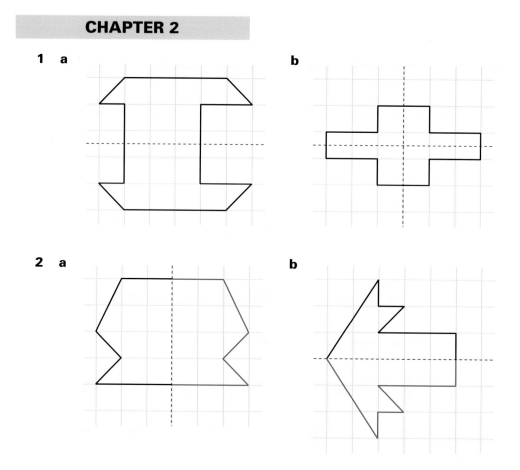

3 **a** W U **b** D **c** J S L

4 **a** 1 **b** 3 **c** 1 **d** None **e** 4

5 **a** 2 **b** 4 **c** 4 **d** 3

6

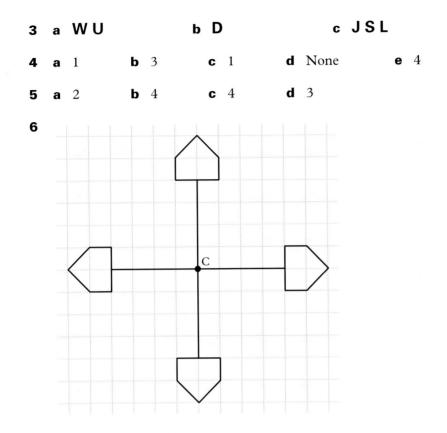

CHAPTER 3

1 **a** 21, 28, 35, 42, 49, 56 The rule is 'add 7'.
   b 100, 90, 80, 70, 60, 50 The rule is 'subtract 10'.
   c 3, 9, 27, 81, 243 The rule is 'multiply by 3'.

2 6, 12, 18, 24, 30

3 **a** 1, 2, 3, 5, 6, 10, 15, 30
       1, 2, 3, 6, 7, 14, 21, 42
   b The highest common factor is 6.

4 **a** The rule is 'add 4'. **c** 1, 21
   b 5, 13, 17 **d** 1, 9, 25

5 **a** 2, 3 **b** 2, 3, 5

6 $54 = 2 \times 3 \times 3 \times 3$

7 $\times 5$

8
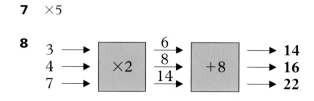

CHAPTER 4

1 **a** 40 since 38 is closer to 40 than to 30.
   b 90 since 85 is half-way between 80 and 90 so we choose the higher.
   c 250 since 253 is closer to 250 than to 260.

2 **a** 400 since 449 is closer to 400 than to 500.
   b 700 since 681 is closer to 700 than to 600.
   c 300 since 250 is half-way between 200 and 300.

3 **a** 79×31 Estimate is $80 \times 30 = 2400$
                       Exact answer = 2449

   b $59 \div 19 \times 38$ Estimate is $60 \div 20 \times 40 = 120$
                       Exact answer = 118

4 $238 \div 7 = 34$ There will be 34 pieces.

5 $3 \times 36\,\mathrm{p}$ each day $= 108\,\mathrm{p}$ 7 days in a week
   Cost for week is: $7 \times 108\,\mathrm{p} = 756\,\mathrm{p}$
                            $= £7.56$

6 50 miles at $28\,\mathrm{p}$ $= £14.00$
   There are $124 - 50$ $= 74$ miles left
   74 miles at $17\,\mathrm{p}$ $= £12.58$
   She will get $£26.58$

7 **a** $3 + 2 \times 7 = 3 + 14$ Do the multiplication first.
                $= 17$

   b $20 \div 2 - 8 = 10 - 8$ Do the division first.
                $= 2$

   c $24 \div 2 + 2 \times 4 = 12 + 8$ Do the division and the multiplication first.
                   $= 20$

8 **a** $(5 + 4) \times 2 = 9 \times 2$ Do the brackets first.
$ = 18$

b $(16 - 11) \times 3 = 5 \times 3$ Do the brackets first.
$ = 15$

c $60 \div (7 + 5) = 60 \div 12$ Do the brackets first.
$ = 5$

9 **a** $32 - (20 + 2) = 32 - 22$ Do the brackets first, then the subtraction.
$ = 10$

b $(13 + 5) \div (14 - 8) = 18 \div 6$ Do the brackets first, then the division.
$ = 3$

c $(25 - 13) + (16 - 4) = 12 + 12$ Do the brackets first, then the addition.
$ = 24$

10 **a** 109
b 8960
c 12

CHAPTER 5

1 **a** and **b**

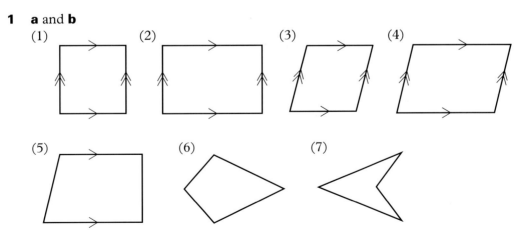

(1) (2) (3) (4)

(5) (6) (7)

c The arrowhead is concave.
d The square is regular (equal sides, all vertices the same shape).

2 a (1) A scalene triangle has no equal sides.
   (2) An isosceles triangle has two equal sides.
   (3) An equilateral triangle has three equal sides.
b (1) A pentagon has five sides.
   (2) A hexagon has six vertices.
   (3) An octagon has eight sides.

3 a The pentagon has rotational symmetry of order five.
b The pentagon has five lines of symmetry.

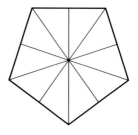

4 a The parallel sides are AB and DC.
b The diagonal is AC.

5

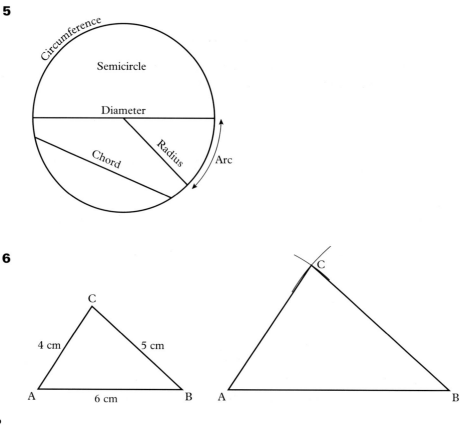

6

A   6 cm   B   A   B

7 a The shapes point in different directions.
There is no regular pattern.
There is a gap in the tessellation.

b Something like:

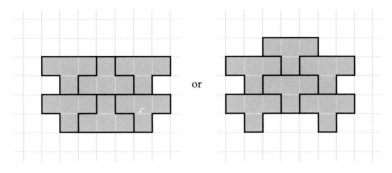

or

CHAPTER 6

1 The 3 is multiplied by 100. It has moved two columns to the left.

2 905   nine hundred and five

3 207 000   two hundred and seven thousand

4 a six tens   **c** no hundredths   **e** one unit
b eight thousandths   **d** three hundredths

5 a 12.9, **13**, 13.1   **c** 2.88, **2.89**, 2.9   **e** 0.5, **0.51**, 0.52
b 7.04, **7.05**, 7.06   **d** 6.7, **6.71**, 6.72

6 a 5.637 × 100 = 563.7. Digits have moved two columns to the left.
b 20.79 ÷ 10 = 2.079. Digits have moved one column to the right.

7 a (1) 4.035, 4.5, 4.53 (All have 4 as the figure in front of the point.
The first figure after the decimal point is 0 or 5, so 4.035 is the
smallest. 4.5 is smaller than 4.53.)
(2) 0.158, 0.18, 0.58 (0.158 is smaller than 0.18 as 5 is less than 8.
0.58 is the largest.)
b 0.5 mm   0.505 mm   0.52 mm   0.525 mm   0.55 mm   0.575 mm
(Apart from 0.52 and 0.525, the numbers have been put into order
using the second decimal place.)

8 a (1) 4.4, 5.6, **6.8**, **8.0**, **9.2**, **10.4**, **11.6**, **12.8**
(2) 0.96, 0.93, **0.90**, **0.87**, **0.84**, **0.81**, **0.78**, **0.75**
b (1) **1**, 0.3, 0.09, 0.027, 0.0081, **0.00243** The rule is 'multiply by 0.3'.
(2) 7.9, **7.4**, 6.9, 6.4, 5.9, 5.4, **4.9** The rule is 'subtract 0.5'.

9 **a**
$$\begin{array}{r} 23.8 \\ +\ 5.91 \\ \hline 29.71 \\ \hline {\scriptstyle 1} \end{array}$$

b
$$\begin{array}{r} 62.9 \\ +\ 7.0 \\ \hline 69.9 \end{array}$$

c
$$\begin{array}{r} {\scriptstyle 4\ 12} \\ 5\cancel{3}.2 \\ -\ 6.8 \\ \hline 46.4 \end{array}$$

d
$$\begin{array}{r} {\scriptstyle 6\ 9} \\ 1\cancel{7}.\cancel{0}\cancel{0} \\ -\ 4.86 \\ \hline 12.14 \end{array}$$

10 **a**
$$\begin{array}{r} 12.8 \\ \times\quad 5 \\ \hline 64.0 \\ \hline {\scriptstyle 1\ 4} \end{array}$$

b
$$\begin{array}{r} 0.000\,46 \\ \times\qquad 6 \\ \hline 0.002\,76 \\ \hline {\scriptstyle 2\ \ 3} \end{array}$$

c $\quad 4\overline{)17.\overset{1}{0}\overset{2}{4}}\ {\scriptstyle 4.26}$

d $\quad 8\overline{)10.\overset{2}{2}\overset{6}{0}\overset{6}{0}}\ {\scriptstyle 1.275}$

11 **a** 2.5 **b** 14.88 **c** 31.98 **d** 6.0

CHAPTER 7

1 **a** **A** hexagonal prism **b** **A** (3)
      B cuboid   **B** (2)
      C cylinder   **C** (1)
      D triangular prism   **D** (4)

  c **E** hexagonal pyramid
      F square pyramid
      G cone
      H tetrahedron or triangular pyramid

  d **C** and **G** are not polyhedrons. They each have a curved face.

2 **a** 4 cm, 3 cm, 1 cm
  b

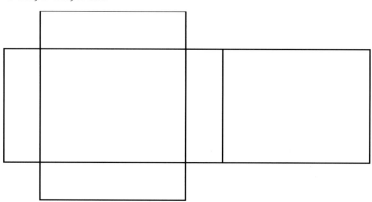

This is one net of the cuboid. There are many other correct arrangements.
To test whether your arrangement is correct, cut it out and fold it.

3 **a** Tetrahedron or triangular pyramid   **e**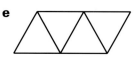
  b 6 edges
  c 4 faces
  d 4 vertices

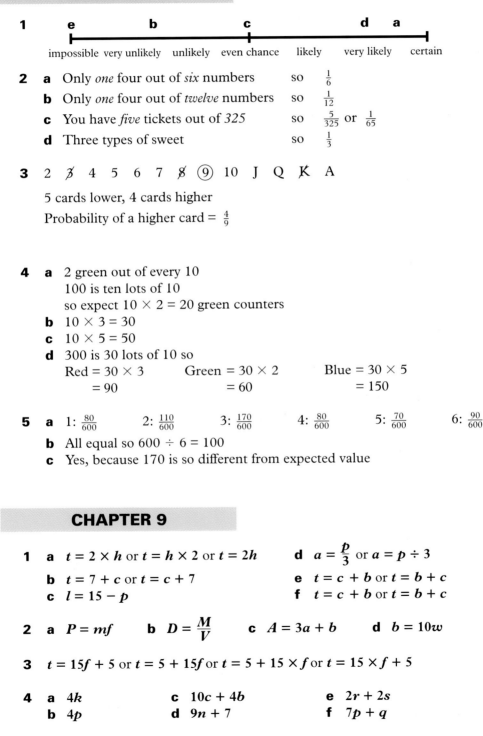

CHAPTER 8

1

e   b   c   d   a

impossible   very unlikely   unlikely   even chance   likely   very likely   certain

2

a Only *one* four out of *six* numbers   so $\frac{1}{6}$

b Only *one* four out of *twelve* numbers   so $\frac{1}{12}$

c You have *five* tickets out of *325*   so $\frac{5}{325}$ or $\frac{1}{65}$

d Three types of sweet   so $\frac{1}{3}$

3   2 $\cancel{3}$ 4   5   6   7 $\cancel{8}$ ⑨   10   J   Q $\cancel{K}$ A

5 cards lower, 4 cards higher

Probability of a higher card = $\frac{4}{9}$

4

a 2 green out of every 10

100 is ten lots of 10

so expect $10 \times 2 = 20$ green counters

b $10 \times 3 = 30$

c $10 \times 5 = 50$

d 300 is 30 lots of 10 so

Red = 30×3 Green = 30×2 Blue = 30×5

      = 90   = 60   = 150

5

a 1: $\frac{80}{600}$ 2: $\frac{110}{600}$ 3: $\frac{170}{600}$ 4: $\frac{80}{600}$ 5: $\frac{70}{600}$ 6: $\frac{90}{600}$

b All equal so $600 \div 6 = 100$

c Yes, because 170 is so different from expected value

CHAPTER 9

1

a $t = 2 \times h$ or $t = h \times 2$ or $t = 2h$ **d** $a = \frac{p}{3}$ or $a = p \div 3$

b $t = 7 + c$ or $t = c + 7$ **e** $t = c + b$ or $t = b + c$

c $l = 15 - p$ **f** $t = c + b$ or $t = b + c$

2   **a** $P = mf$ **b** $D = \frac{M}{V}$ **c** $A = 3a + b$ **d** $b = 10w$

3 $t = 15f + 5$ or $t = 5 + 15f$ or $t = 5 + 15 \times f$ or $t = 15 \times f + 5$

4

a $4k$ **c** $10c + 4b$ **e** $2r + 2s$

b $4p$ **d** $9n + 7$ **f** $7p + q$

5 **a** $f^2 = f \times f$ **c** $\dfrac{g}{f} = g \div f$ **e** $3(f + g) = 3(2 + 4)$

   $\qquad = 2 \times 2$ $\qquad = 4 \div 2$ $\qquad\qquad = 3 \times 6$

   $\qquad = 4$ $\qquad = 2$ $\qquad\qquad = 18$

   b $fg = f \times g$ **d** $2f + 3g = 2 \times 2 + 3 \times 4$ **f** $g^2 - 5f = g \times g - 5 \times f$

   $\qquad = 2 \times 4$ $\qquad\qquad = 4 + 12$ $\qquad\qquad = 4 \times 4 - 5 \times 2$

   $\qquad = 8$ $\qquad\qquad = 16$ $\qquad\qquad = 16 - 10$

   $\qquad\qquad\qquad\qquad\qquad = 6$

6 **a** $A = \dfrac{b \times h}{2}$ **b** $M = m(v - u)$

   $\qquad = \dfrac{6 \times 10}{2}$ $\qquad = 4(2 - 0)$

   $\qquad = 30$ $\qquad = 8$

7 **a** $p = 5s$ or $p = 5 \times s$

   $p = 5 \times 6$

   $\quad = 30$ **cm**

   b $k = \dfrac{8m}{5}$ or $\dfrac{8 \times m}{5}$ or $\dfrac{m \times 8}{5}$ or $m \times 8 \div 5$

   $\quad = \dfrac{8 \times 20}{5}$

   $\quad = \dfrac{160}{5}$

CHAPTER 10

1 **a** and **b**

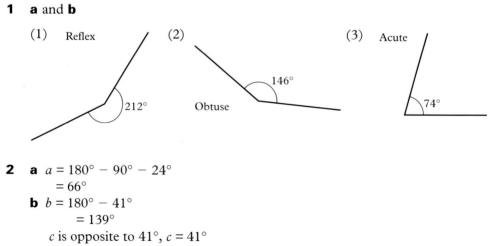

(1) Reflex   (2)   (3) Acute

$212°$ $146°$ $74°$

Obtuse

2 **a** $a = 180° - 90° - 24°$

   $\quad = 66°$

   b $b = 180° - 41°$

   $\qquad = 139°$

   c is opposite to $41°$, $c = 41°$

   d is opposite to b, $d = 139°$

c

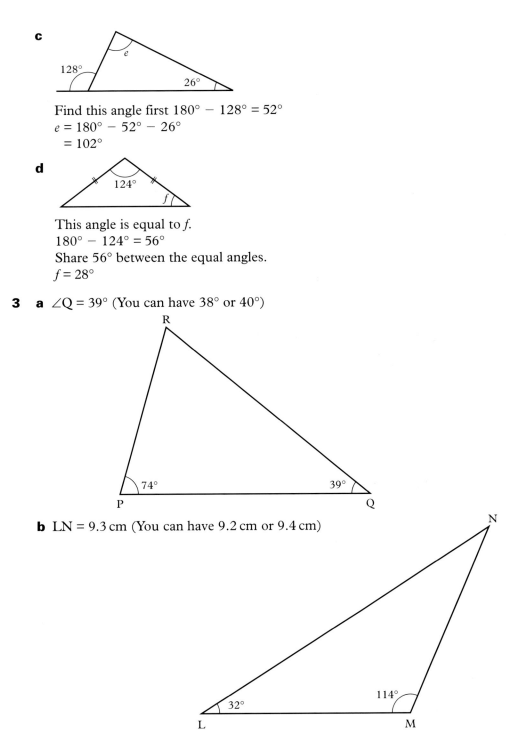

Find this angle first $180° - 128° = 52°$
$e = 180° - 52° - 26°$
$ = 102°$

d

This angle is equal to f.
$180° - 124° = 56°$
Share $56°$ between the equal angles.
$f = 28°$

3 **a** $\angle Q = 39°$ (You can have $38°$ or $40°$)

b $LN = 9.3\,cm$ (You can have $9.2\,cm$ or $9.4\,cm$)

4 **a** The red angle is $\angle ABD$ (or $\angle DBA$).

b The blue angle is $\angle DBC$ (or $\angle CBD$).

CHAPTER 11

1 Find the temperatures on a thermometer scale.
Warmer temperatures are higher up on the scale.
$-18\,°C, -11\,°C, -6\,°C, 0\,°C, 4\,°C, 25\,°C$

2 **a** From $-25\,°C$ to $-18\,°C$ is $7\,°C$ counted up a thermometer scale.
On a calculator [1][8][+/−][−][2][5][+/−][=]

b From $-18\,°C$ to $19\,°C$ is $37\,°C$ counted up a thermometer scale.
On a calculator [1][9][−][1][8][+/−][=]

3 **a** $A\,(6, 2), B\,(6, -2), C\,(4, -4),$
$D\,(0, -4), E\,(-2, -2),$
$F\,(-2, 2), G\,(0, 4), H\,(4, 4)$
b F has a negative x co-ordinate
and a positive y co-ordinate.
c B and C are in the fourth
quadrant.
d DC is a reflection of GH in the
x axis.

Second quadrant | First quadrant
Third quadrant | Fourth quadrant

4 **b**

x	-5	-4	-3	-2	-1	0	1
y	-1	0	1	2	3	4	5

$y = x + 4$

c and **d**

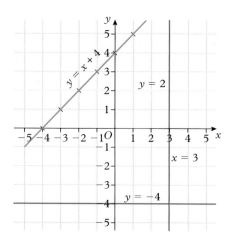

e $(-2, 2)$ is the point where the line $y = 2$ crosses $y = x + 4$.

418

CHAPTER 12

1 **a** 3 ft $= 3 \times 12$ in
$= 36$ in

b 60 in $= 60 \div 12$ ft
$= 5$ ft

c 5 yd $= 5 \times 3$ ft
$= 15$ ft

d 24 ft $= 24 \div 3$ yd
$= 8$ yd

2 **a** 48 mm = 4.8 cm **d** 3.7 cm = 37 mm
b 240 cm = 2.4 m **e** 4.6 m = 460 cm
c 3700 m = 3.7 km **f** 0.4 km = 400 m

3 **a** 50 km **b** 35 km

4 Any answer between 17 km and 23 km

5 **a** ─────────────────────── $(5\frac{1}{2}$ cm)
b ──────────── $(2\frac{1}{2}$ cm)

6 10 miles

7 **a** (1) 8 inches $= 8 \times 2\frac{1}{2}$ cm
$= 20$ cm
(2) 25 yd is a bit less than 25 m, about 22 to 23 m
(3) 20 miles are a bit less than $1\frac{1}{2} \times 20$ km $= 30$ km, about 31 to 33 km.

b (1) 24 in $= 24 \times 2.5$ cm
$= 60$ cm
(2) 8 yd $= 8 \times 0.9$ m
$= 7.2$ m
(3) 30 miles $= 30 \times 1.6$ km
$= 48$ km

8 **a** 240 (5 divisions, count in 20s)
b 3500 (halfway between 3000 and 4000)
c (1) 4 km ≈ 2.5 miles
(2) 6 miles ≈ 9.5 km

CHAPTER 13

1

$$\longleftarrow \boxed{-2} \longleftarrow \boxed{\div 10} \longleftarrow$$

2

$$\longleftarrow \boxed{\times 8} \longleftarrow \boxed{+2} \longleftarrow$$

3
$$5y = 30$$
$$\frac{5y}{5} = \frac{30}{5}$$
$$y = 6$$

4
$$\frac{c}{4} = 8$$
$$\frac{c}{4} \times 4 = 8 \times 4$$
$$c = 32$$

5
$$2x - 13 = 17$$
$$2x - 13 + 13 = 17 + 13$$
$$2x = 30$$
$$\frac{2x}{2} = \frac{30}{2}$$
$$x = 15$$

6
$$\frac{x}{2} - 5 = 12$$
$$\frac{x}{2} - 5 + 5 = 12 + 5$$
$$\frac{x}{2} = 17$$
$$\frac{x}{2} \times 2 = 17 \times 2$$
$$x = 34$$

7
$$\frac{x}{4} + 8 = 14$$
$$\frac{x}{4} + 8 - 8 = 14 - 8$$
$$\frac{x}{4} = 6$$
$$\frac{x}{4} \times 4 = 6 \times 4$$
$$x = 24$$

8
$$x + 135 = 180$$
$$x + 135 - 135 = 180 - 135$$
$$x = 45$$

9
$$2x - 10 = 130$$
$$2x - 10 + 10 = 130 + 10$$
$$2x = 140$$
$$\frac{2x}{2} = \frac{140}{2}$$
$$x = 70$$

10
$$p = r + 15$$
$$r + 15 = p$$
$$r + 15 - 15 = p - 15$$
$$r = p - 15$$

11
$$a = b - 5$$
$$b - 5 = a$$
$$b - 5 + 5 = a + 5$$
$$b = a + 5$$

12
$$y = 4x - 5$$
$$4x - 5 = y$$
$$4x - 5 + 5 = y + 5$$
$$4x = y + 5$$
$$\frac{4x}{4} = \frac{y + 5}{4}$$
$$x = \frac{y + 5}{4}$$

13
$$f = 6g + 10$$
$$6g + 10 = f$$
$$6g + 10 - 10 = f - 10$$
$$6g = f - 10$$
$$\frac{6g}{6} = \frac{f - 10}{6}$$
$$g = \frac{f - 10}{6}$$

14 $7x + 153 = 384$

Value of x	Value of $7x + 153$	
20	293	too small
30	363	too small
40	433	too big
35	398	too big
34	391	too big
33	384	correct

Answer: $x = 33$

CHAPTER 14

1 **a** The length of the rectangle is 6.5 cm, width 3 cm.

b $A = lw$
$$= 6.5 \times 3$$
$$= 19.5 \text{ cm}^2$$

c Perimeter = 6.5 + 3 + 6.5 + 3 = 19 cm
This is the distance around the outside of the rectangle.

2 **a** $A = lw$
$$= 50 \times 50$$
$$= 2500 \text{ cm}^2$$

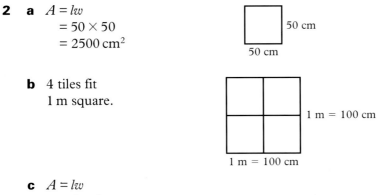

50 cm

50 cm

b 4 tiles fit
1 m square.

1 m = 100 cm

1 m = 100 cm

c $A = lw$
$$= 4 \times 6$$
$$= 24 \text{ m}^2$$

Since   4 tiles are needed for 1 m²
       $4 \times 24 = 96$ tiles are needed for 24 m²

3 Perimeter = 36 cm
Half the perimeter = 18 cm
Length of rectangle = 18 − 3 cm
                = 15 cm

4 **a** Area of triangle $= \dfrac{bh}{2}$
$$= \dfrac{16 \times 10}{2}$$
$$= 80 \text{ cm}^2$$

b Area of parallelogram $= bh$
$$= 13 \times 12$$
$$= 156 \text{ m}^2$$

5 Width of $A = 22 - 12$
$= 10\,\text{m}$

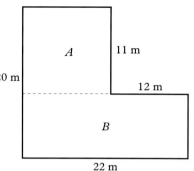

    a   Area of A $= 11 \times 10$
                              $= 110\,\text{m}^2$
        Area of B $= 22 \times 9$
                              $= 198\,\text{m}^2$
        Area of shape $= 110 + 198$
                              $= 308\,\text{m}^2$

    b   Area of large rectangle $= 10 \times 19$
                                  $= 190\,\text{cm}^2$
       Area of small rectangle $= 7 \times 8$
                                  $= 56\,\text{cm}^2$
       Area coloured green $= 190 - 56$
                                  $= 134\,\text{cm}^2$

CHAPTER 15

1   **a, b,**   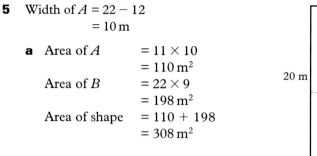   The rectangle is split into 5 equal parts
                                         2 parts are shaded.

2   **a** $\frac{1}{3}$ of $15 = 15 \div 3 = 5$
      b $\frac{1}{5}$ of $20 = 20 \div 5 = 4$
          $\frac{2}{5}$ of $20 = 4 \times 2 = 8$

3 $5 \div 3 = 1\frac{2}{3}$

4 $\overset{\div 2}{\frac{10}{24}} = \underset{\div 2}{\frac{5}{12}}$

5   17 squares are shaded out of 100   **a** $\frac{17}{100}$ **b**   17%

6 a 1 hour = 60 mins so 10 mins = $\frac{10}{60}$ of an hour

b $\frac{10}{60} = \frac{1}{6}$

7 a $\frac{2}{5} + \frac{2}{5} = \frac{4}{5}$

b $\frac{2}{5} + \frac{1}{10} = \frac{4}{10} + \frac{1}{10} = \frac{5}{10} = \frac{1}{2}$

c $\frac{5}{6} - \frac{1}{3} = \frac{5}{6} - \frac{2}{6} = \frac{3}{6} = \frac{1}{2}$

8 a $\frac{2}{3} \times \frac{4}{5} = \frac{8}{15}$

b $\frac{5}{7} \div \frac{5}{6} = \frac{5}{7} \times \frac{6}{5} = \frac{30}{35} = \frac{6}{7}$

c $1\frac{1}{4} \times \frac{7}{9} = \frac{5}{4} \times \frac{7}{9} = \frac{35}{36}$

9 a $\frac{4}{5} = 5\overline{)4.^40}$ quotient 0.8

b $\frac{5}{16} = 16\overline{)5.^50^20^40^80}$ quotient 0.3125

c $\frac{5}{6} = 6\overline{)5.^50^20^20}$ quotient $0.833\ldots$ $= 0.8\dot{3}$

10 a $0.4 = \frac{4}{10} = \frac{2}{5}$

b $0.56 = \frac{56}{100} = \frac{14}{25}$

c $0.175 = \frac{175}{1000} = \frac{7}{40}$

11 $\frac{3}{11} = \frac{39}{143}$ $\frac{4}{13} = \frac{44}{143}$

So $\frac{4}{13}$ is the bigger.

12 $\frac{1}{5}$ $\frac{2}{7}$ $\frac{1}{2}$ $\frac{2}{3}$ $\frac{3}{4}$

CHAPTER 16

1 £45

2 **a** 30 g   **b** Yes   **c** 30 g   **d** Yes

3 **a** 0.41 − 0.21 = 0.20
 b Mean = 0.293, 9 results are below the mean.
 c 0.29

4 **a** From the graph it looks as if the sales figures are hardly changing.
 b

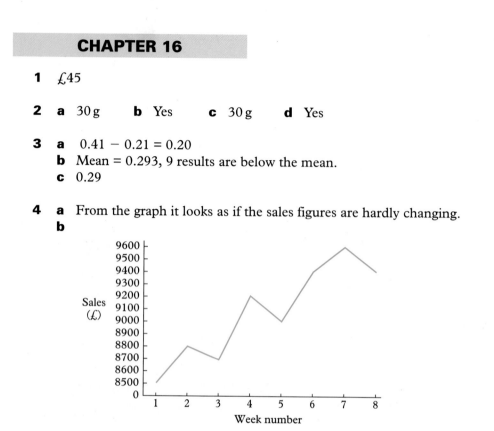

 c The sales figures now seem to be rising dramatically.